1973

be kept

CREATING A ROLE

Also by Constantin Stanislavski

AN ACTOR PREPARES

AN ACTOR'S HANDBOOK

BUILDING A CHARACTER

MY LIFE IN ART

The Seagull PRODUCED BY STANISLAVSKI

STANISLAVSKI PRODUCES *Othello*

STANISLAVSKI'S LEGACY

CREATING
A ROLE

Constantin Stanislavski

TRANSLATED BY ELIZABETH REYNOLDS HAPGOOD

EDITED BY HERMINE I. POPPER

FOREWORD BY ROBERT LEWIS

THEATRE ARTS BOOKS • *New York*

Published by

THEATRE ARTS BOOKS
333 Sixth Avenue, New York 14, N.Y.

PUBLISHED SIMULTANEOUSLY IN CANADA BY
AMBASSADOR BOOKS LTD., 370 ALLIANCE AVENUE, TORONTO 9

PRINTED IN THE UNITED STATES OF AMERICA

Foreword

by Robert Lewis

HERE, almost a quarter of a century after his death, are some more nuggets dug up from the vast gold mine of Stanislavski's continuous search for a truthful and artistic method of training actors and working on roles. So rich is the substance of *Creating a Role*, so provocative, that one feels it is possible to take many of the ideas presented and expand them into essays or books.

The first of the three parts of this book is a particularly brilliant break-down of how to work on a part. It will confirm, or clarify, many points for those actors and directors who already work along these lines. For those who don't, this study of Stanislavski's approach to his role of Chatski in *Woe From Wit* will be a revelation. This section, without the device of the teacher-pupil dialogue used in the rest of the book, seems to me to be the most lucid presentation of Stanislavski's aims so far.

Here we have a logical break-down of the rehearsal period from the first reading on. "Beginnings" being so important, Stanislavski tells us why it is advisable for the play first to be read to the cast by one person. He shows us how to recount the story of a play in actors' terms, how to analyze the play and the roles, being careful to distinguish between intellectual and artistic analysis. He teaches us how to create a logical subtext to create an inner life which will give substance to the author's words. The most important, and least understood, aspect of the work, the search into one's own experience to arouse feelings analogous to those required in the part, gets a thorough airing.

Don't think that "feeling" is all that is stressed here. Unlike

v

some modern self-styled practitioners of what they call "The Method" (no such arrogance will be found in Stanislavski's own writings) there is more than lip-service paid to beauty of language, lightness of verse, rhythm, imagination, and all the theatrical and artistic means of expression. Stanislavski was not unaware that although it is true that if your intention "to not disturb those inside" makes you knock on the door timidly, it is also true that a careful, delicate knock on the door creates a sense of timidity in you. He constantly stresses the choice of "physical actions," a process he keeps intertwining with his "internal actions" as he works on a role. The question always asked in making the part true to himself is, "What would I *do* if I were in so-and-so's [the character's] situation?" Yes, always the *character's* situation: *his* life in *his* city in *his* time, and so forth; not *my* life in *my* city in *my* time, as we sometimes suspect modern "methodists" are thinking.

In Chapter Three, Stanislavski speaks clearly of the *physical embodiment* of the part. Here you will find such phrases as "subtle means of expression of your eyes and face," "use your voice, sounds, words, intonations, and speech." True, he rightly maintains that "voice and speech remain in complete dependence on inner feelings and are their direct, exact, and subservient expression." But he also knew the *importance* of voice, speech, movement, and so forth. If it ever was needed, here is proof that gives the lie to the argument that anything in Stanislavski's method leads perforce to sloppy speech and slouching. "Every living organism," he says, "has an outer form as well, a physical body which uses make-up, has a typical voice as to manner of speech and intonation, typical way of walking, manners, gestures, and so forth." What a blow to self-indulgent actors busy squeezing out a bit of private feeling, who care not a jot how they look, whether they can be heard, and so forth. Let this once and for all answer those who mistakenly, or deliberately, accept this lunatic fringe as exponents of the theories of a man who, for half a century, produced with distinction everything from realistic plays to opera, and in every style. It cannot be said too often that Stanislavski's method is not a style and not applicable to one particular style of theatre, but is an attempt to find a logical approach to the training of actors for any play, and an artistic way of preparing for any role.

Parts II and III of *Creating a Role* revert to the style of writing used in *An Actor Prepares* and *Building a Character*. We have that mythical classroom with Tortsov, the teacher, instructing a group of students. This form of presentation may seem a bit murky and not as forthright and crystal clear as the more direct approach of Part I. But we do have a chance to see Stanislavski trying his rehearsal procedure on two other roles: Othello, and Khlestakov in *The Inspector General*. Again he approaches these parts from the "inside" and the "outside" simultaneously. He discovers, in fact, that finding the correct physical truth of the part feeds his inner truth better, as he says, than "forcing" feeling. He pursues the character by his use of the justification of the physical acts of the part, by placing himself in the circumstances of the character through the celebrated "magic if," and by breaking down the inner line of the part into logical objectives; in other words, an interior and exterior analysis of himself as a human being in the circumstances of the life of his role, his "own" feelings always chosen to be analogous to the feelings inherent in the part. This makes for the "truthful playing of the life of the part in the play."

Of particular interest to directors, there is, in the appendix, a twenty-five point summing-up of a plan of rehearsal from the first reading to the final characterization. There are certain suggestions, such as asking the actors where they would like to be on the stage at given moments, that are the privileges of directors with permanent theatres. In show-business, that is to say, doing one isolated production at a time, with newly assembled actors, all from different backgrounds, with limited rehearsal time, the director may want to forget that indulgence!

All through the three sections of this book you get a picture of a real artist at work, sometimes failing, but without despair, and always seeking truthful answers. (He reworked his role of Satin in *The Lower Depths* after playing it eighteen years!) Admirers of *An Actor Prepares* and *Building a Character* will relish *Creating a Role*. Those being introduced to Stanislavski's writings with this book will want to examine the other two. A thorough study of all three books will reveal the all-important point of how to apply the technique studied in the classroom to the preparation of roles.

Here, then, is more word from the master, rather than from his disciples. It is a book for all theatre professionals as well as students. Whether you are in agreement or disagreement with all, or parts, of it, you cannot help being stimulated and enriched by it.

Translator's Note

Creating a Role is the third volume of Stanislavski's planned trilogy on the training of an actor. The first two, *An Actor Prepares* and *Building a Character*, although published thirteen years apart, were intended to describe the young actor's regime at much the same period in his development: while training his inner qualities of emotion memory, imagination and concentration, he was also developing his physical means by rigorous work on his voice and body, the very instruments for putting into vivid and convincingly concrete form what the inner life might develop. Now, another twelve years later, we are able to issue the projected third volume. This phase in Stanislavski's teaching, which he believed an actor should come to after mastery of the other two, is the preparation of specific roles, beginning with the first reading of a play and the development of the first scene. The English title is as close as possible to the rather longer Russian one, literally *The Work of an Actor on a Role*.

When I was working with Stanislavski on *An Actor Prepares* and *Building a Character* (for which he had a contract in America) in France and Germany during 1929 and 1930, he spoke of his idea of having all three of his books on acting technique centered on Shakespeare's *Othello*. He felt that this play, with which he had long been preoccupied, would be accessible to students of many nationalities, especially the English-speaking ones. Indeed at this very time in France, he was sending back to Moscow suggestions for the production of *Othello*, the direction of which he was forced to relinquish because of his serious illness in 1928. These suggestions are the basis for *Stanislavski Produces Othello*, a director's promptbook, with his instructions published opposite the text of the play, a volume of enormous value as a demonstration of how this great director worked on a play. But in this present book we see how his mind also turned to *Othello* as an exercise through which actors themselves could enter into their roles to create characters of truth and a memorable vividness.

Stanislavski died in August 1938. Only *An Actor Prepares* had been published in the United States and England (1936) and it had not yet appeared in the Soviet Union. He had collected all the material for *Building a Character* but the Second World War postponed its publication. Now with the official publication in Russian of all of Stanislavski's manuscripts, we find that he had actually drafted three versions of the third book. The first had been done years earlier (1916-1920), before he had invented the semi-fictional form of a teacher and his students used in *An Actor Prepares* and *Building a Character*. The other two are dated in the 1930's after he had prepared *An Actor Prepares* for publication and completed the material that was published as *Building a Character*.

The first version presented problems. It deals specifically with a classic Russian satirical comedy, Griboyedov's *Woe from Wit* (also called *The Misfortune of Being Clever*), which after 150 years still defies translation. Although line after line of this play has been incorporated into literary Russian much as Shakespeare's phrases have in English, no translator has as yet succeeded in conveying Griboyedov's witty verse in a Western European language. The situations and the satirical darts even seem to lie beyond the comprehension of all except specialists. Yet in its humanity it is universal and thus a meaningful framework for Stanislavski's search for ways to help an actor perfect his art. In order to make this first version of *Creating a Role* accessible to English-speaking actors we have resorted to minor cuts and some brief elucidations always clearly marked as such.

It is interesting that in his work on *Woe from Wit* Stanislavski demonstrates the methods he describes early in *My Life in Art*, and the emphasis is on the actor's psycho-technique, on the preparation of the inner pattern of a role as a starting point. In the two other versions, based on *Othello* and Gogol's *Inspector General*, one sees how Stanislavski was always revising his methods, how he persisted in his search for better ways. His approach to certain problems did change toward the end of his life and if he here revises some of the practices in the *Woe from Wit* section, so much the truer it is of Stanislavski's real method. In publishing all three we believe the reader has the advantage of seeing Stanislavski treat a variety of roles, of comparing his sensitive adjustment to given material in three different plays, of realizing that his lifelong goal remained the same: the creation of life on the stage in terms of what he called *spiritual* naturalism.

These three versions were sent to me for translation and publication by Stanislavski's son and I believe that in preparing them for use by English-speaking actors I have carried out once more the task entrusted to me by Stanislavski himself, to eliminate duplications and cut whatever was meaningless for non-Russian actors. There has been some slight rearrangement of sections within the versions where we think Stanislavski would have done the same himself had he had the chance to work over his manuscripts. Editor's notes have been added, giving needed information from *An Actor Prepares* and *Building a Character* and background which Mrs. Popper and I hope will make *Creating a Role* more rewarding for all who read it.

Elizabeth Reynolds Hapgood

New York City
June 1st, 1961

Contents

FOREWORD by Robert Lewis   v

TRANSLATOR'S NOTE   ix

Part I. Griboyedov's *Woe from Wit*   I

    I. The Period of Study   3
         First Acquaintance with a Part   3
         Analysis   8
         Studying the External Circumstances   12
         Putting Life into External Circumstances   18
         Creating Inner Circumstances   25
         Appraising the Facts   34
   II. The Period of Emotional Experience   44
         Inner Impulses and Inner Action   44
         Creative Objectives   51
         The Score of a Role   56
         The Inner Tone   62
         The Superobjective and Through Action   77
         The Superconscious   81
  III. The Period of Physical Embodiment   85

Part II. Shakespeare's *Othello*   107

   IV. First Acquaintance   109
    V. Creating the Physical Life of a Role   131
  VI. Analysis   151
 VII. Checking Work Done and Summing Up   194

CONTENTS

Part III. Gogol's *The Inspector General*   211

VIII. From Physical Actions to Living Image   213

Appendices   251

a. Supplement to *Creating a Role*   253
b. Improvisations on *Othello*   256

Part I

Griboyedov's *Woe from Wit*

The following study in the preparation of a role, with a focus on Griboyedov's comic classic, *Woe from Wit*, was written between 1916 and 1920. It is thus Stanislavski's earliest known exploration of a theme that was to preoccupy him in its various aspects for the rest of his life. Although he had not yet settled on the semi-fictional form of *An Actor Prepares* and *Building a Character*, the student of those later works will find here the original statement of many ideas already familiar to him. In some cases, those ideas remained stable in subsequent years; in others, they underwent a subtle sea-change as Stanislavski continued to throw the light of his free and restless creative imagination on the actor's problem.

—EDITOR

CHAPTER ONE

The Period of Study

THE PREPARATORY WORK on a role can be divided into three great periods: studying it; establishing the life of the role; putting it into physical form.

First Acquaintance with a Part

Becoming acquainted with a part is a preparatory period in itself. It begins with one's very first impressions from the first reading of the play. This all-important moment can be likened to the first meeting between a man and a woman, the first acquaintanceship between two people who are destined to be sweethearts, lovers, or mates.

First impressions have a virginal freshness about them. They are the best possible stimuli to artistic enthusiasm and fervor, states which are of great significance in the creative process.

These first impressions are unexpected and direct. They often leave a permanent mark on the work of the actor. They are unpremeditated and unprejudiced. Unfiltered by any criticism, they pass freely into the depths of an actor's soul, into the wellsprings of his nature, and often leave ineradicable traces which will remain as a basis of a part, the embryo of an image to be formed.

First impressions are—seeds. Whatever variations and alterations an actor may make as he proceeds with his work, he often is so attracted by the deep effect of his first impressions that he yearns to hold on to them even when he finds he cannot apply them to his part as it develops. The power, depth, and permanence of these impressions is such that the actor must be particularly careful about his first acquaintance with a play.

In order to register these first impressions actors must be in a receptive frame of mind, a proper inner state. They must have the emotional concentration without which no creative process is possible. An actor must know how to prepare a mood to incite his artistic feelings, to open his soul. Moreover, the external circumstances for the first reading of a play should be properly set. One must know how to choose the time and place. The occasion should be accompanied with a certain ceremoniousness; if one is to invite one's soul to buoyancy, one must be spiritually and physically buoyant.

One of the most dangerous obstacles to the receiving of pure and fresh impressions is any kind of prejudice. Prejudices block up the soul like a cork in the neck of a bottle. Prejudice is created by the opinions that others foist upon us. In the beginning and until such time as the actor's own relationship to the play and his part is defined and set in concrete emotions or ideas, he is in danger of being influenced by the opinions of others, especially if they are false. Another's opinion can distort a naturally established relationship of an actor's emotions toward his new part. Therefore during his first acquaintance with a play, an actor should try not to come under outside influences that might create a prejudice and throw his own first impressions, as well as his will, his mind, and his imagination out of line.

If an actor is impelled to seek help to clarify the external and internal circumstances and conditions of life of the characters in the play, let him, to begin with, try to answer his questions himself; because only then can he sense what questions he can put to others without doing violence to his individual relation to his own part. Let the actor for the time being keep to himself, store up his emotions, his spiritual materials, his reflections about his part, until his feelings and a definite, concrete, creative sense of the image of his part have become crystallized. It is only with time, when an actor's own attitude toward his part has become established, has matured, that he can make wide use of outside advice and opinions without running the risk of infringing on his own artistic independence. Let an actor remember that his own opinion is better than that of an outsider, better even than an excellent one, if only because another's opinion can only add to his thoughts without appealing to his emotions.

Since, in the language of an actor, *to know* is synonymous with *to feel*, he should give free rein, at a first reading of a play, to his creative emotions. The more warmth of feeling and throbbing, living emotion he can put into a play at first acquaintance, the greater will be the appeal of the dry words of the text to his senses, his creative will, mind, emotion memory, the greater will be the suggestiveness of this first reading to the creative imagination of his visual, auditory, and other faculties, of images, pictures, sensation memories. The imagination of the actor adorns the text of the playwright with fanciful patterns and colors from his own invisible palette.

It is important for actors to find the angle of vision from which the playwright views his work. When this is achieved they are carried away by the reading. They cannot control the muscles of their faces, which oblige them to grimace or mime in accordance with what is being read. They cannot control their movements, which occur spontaneously. They cannot sit still, they push closer and closer to the person reading the play.

As for the reader who is presenting the play for the first time, there are a few practical suggestions which can be made to him.

In the first place he should avoid too illustrative a manner, which might force his personal interpretation of parts and images on the actors. Let him limit himself to a clear exposition of the basic idea of the play, the main line of the development of the inner action, with the help of such technical aids as are inherent in the play.

At the first reading the play should be presented simply, clearly, with understanding of its fundamentals, its essence, the main line of its development, and its literary merit. The reader should suggest the playwright's point of departure, the thought, the feelings, or experiences for the sake of which he wrote the play. At this first presentation the reader should push or lead each actor along the main line of the unfolding life of a human spirit in the play.

Let the reader learn from experienced literary people how to pick out at once the heart of a work, the fundamental line of the emotions. A person trained in literature, who has studied the basic qualities of literary works, can instantly grasp the structure of a play, its point of departure, the feelings and thoughts which impelled the playwright to put pen to paper. This capacity is very helpful to an actor, so long as it does not interfere with his seeing for himself into the soul of the play.

It is a great piece of good fortune when an actor can instantly grasp the play with his whole being, his mind and his feelings. In such happy but rare circumstances it is better to forget about all laws and methods, and give himself up to the power of creative nature. But these instances are so rare that one cannot count on them. They are as rare as the moments when an actor immediately grasps an important line of direction, a basic section of the play, important elements out of which its fundamentals are woven or shaped. It is much more usual for a first reading to leave only individual moments fixed in an actor's emotions while all the rest is vague, unclear, and extraneous. The snatches of impressions, bits of feelings, that do remain are like oases in a desert, or points of light in surrounding darkness.

Why is it that some parts of a play come to life, are warmed by our feelings, while others remain fixed only in our intellectual memory? Why is it that when we recall the former we have a sense of excitement, joy, tenderness, buoyancy, love, while the recollection of the latter leaves us without feeling, cold, and lacking in expression?

That happens because the places which are infused with immediate life are congenial to us, familiar to our emotions; whereas the dark places are alien to our natures.

Later on, as we become better acquainted with and feel closer to the play, which at first we accepted only in fragments, we shall find that the points of light grow and spread, coalescing with one another until finally they fill out our entire role. They are like the rays of the sun coming through a narrow chink in a blind, they throw only a few bright spots in the dark. But when the blinds are opened the whole room is flooded with light and the darkness is banished.

We seldom come to know a play from one reading. Often it has to be approached in different ways. There are plays whose spiritual essence is so deeply embedded that it takes great effort to dig it out. Perhaps its essential thought is so complex that it must be decoded. Or the structure is so confused and intangible that we only come to know it bit by bit, by studying its anatomy piecemeal. You approach such a play as you do a puzzle, and it does not offer much interest until it is solved. It must be read over and over, and with each additional reading we must guide ourselves by what was established the time before.

Unfortunately, many actors do not realize the importance of their first impressions. Many do not take them seriously enough. They approach this stage in their work carelessly and do not consider it part of the creative process. How many of us make serious preparation for the first reading of a play? We read it hurriedly, wherever we happen to be, in a railroad train, in a cab, during intermissions, and we do it not so much because we want to come to know the play but because we want to imagine ourselves in some fat part or other. Under such circumstances we lose an important creative occasion—an irreparable loss, because later readings are deprived of the element of surprise which is so essential to our creative intuition. You cannot erase a spoiled first impression any more than you can recover lost maidenhood.

Analysis

The second step in this great preparatory period is the *process of analysis*. Through analysis the actor becomes further acquainted with his role. Analysis is also a method of becoming familiar with the whole play through a study of its parts. Like a person engaged in restoration, analysis guesses at the whole by bringing various segments of it to life.

The word "analysis" usually connotes an intellectual process. It is used in literary, philosophical, historical, and other types of research. But in art any *intellectual* analysis, if undertaken by itself and for its own sake, is harmful because its mathematical, dry qualities tend to chill an impulse of artistic élan and creative enthusiasm.

In art it is the feeling that creates, not the mind; the main role and the initiative in art belong to feeling. Here the role of the mind is purely auxilliary, subordinate. The analysis made by an artist is quite different from one made by a scholar or a critic. If the result of a scholarly analysis is *thought*, the result of an artistic analysis is *feeling*. An actor's analysis is first of all an analysis of feeling, and it is carried out by feeling.

This role of knowledge through feeling, or analysis, is all the more important in the creative process because only with its aid can one penetrate the realm of the subconscious, which constitutes nine-tenths of the life of a person or a character, its most valuable part. In contrast with the nine-tenths that the actor uses through his creative intuition, his artistic instinct, his supersensory flair, only one-tenth remains for the mind.

The creative purposes of an analysis are:

1. The study of the playwright's work.

2. The search for spiritual or other material for use in creative work, whatever the play and one's own part in it contain.

3. The search for the same kind of material in the actor himself

8

(self-analysis). The material considered here consists of living, personal memories related to the five senses, which have been stored up in an actor's emotion memory, or acquired through study and preserved in his intellectual memory, and which are analogous to feelings in his role.

4. The preparation in an actor's soul for the conception of creative emotions—both conscious and especially unconscious feelings.

5. The search for creative stimuli that will provide ever new impulses of excitement, ever new bits of live material for the spirit of a role in the places that did not immediately come to life in the first acquaintance with the play.

* * *

Pushkin asks of the dramatist, and we ask of the actor, that he possess "sincerity of emotions, feelings that seem true in given circumstances." Therefore, the purpose of analysis should be to study in detail and prepare *given circumstances* for a play or part so that through them, later on in the creative process, the actor's emotions will instinctively be sincere and his feelings true to life.

What is the point of departure for an analysis?

Let us make use of the one-tenth part of ourselves which in art as in life is attributed to the mind, so that with its aid we can appeal to the work of our feelings, and after that, when our feelings reach the point of expression, let us try to understand their direction and unobtrusively guide them along the true creative path. In other words, let our unconscious, intuitive creativeness be set into motion by the help of conscious, preparatory work. Through the conscious to the unconscious—that is the motto of our art and technique.

How do we use the mind in this creative process? We reason this way: The first friend and best stimulant for intuitive emotion is *artistic enthusiasm, ardor*. Let it then be the first means used in analysis. Ardor can penetrate to what is not accessible to sight, sound, consciousness, or even the most refined awareness of art. An analysis made by means of artistic enthusiasm and ardor acts as the best means to search out *creative stimuli* in a play, and they in turn provoke an actor's creativeness. As an actor is enthused he comes to understand a part, as he understands it he is even more enthused; the one evokes and reinforces the other.

Artistic ardor is at its most expansive at the time of first acquaintance with a play. That is why an actor should repeatedly enjoy and relish the places in his role that aroused his enthusiasm at the first reading, the things that struck him and to which he felt his emotions respond from the outset. An actor's nature is responsive to everything that possesses artistic beauty, elevation, emotion, interest, gaiety; he is instantly transported by the playwright's flashes of talent, scattered either on the surface or in the depths of the play. All these places have the explosive quality that arouses artistic ardor.

But what is the actor to do about the portions of the play which did not evoke the miracle of instant intuitive comprehension? All such portions must then be studied to disclose what materials they possess to incite him to ardor. Now, since our emotions are silent, we have no recourse except to turn to the nearest aid and adviser of the emotions—the mind. Let it be a scout, to hunt through the play in all directions. Let it be a pioneer, cutting new paths for our principal creative forces, our intuitions and feelings. In their turn, let our feelings seek out fresh stimulants to enthusiasm, let them call on intuition to search out and find more and more new bits of live material, parts of the spiritual life of the role, things which are not reached by conscious means.

The more detailed, varied, and profound an actor makes this analysis by the mind, the greater his chances of finding stimulants for his enthusiasm and spiritual material for unconscious creativeness.

When you look for something you have lost, more often than not you find it in an unexpected place. The same is true with creativeness. You must send your scouting mind off in all directions. You must search everywhere for creative stimuli, leaving it to your feelings and their intuition to choose whatever is most appropriate for their enterprise.

In the process of analysis searches are made, as it were, in the width, length, and depth of a play and its roles, its separate portions, its component strata, all its planes beginning with the external, more obvious ones, and ending with the innermost, profoundest spiritual levels. For this purpose one must dissect a play and its roles. One must plumb its depths, layer by layer, get down to its essence, dismember it, examine each portion separately, go over all parts that were not carefully studied before, find the stimuli to creative ardor, plant, so to say, the seed in an actor's heart.

*   *   *

A play and its roles have many planes, along which their life flows. First there is the *external plane* of facts, events, plot, form. This is contiguous with the *plane of social situation*, subdivided into class, nationality, and historic setting. There is a *literary plane*, with its ideas, its style, and other aspects. There is an *aesthetic plane*, with the sublayers of all that is theatrical, artistic, having to do with scenery and production. There is the *psychological plane* of inner action, feelings, inner characterization; and the *physical plane* with its fundamental laws of physical nature, physical objectives and actions, external characterization. And finally there is the plane of *personal creative feelings* belonging to the actor.

Not all of these planes are of equal significance. Some of them are basic in creating a life and a soul for a part, while others are subordinate, providing characterization and additional material for the body and spirit of the image to be created.

Nor are all of these planes immediately accessible; many of

them have to be searched out, one by one. Eventually all of the planes coalesce in our creative feelings and presentation, and then they provide for us not only an external form but also an inner spiritual configuration of part and play, containing all that is accessible and also inaccessible to our conscious approach.

The conscious levels of a play or part are like the levels and strata of the earth, sand, clay, rocks, and so forth, which go to form the earth's crust. As the levels go deeper down into one's soul they become increasingly unconscious, and down in the very depths, in the core of the earth where you find molten lava and fire, invisible human instincts and passions are raging. That is the realm of the superconscious, that is the lifegiving center, that is the sacrosanct "I" of the actor, the artist-human, that is the secret source of inspiration. You are not conscious of these things but you feel them with your whole being.

Studying the External Circumstances

Thus the line of an analysis takes its point of departure from the external form of the play, from the printed text of the playwright, which is accessible to our consciousness, and it goes from there to the inner spiritual essence of the play, that invisible something which the playwright put inside his work, and which is largely accessible only to our subconscious. So we go from the periphery to the center, from the external literal form of the play to its spiritual essence. In this way we come to know (feel) the circumstances proposed by the playwright in order, later on, to feel (know) sincere emotions or at least feelings that appear to be true.

I begin my analysis with the *externals of a play* and take up the verbal text in order to draw from it, in the first instance, the external circumstances suggested by the playwright. At the start of my analysis, I am not interested in feelings—they are intangible and

difficult to define—but in the circumstances, suggested by the playwright, that can give rise to feelings.

Among the external circumstances of life in a play the easiest
to study is the plane of facts. When the playwright created his
work, every tiniest circumstance, every fact, was important. Each
was a necessary link in the unbroken chain of the life of the play.
Yet we are far from grasping all the facts at once. The facts which
we do comprehend in their essence, and at once, etch themselves
intuitively on our memory. Others which we do not sense at once,
which are not discovered or corroborated by our feelings, remain
unnoticed, unappreciated, forgotten, or hang in the air, each one
separately, a burden on the play. We become confused by them
and can find no truth of living reality in them. All this interferes
with our receiving and absorbing our first impressions of the play.

What is one to do in such cases? How can one find one's way
around in the external factors of a play? Nemirovich-Danchenko
has offered an extremely simple and intelligent device. It consists
of retelling the contents of the play. Let the actor learn by heart
and write down the existing facts, their sequence, and their external physical connection with one another. In the stage of early
acquaintance with the play, one is not able to retell its contents
much better than it is done in the advertisements or the condensed
librettos. But with growing experience of the play and its contents
this method helps not only to pick out the facts and orient oneself
in relation to them but also to get at that inner substance, their
interrelationships and interdependence.

As an example, I shall try to do this with Russia's most popular
play, Griboyedov's *Woe from Wit*.

[EDITOR'S NOTE: *The principal characters in this classic verse-play
are:* FAMUSOV, *a wealthy land- and serf-owner, not of the high
aristocracy. He has a large house in Moscow, where the scene of
the play is laid in the 1820's. He is the father of* SOPHIA, *a young
girl brought up on European literature, especially sentimental*

and romantic novels. She likes to have men in love with her and is flattered by the courtship of her childhood friend CHATSKI. *But while he is away abroad she discovers that the adoration of her father's secretary* MOLCHALIN *is much more slavish than that of the independent Chatski. She encourages Molchalin's attentions. They have just spent the night together playing duets and reciting poetry when the play opens.* LIZA *is Sophia's confidential maid, a peasant and a household serf. Famusov pesters her with his attentions, but she is in love with the footman* PETRUSHKA. *Molchalin, a yes-man in love with Sophia, toadies to anyone farther up in the social scale than he is. Though anxious to keep in Famusov's good graces, he eventually insults Sophia and is dismissed by Famusov. He is a milksop and foil to Chatski, a handsome, brilliant, educated man who was almost like a brother to Sophia before he went abroad. As soon as he returns he comes to call on her, only to find that she has now grown up and he is in love with her. She receives him coolly and he is revolted to find that she prefers the insignificant Molchalin to him. He is further indignant at the superficiality of the culture he finds in Moscow. He feels that Sophia has been corrupted by all this. His biting denunciation of Moscow society results in Sophia's starting the rumor that he is insane. At the end of the play he leaves the country once more.* PRINCESS MARIA ALEXEYEVNA, *the eldest of the family, is the arbiter of Moscow conservative society manners and traditional spirit. The phrase that ends* Woe from Wit—*"What will Maria Alexeyevna say?"—became a household word in Russia.* SKALOZUB *is an army man whom Famusov favors as a prospective son-in-law. He is very rich and of good family, is likely to reach the highest rank in the army; but he is gruff and military in manner, of limited intelligence, and is scorned by Sophia.*]

Here are the facts of the first act:

1. A meeting between Sophia and Molchalin has continued all night.

2. It is dawn. They are playing a duet of flute and piano in the next room.

3. Liza, the maid, is asleep. She is supposed to be keeping watch.

4. Liza wakes up, sees that day is breaking, begs the lovers to separate quickly.

5. Liza sets the clock ahead to frighten the lovers and turn their attention to danger.

6. As the clock strikes, Sophia's father, Famusov, enters.

7. He sees Liza, flirts with her.

8. Liza cleverly evades his attention and persuades him to go away.

9. At the noise Sophia enters. She sees the dawn and is astonished at how quickly her night of love has passed.

10. The lovers have not had time to separate before Famusov confronts them.

11. Astonishment, questions, angry uproar.

12. Sophia cleverly extricates herself from embarrassment and danger.

13. Her father releases her, while he goes off with Molchalin to sign some papers.

14. Liza upbraids Sophia and Sophia is depressed by the prose of daytime after the poetry of her nighttime meeting.

15. Liza tries to remind Sophia of her childhood friend Chatski, who apparently is in love with Sophia.

16. This angers Sophia and causes her to think all the more about Molchalin.

17. The unexpected arrival of Chatski, his enthusiasm, their meeting. Sophia's embarrassment, a kiss. Chatski's bewilderment, he accuses her of coldness. They speak of old times. Chatski is witty in his friendly chatter. He makes a declaration of love to Sophia. Sophia is caustic.

18. Famusov returns. He is astonished. His meeting with Chatski.

19. Exit Sophia. She makes a sly remark about being out of her father's sight.

20. Famusov cross-examines Chatski. His suspicions about Chatski's intentions with regard to Sophia.

21. Chatski is lyrical in praise of Sophia. He leaves abruptly.

22. The father's bewilderment and suspicions.

There you have a list of the facts in the first act. If you use that as a pattern to write down the facts of the following acts you would have a catalogue of the external life of the Famusov household on a given day.

All these facts taken together give the *present tense of the play*.

There can be no present, however, without a past. The present flows naturally out of the past. The past is the roots from which the present grew; the present without any past wilts like a plant with its roots cut off. An actor must always feel that he has the *past* of his role behind him, like the train of a costume he carries along.

Neither is there a present without a *prospect of the future*, dreams of it, guesses and hints about it.

The present deprived of past and future is like a middle without beginning or end, one chapter of a book, accidentally torn out and read. The past and the dreams about the future make up the present. An actor should always have before him thoughts about the future which excite his ardor and which are at the same time compatible with the dreams of the character he is portraying. These dreams about the future should beckon to the actor, should lead him on through all his actions on the stage. He must choose from the play hints, dreams, of the future.

A direct connection between the present tense of a role with its past and future gives bulk to the inner life of a character to be portrayed. If he supports himself with the past and the future of his role, an actor will be able to appreciate its present with greater power.

Often the facts of a play derive from a way and kind of life, a

16

social situation; therefore it is not difficult to push down from them into a deeper level of existence. At the same time the circumstances which make up a way of life must be studied not only in the actual text but also in a variety of commentaries, pieces of literature, historical writings concerning the period, and so forth.

Thus in *Woe from Wit,* on the *social level,* here is a list of facts that need study:

1. The rendezvous between Sophia and Molchalin. What does it show? How did it come about? Is it due to the influence of French education and books? Sentimentality, languor, tenderness, and purity on the part of a young girl; yet at the same time, her laxity of morals.

2. Liza watches over Sophia. You must understand the danger which threatens Liza: She could be sent to Siberia or demoted to farm work. You must understand Liza's devotion.

3. Famusov flirts with Liza at the same time that he poses as being monk-like in behavior. This is an example of a Pharisee of those times.

4. Famusov is afraid of any misalliance; there is Princess Maria Alexeyevna to be considered. What is the position of Maria Alexeyevna? Her family are afraid of her criticism. One can lose one's good name, prestige, and even one's place.

5. Liza favors Chatski; she will be ridiculed if Sophia marries Molchalin.

6. Chatski arrives from abroad. What does it mean to come home in those days, traveling by coaches with relays of horses?

As we probe deeper into a play we come to the *literary plane.* It is not something we can grasp at once; that comes with further study. To begin with, however, we can appreciate, in general terms, the form, style of writing, the formulation in words, the verse. We can appreciate, for example, the beauty of Griboyedov's language, the lightness of his verse, the sharpness of his rhythm, the aptness of his words.

We can dissect a play into its component parts, in order to

understand its structure, to admire the harmony and combination of its various parts, its elegance, smoothness, logic of development, the scenic quality of its action, the inventiveness of exposition, the characterization of the dramatis personae, their pasts, the hints at their future.

We can appreciate the originality of the playwright in contriving motives, reasons for precipitating actions, which in turn reveal the inner essence and human spirit in the play. We can contrast and evaluate the outer form in relation to the inner content of the play.

Digging down still further we come to the *aesthetic plane*, with the sublayers of all that is theatrical, artistic, having to do with scenery and the production, whatever is plastic, musical. You can discover and make a note of whatever the playwright tells you about the scene, the setting, the position of rooms, architecture, lighting, groupings, gestures, manners. Moreover you can hear what the director of the play and the scene designer say on the subject. You can look at the various materials collected for use in the production, and participate in the gathering of these materials by accompanying the director and the scene designer to museums, picture galleries, old private homes of the period. And finally you can look through the diaries and engravings of the period. In other words you yourself can study the play in relation to its artistic, plastic, architectural, and other factors.

All the notes you have taken on the external circumstances constitute a great bulk of material, which will be grist to your forthcoming creative work.

Putting Life into External Circumstances

So far, we have merely established the existence of certain facts. Now it is necessary to find out what underlies them, gave rise to them, is hidden behind them. We have accumulated material on the external circumstances of a play by rather extended intellectual analysis. Up to now it has consisted of little more than the listing of facts—past, present, and future—excerpts from the text of the play, commentaries, really just a *record of the given circumstances of the life in the play and its parts*. In any such intellectual study, the events of a play lack living, authentic meaning; they remain inert, merely theatrical actions. With any such purely external attitude toward the given circumstances of a play it would be impossible to react with "sincere emotions" or "feelings that seem true to life."

In order to mold this dry material to creative purposes, we must give it spiritual life and content, the theatrical facts and circumstances must be transformed from dead factors into live and life-giving ones; our attitude toward them must be shifted from the *theatrical* to the *human*. The dry record of facts and events must be infused with the spirit of life, because only that which is living can generate life. Thus we must recreate in living form the circumstances proposed by the playwright.

This transformation is accomplished by the help of one of the principal creative forces in our art, *artistic imagination*. At this point our work is lifted from the plane of reason into the sphere of artistic dreams.

Every human being lives a factual everyday life, but he can also live the life of his imagination. The nature of an actor is such that often this life of imagination is much the more agreeable and interesting one. An actor's imagination can draw to itself the life of another person, adapt it, discover mutual and exciting qualities and features. It knows how to create a make-believe existence to its own taste, therefore close to the heart of the actor, a life that thrills him, one that is beautiful, full of inner meaning especially for him, a life closely akin to his own nature.

This imaginary life is created at will by the help of the actor's own desire and in proportion to the creative intensity of the spiritual material he possesses or has accumulated in himself; it is therefore close to and cherished by him because it is not taken casually from the outside. It is never in conflict with his inner desires nor the result of any evil blow of fate, as often happens in real life. All this makes his imaginary life much more attractive to the actor than everyday reality; it is not surprising therefore that his dream arouses a genuinely ardent response in his creative nature.

An actor must love dreams and know how to use them. This is one of the most important creative faculties. Without imagination there can be no creativeness. A role that has not passed through the sphere of artistic imagination can never become engaging. An actor must know how to use his fancy on all sorts of themes. He must know how to create in his imagination a true life out of any given materials. Like a child, he must know how to play with any toy and find pleasure in his game. An actor is completely free in creating his dream, as long as it does not stray too far from the playwright's basic thought and theme.

There are various aspects of the life of the imagination and its artistic functioning. We can use our inner eye to see all sorts of visual images, living creatures, human faces, their features, landscapes, the material world of objects, settings, and so forth. With our inner ear we can hear all sorts of melodies, voices, intonations, and so forth. We can feel things in imagination at the prompting of our sensation and emotion memory.

There are actors of things seen and actors of things heard. The first are gifted with an especially fine inner vision and the second with sensitive inner hearing. For the first type, to which I myself belong, the easiest way to create an imaginary life is with the help of visual images. For the second type it is the image of sound that helps.

We can cherish all these visual, audible, or other images; we can enjoy them passively from the sidelines, without feeling any impulse to direct action; in a phrase, with *passive imagining*, we can be the audience of our own dreams. Or we can take an active part in those dreams by *active imagining*.

I shall begin with passive imagining. With my inner eye I shall try to visualize Pavel Famusov, at the point where he first appears in *Woe from Wit*. The material I amassed in my analysis of facts about the architecture and furnishings of the 1820's now comes into use.

Any actor who has powers of observation and a memory for impressions received (alas for the actor who does not have these qualities!), any actor who has seen, studied, read, traveled extensively (alas for the actor who has not done this!) can put together in his own imagination, let us say, the house in which Famusov lived. We Russians, especially those of us who come from Moscow, know such houses—if not as whole buildings, at least in part—as remnants of the times of our ancestors.

In one of these old private houses in Moscow let us suppose we have seen a vestibule with the front staircase of the epoch. In another we may remember having seen columns. In a third we retain the image of a Chinese whatnot, an engraving, say of an interior in the 1820's, an armchair in which Famusov might have sat. Many of us may still possess old pieces of handwork, a bit of material embroidered with beads and silk. As we look at it admiringly we think of Sophia: Could she perhaps have embroidered some such thing down in the country, where she was obliged to "languish, to sit with her embroidery frame and yawn at the church calendar"?

All our memories, gathered during the analysis of the play and at various other times and places, memories of real or imaginary life, all come back to us at our summons and take up their places, restoring for us a lordly old private house of the 1820's.

After several sessions of this kind of work we can mentally erect an entire house, and having built it, we can study it, admire its architecture, examine the arrangement of the rooms. As we do this the imaginary objects take their places and gradually the whole place acquires the atmosphere of something dear, familiar; everything comes together to form unconsciously an inner life of the house. If anything in this imaginary life does not seem right, if it is a cause of boredom, we can instantly reconstruct a new house, or remodel the old one, or simply repair it. The life of the imagination has the advantage of knowing no obstacles, no delays; it does not recognize the impossible. Anything that pleases it is available; whatever it desires is instantly executed.

By passively admiring this house several times a day the actor comes to be familiar with it down to its last detail. Habit, which is our second nature, does the rest.

However, an empty house is a bore; we must have people inside it. Imagination will attempt to create them too. First of all the setting itself tends to produce people. The world of things often reflects the soul of those who created this world—the inhabitants of the house.

To be sure, our imagination does not at once produce these people, or even their personal appearance; all it does is show their costumes, perhaps the way they wear their hair. With our inner vision we see how they move around in the costumes even though they have as yet no faces. Sometimes we fill in the blank with a vague sketch.

Yet, as I watch, one of the footmen comes out with extraordinary sharpness. With my inner eye I clearly see his face, eyes, manners. Can it be the footman Petrushka? Nonsense, it is that jolly sailor I once saw sailing out of the harbor of Novorossiisk. How did he get here, into the house of Famusov? Extraordinary! Will there be other such amazing events in the imagination of an actor?

Other characters are still lacking in personality, individual peculiarities, and qualities. Their social position and place in life is only vaguely reflected in general terms: a father, mother, lady of the house, daughter, son, governess, houseman, footman, maid servant, and so forth. Nevertheless these shades of people fill out the picture of the house, they help to convey a general mood, lend atmosphere, although for the time being they are merely accessories.

In order to look more closely at the life of the house, I must open a door slightly into one or another of the rooms; I must enter one of the halves of the house, going into, shall we say, the dining room and its dependencies: down the corridor, through the pantry, into the kitchen, up the stairs. Around dinner time, I see the maids, who have removed their shoes in order not to mar the master's floors, running in all directions with plates and dishes. I see the butler's costume, even though he has no face, as he importantly receives dishes from an underling, tasting them with all the airs of a gourmet before taking them in and serving them to the master. I see the costumes of the footmen and scullery boys darting along the corridor, on the stairs. One of them may snatch a hug, just for fun, from one of the passing maids.

Then I see the living costumes of guests, poor relations, godchildren who come to call. They are taken in to bow to Famusov in his study, to kiss the hand of their benefactor. The children recite verses they have learned for the occasion and their benefactor-godfather distributes sweets and gifts. Then everyone gathers again for tea in the corner or green room. Still later when they have all gone home and the house is quiet once more I see the lamps being carried into all the rooms on a large tray; I hear the scraping noises as they are turned up ready to light, I hear the servants bring in stepladders to climb up and put oil lamps in the chandeliers.

Now the silence of night falls; I hear slippered feet in the hall. Someone slips by and all is dark and silent. Only from a distance, now and then, comes the call of a watchman, the crunching noise of a late arrival in a carriage. . . .

So far the life of the Famusov household has developed only as far as its external habits and ways are concerned. To give an inner spirit and thought to the life of the house one must have human beings, yet in addition to myself and the surprising phenomenon of Petrushka there is not a living soul in all the household. In a concerted effort to put life into the costumes as they are moved about by people I try to imagine myself in them. This device works well enough for me. I see myself in the hairdress and costume of the times walking through the house, in the vestibule, the ballroom, the living room, the study; I see myself seated at the dinner table next to the enlivened costume of the lady of the house, and I am delighted to be put in a place of such honor; or when I see I have been put way down at the foot of the table beside the costume of Molchalin I am upset at having been thus demoted.

In this way I acquire a feeling of sympathy for the people of my imagination. That is a good sign. Of course, sympathy is not feeling; nevertheless, it is a step in that direction.

Encouraged by my experiment I try to imagine my head on the shoulders of the costumes of Famusov and others. I try to recall myself as a young man and I put my youthful head on the shoulders of Chatski's costume, and Molchalin's, and to a certain degree, I enjoy success. I apply make-up, mentally, and adapt it to a variety of characters in the play, trying to visualize them as the inhabitants of this house introduced to me by the playwright. But although I succeed somewhat with this, it does not offer me any substantial help. Later on I recall a whole gallery of faces of living people with whom I am acquainted. I look at all kinds of pictures, engravings, photographs. I make the same kind of experiment with heads of people living and dead, but they all end in failure.

This unsuccessful experiment with other people's heads persuades me that this is a fruitless kind of work. I have come to realize that the point of my work is not to be able to visualize make-ups, costumes, the external appearance of the inmates of the Famusov household from the point of view of a passive observer, but to feel that they are actually present, feel them right beside me. It is not sight and sound but the sense of nearness of an object that helps to make us feel existing reality. More than that I realize that I cannot achieve this sense of nearness, really feel it, by digging in the text of the play while sitting at my desk; it is necessary to make a mental picture of Famusov's personal relationship to the people of his family.

How can I accomplish this shift? It also is done with the help of imagination—but this time, the imagination plays an *active* rather than a passive role.

You can be the observer of your dream, but you can also take an active part in it—that is you can find yourself mentally in the center of circumstances and conditions, a way of life, furnishings, objects, and so forth, which you have imagined. You no longer see yourself as an outside onlooker, but you see what surrounds you. In time, when this feeling of "being" is reinforced, you can become the main active personality in the surrounding circumstances of your dream; you can begin, mentally, to act, have desires, make an effort, achieve a goal.

This is the active aspect of imagination.

Creating Inner Circumstances

The creation of the inner circumstances of the life of a play is a continuation of the general process of analysis and infusing life in the material already accumulated. Now the process goes deeper, it goes down from the realm of the external, the intellectual, into that of the inner, spiritual life. And this is brought about with the help of an actor's creative emotions.

The difficulty of this aspect of emotional perception is that the actor is now coming to his part not through the text, the words of his role, nor by intellectual analysis or other conscious means of knowledge, but through his own sensations, his own real emotions, his personal life experience.

To do this he must set himself at the very center of the household, he must be there in person, not seeing himself as an observer, as I was doing earlier; his imagination must be active, not passive as before. This is a difficult and important psychological moment in the whole period of preparation. It requires exceptional attention. This moment is what we in actor's jargon call the state of "I am," it is the point where I begin to feel myself in the thick of things, where I begin to coalesce with all the circumstances suggested by the playwright and by the actor, begin to have the right to be part of them. This right is not won immediately, it is achieved gradually.

At this stage in the preparation of *Woe from Wit*, for example, I try to transfer myself from the place of observer to that of active participant, a member of the Famusov family. I cannot pretend that I can accomplish this at once. What I can do is to shift my attention from myself to what is surrounding me. I begin again to go through the house. Now I am entering the doorway, going up the staircase, I have opened the door to the row of living rooms; now I am in the reception room, I push a door open into an antechamber. Someone has blocked the door with a heavy armchair which I push aside to walk on into the ballroom.

But enough of that! Why fool myself? What I am feeling as I take this walk is not the result of active imagining or a real sense of being in the situation. It is nothing more than self-deception. I am only forcing myself to have emotions, forcing myself to feel I am living something or other. Most actors make this mistake. They only imagine they are alive in a situation, they do not really feel it. One must be extraordinarily strict with oneself in this matter of feeling "I am" on the stage. There is a vast difference between the true feeling of the life of the part and some accidentally imagined emotions. It is dangerous to be trapped by such false illusions; they tend to mislead the actor into forced and mechanical acting.

Nevertheless, in the course of my fruitless walk through Famusov's house there has been one instant when I really felt that I was there and believed in my own feelings. This was when I opened the door into the antechamber and pushed aside a large armchair; I really felt the physical effort entailed in this act. It lasted for several seconds; I felt the truth of my being there. It was dissipated as soon as I walked away from the armchair and I was again walking in space, amid undefined objects.

This experience teaches me the exceptional importance of the part played by an *object* in helping me to get into the state of "I am."

I repeat my experiments with other inanimate objects. Mentally I change about all the furniture in various rooms, I carry objects back and forth, I dust them, examine them. Encouraged, I push the test a step farther; I now come into closer contact with animate objects. With whom? With Petrushka, of course, since he is so far the only living personality in this house of phantoms and moving costumes. So we meet, let us say, in the dimly lighted corridor near the staircase leading to the upper floor and the girls' quarters.

"Perhaps he is waiting for Liza?" I think, as I jokingly wag my finger at him.

He smiles a pleasant, engaging smile. At this moment I not only feel his actual presence among all the imagined circumstances but I also feel keenly that the world of things has, as it were, come to life. The walls, the air, things are bathed in a living light. Something true has been created and I believe in it, and as a result my feeling of "I am" is further strengthened. At the same time I am aware of a kind of creative joy. It turns out that a live object is a force in creating the sense of being. It is quite clear to me that this situation has not created itself directly, but through my feeling concerning an object, especially a live one.

The more I experiment with creating people mentally, meeting them, feeling their nearness, their actuality, the more I become convinced that in order to reach the state of "I am," the external, physical image (the vision of a head, body, manners, of a person) is not so important as its inner image, the tenor of its inner being.

I also come to realize that in any interchange with other people it is important not only to know their psychology but also to know one's own.

That is why my meeting with Petrushka was successful. I sensed what he was like inside; I could see his inner image. I recognized the sailor in the image of Petrushka not because of any external likeness but because of what I imagined his inner nature was like. I would like to say about the sailor what Liza said about Petrushka: "How could one not fall in love with him!"

The next question is how to use one's own life experience to feel what the life of all the other inmates of the Famusov household is like, and especially to establish one's own relationship to them. That, it would seem, is a complex task; to accomplish it would be almost the same as creating a whole play. My intentions do not go that far. They are much simpler in scale. It will be sufficient to find living souls among the phantoms in the house of Famusov. There is no need for them to be exactly the creatures intended by Griboyedov. Yet since I believe that my own feelings, my imagination, and my whole artistic nature will be influenced by the work already done, I am convinced that these living objects will, if only partially, have some of the traits which should animate Griboyedov's characters.

In order to train myself in meeting these live objects, I undertake a whole series of imaginary visits to the members of the Famusov household, family, and friends. I am now prepared to knock at any door in the house for permission to enter.

Under the fresh impact of having just read the play I naturally wish to call, first of all, on the inmates of the Famusov household with whom the author has acquainted me. I wish to see especially the head of the house, Pavel Famusov himself, then the young lady of the house, Sophia, then Liza, Molchalin, and so forth. I go down the familiar corridor, trying not to stumble over anything in the dim light; I count off the doors to the third on the right. I knock and cautiously open the door.

Thanks to acquired habit I am quick to believe in what I am doing, in my actually being there. I enter Famusov's room and what do I see? In the middle of the room stands the head of the house dressed in his nightshirt and singing a Lenten song, "Oh, my prayer is to become a better boy," and all the while making the gestures of a choir master. In front of him stands a small boy whose face is contorted with fruitless efforts at understanding. He squeaks in a thin, childish treble, trying to catch and retain the words of the prayer. There are traces of tears in his eyes. I take a seat off to one side of the room. The old man is not in the least embarrassed by his semi-nude state, and continues to sing. I hear him with my inner ear and seem to sense his physical nearness. However the physical sense is not enough, I must try to feel his soul.

Since this cannot be done in a physical way, I must use other avenues of approach. After all, people commune with each other not just by means of words and gestures but mainly through the invisible radiations of will, vibrations which flow back and forth between two souls. Feeling finds out feeling, as one soul does another. There is no other way. To try to get at the soul of my living object I must find out its quality and, above all, my relationship to it.

I attempt to direct the rays of my will or feelings, a part of my own self, toward him and to take back a part of his soul. In other words I am doing an exercise in giving out and receiving rays. Yet what can I take from or give him, when Famusov himself does not as yet exist for me, is still without soul? Yes, he does not exist, that is true, but I know his position as head of the household, I know his kind, his social group, even if I do not know him as an individual. This is where my personal experience helps me; it reminds me that judged by his external appearance, manners, habits, his childlike seriousness, his deep faith, his reverence for sacred music, he must be a familiar type of good-natured, amusing, stubborn eccentric, who includes in his make-up the barbarous fact of being a serf-owner.

Even though this may not help me to penetrate to the soul of a person and understand it, it nevertheless enables me to find inside myself the correct attitude toward Famusov. Now I know how to take his sallies and acts. For a while these observations engross me, but then they begin to pall. My attention wanders, I take myself in hand and concentrate again, but soon I am off woolgathering and my thoughts leave Famusov, I have nothing more to do with him. Nonetheless, I consider this experiment somewhat successful, and being thus encouraged I go on to Sophia.

I run into her in the vestibule. She is all dressed up and is hurriedly putting on a fur coat to go out. Liza is fluttering around her, helping to button up her coat, and running around with all the little packages that a young lady is likely to take with her. Sophia herself is prinking in front of a mirror. The father has gone to his office in the ministry—so I have reasoned—and the daughter is hurrying downtown to the French stores to look at "hats, bonnets, needles, and pins," to "book and cake shops," and perhaps "on other errands."

This time the result is the same: My object of attention gives me a lively feeling of "being"; yet I cannot retain it for long, my thoughts are soon distracted. I concentrate again and then in the end, having nothing to do, I leave Sophia and go off to Molchalin.

As long as he is writing, at my request, the list of relatives and friends of Famusov on whom I plan to call, I feel at ease. I am entertained by the florid penmanship with which Molchalin forms his letters. But when he has finished I am bored and set off to make my calls. . . .

All you have to do is to imagine you have left home and the curiosity of your artistic nature will know no bounds. Everywhere I go on my imaginary visits I feel the presence of animated objects and am able to communicate with them if there is any basis for it; and each time, this reinforces my sense of being. But unfortunately each new acquaintance holds my attention only briefly. Why is that? It is easy to understand: All of these meetings lack purpose. They are created as exercises and to feel the physical presence of the objects chosen. This feeling has been acquired for its own sake, and one cannot be interested for long in mere physical sensation. It would be quite different if these visits had a purpose, even an external one. So I repeat my experiments, after first formulating a definite purpose. I go into the ballroom and I say to myself: The marriage of Sophia and Skalozub will soon take place and I have been commissioned to get up a great wedding breakfast for a hundred guests. What is the best way to arrange the silver, the tables, and so forth?

This brings all sorts of considerations to mind: For instance, the colonel of Skalozub's regiment and perhaps his whole staff will be present at the wedding. They will have to be seated by rank so that no one will be offended by not being as near as possible to the place of honor, nearest to the bride and groom. The same problem applies to relatives. They may be all too easily offended. Having collected so many honored guests I am in a quandary as I do not have enough places for them. How about putting the bridal couple in the center and radiating the other tables from there in all directions? That would automatically increase the number of places of honor.

And the more places one has, the easier it is to seat people according to rank. I am preoccupied for a long time with this problem, and when it begins to lose interest something else is ready to take its place—the preparation of the food, this time for Sophia's wedding not with Skalozub but with Molchalin.

That changes everything! Marrying her father's secretary would be a misalliance, the wedding would be much quieter, only the immediate family would come, and indeed not all of them would be willing to grace the occasion. There would be no colonel since Molchalin's chief is Famusov himself.

New combinations ferment inside me, and I no longer think

about the closeness of the objectives, or about being in communication with my object. I am in *action!* My head, my feelings, will, imagination all are as busily at work as if this were all happening in real life. Encouraged by my experiment I decide to try one more, this time not with inanimate objects but with living ones.

To do this I go once more to Famusov's. He is still teaching the boy to sing a hymn and is still conducting the music dressed only in his nightshirt.

I decide to aggravate this old eccentric. I enter, I sit down at the other end of the room, I draw my bead, as it were, on him and seek a pretext to argue in order to tease the old gentleman.

"What is that you are singing?" I ask.

But Famusov does not deign to reply, perhaps because he has not reached the end of the prayer. Finally he finishes.

"A very nice melody," I announce calmly.

"That was not a melody, but a sacred prayer," he replies with emphasis.

"Oh, excuse me, I had forgotten! . . . When is it sung?"

"If you went to church, you'd know."

The old man is already annoyed, but that only amuses me and incites me to bait him further.

"I'd go except that I can't stand for so long," I say mildly. "Besides it's so hot there!"

"Hot?" retorts the old gentleman. "What about Gehenna? Isn't it hot there?"

"That's different," I reply with even greater mildness.

"How so?" demands Famusov, taking a step in my direction.

"Because in Gehenna you can walk around without clothes, just as God made you," I say with pretended stupidity, "and you can lie around, and steam yourself as in a Russian bath; but in church they make you stand and sweat in your fur coat."

"Oh you . . . you're a terrible sinner," and the old gentleman hurries off lest he "rock the foundations" by laughing.

This new work seems to me so important that I decide to confirm it. I again set off to make a round of calls, but this time I have the definite purpose in mind of announcing to the relatives and friends of Famusov the forthcoming marriage of Sophia and Skalozub. The experiment is successful, though not always in equal degree; still I am aware of the living soul of the objects with whom I have been communicating. And my own sense of being in the picture is fortified by each new test.

As my work develops, my ultimate purpose and the ensuing circumstances become more difficult and complex. Whole events take place. For example, in my imagination Sophia is sent away, far down into the country. What is her secret fiancé, Molchalin, to do? In casting around for a solution I go so far as to plan her abduction. At another time I undertake to defend Sophia in the family meeting after she has been discovered with Molchalin. The family judge on this occasion is that pillar of convention, Princess Maria Alexeyevna. It is not easy to argue with this formidable representative of family traditions. On a third occasion I am present at the surprise announcement of Sophia's engagement to Skalozub. I rack my brains to think of how to avert such a catastrophe. Things reach the point of my becoming involved in a duel with Skalozub himself and . . . I shoot him!

As I did these test experiments in achieving the state of "I am" I became convinced that simple action is not enough; there must be incidents. In this way you not only begin to exist in your imagined life, you also are more keenly aware of the feelings of other people, of your relations with them and theirs with you. You come to know people when they are happy or unhappy. Meeting people, day by day in the thick of life, going forward together to face events, facing each other, making efforts, struggling, reaching your goal or abandoning it, you are not only aware of your own existence but also of your relationship to these others and to the very facts of life.

When I found myself able to become wholly involved in imaginary action and my struggles with oncoming events, I felt that some miraculous metamorphosis had taken place in me. . . .

At this point one comes to appreciate inner circumstances at their full value. They are compounded of personal attitudes toward events of external and internal life and of mutual relationships with other people. If an actor possesses the technique of the creative inner state, that state of "I am," if he has the real feel of an animate object of attention, and can move among and communicate with the phantoms of his imagination, then he is able to infuse life into external and internal circumstances, breathe a living spirit into a part; in other words, he can accomplish the work we set out to do in the first phase of studying a new play. Facts and people may change; instead of those he creates with his own imagination an actor may be offered other, new ones; still, his ability to put life into them is an important factor in his further work.

With this moment of miraculous metamorphosis our first phase of work is temporarily concluded. This working over, plowing up of the actor's soul, has prepared the ground for producing creative emotions and experiences. The actor's analysis of the play has brought to life for him the circumstances proposed by the playwright, in which "sincerity of emotions" can now grow in a natural way. This does not mean that an actor does not have to come back later to what has already been done. All this work will continue, be developed, endlessly enlarged until he is in full contact with his role.

Appraising the Facts

Appraising the facts of a play is actually the continuation, indeed the repetition, of what we have just finished doing, the result of which was an inner transformation. The difference is that the earlier work was done on an *ad libitum* basis, in the form of variations on and about the play, whereas now we are to deal with the play itself in the form in which the playwright created it.

There is a direct bond between the internal and external circumstances of a play. Indeed the inner life of the characters is concealed in the outer circumstances of their life, therefore in the facts of the play. It is difficult to assess them separately. If you penetrate through the external facts of a play and its plot to their inner essence, going from the periphery to the center, from form to substance, you inevitably enter the inner life of the play.

So we must go back to the external facts of *Woe from Wit*, not for their own sake but for the sake of what they conceal. We must consider them from a fresh angle of vision, in a new light; we must see a new state in the Famusov house in view of our own new creative state of "I am." But we go back to the facts with considerably more preparation and practical experience than we started with.

Although I am going to play Chatski, I approach the appraisal of the facts of my own part gradually; for I must know (feel) all the life in the Famusov household, and not just that part of it which directly concerns my role.

First we have the lovers' meeting, Sophia with Molchalin. In order to weigh this fact in the scales of my own emotions, my own experience in life, I try mentally to put myself in the place of the actress who is to play Sophia, and in her name I try to *exist* in the role. As part of my state of "I am," I ask myself: "What are the circumstances of my inner life, what are my personal, living thoughts, desires, capacities, if I am a woman and stand in the relationship to Molchalin that Sophia does?"

But everything inside me protests: "He's just a cardboard lover —an opportunist, an underling!" I am revolted by him. No possible circumstances could force me, were I a woman, to have the attitude toward Molchalin that Sophia has. Obviously, if I were a woman I would be unable to summon up emotions, memories, or any affective materials with which to bring the role of Sophia to life; I would have to abandon my part in *Woe from Wit*.

35

While my reason is working, however, my imagination is not asleep. Imperceptibly it envelops me with the familiar surroundings of life in the Famusov household; it makes me live in the circumstances of Sophia's life; it pushes me into the thick of the facts, so that being in the center of things, the impulses of my own will, my own feelings, my own reason and experience force me to assess the importance and significance of these factors. And from this fresh angle, my imagination seeks a new justification, inner explanation, and approach of feeling for the facts as given by the playwright.

"And what if Sophia," suggests my imagination, "is so corrupted by her upbringing, by French novels, that the very kind of love she would prefer is that of an insignificant creature like this underling Molchalin?"

"How revolting! How pathological," say my feelings indignantly; "where can you find any inspiration for such emotions?"

"In the very revulsion which they cause," comes the cold comment of my mind.

"What about Chatski?" my feelings protest. "Is it possible that he could love such a perverse Sophia? I do not want to believe it. It ruins the image of Chatski and the whole play."

When I see that I can find no avenue of approach for my feelings from this angle, my imagination seeks out fresh motives, other circumstances which will evoke different reactions.

"What if Molchalin," says my imagination temptingly, "is really an extraordinary person, indeed just what Sophia describes him as being—poetic, gentle, affectionate, considerate, sensitive, and above all, easy and compliant?"

"Then he would not be Molchalin but someone else and very nice," replies my feeling captiously.

"Very well then," agrees my imagination. "But is it possible to fall in love with such a person?"

Of course my emotions are routed.

"Besides," insists my imagination without allowing my emotions to recover their balance, "one must not forget that every human being, especially a spoiled woman, tends to self-admiration, and to that end is obliged to imagine herself as she would like to be, not as she actually is. If this game is played when she is alone, how much more agreeable it is when played with someone else, someone like Molchalin, who evidently sincerely believes anything anyone wants him to believe. What a pleasure it is for a woman to pose as a kindly, high-minded, poetic creature, humiliated by everyone! How pleasant to pity oneself and to arouse the pity and enthusiasm of others. The presence of an audience impels her to further tricks, to playing another beautiful role, to admire herself afresh; especially if the onlooker is someone who knows how, as Molchalin does, to give her encouraging replies."

"Yes, but this interpretation of Sophia's feelings is arbitrary and runs counter to Griboyedov."

"Not in the least. Griboyedov is intent on Sophia's self-deception, on Molchalin's brazen falseness," concludes my mind.

"Do not believe the teachers of literature," urges my imagination even more strongly. "Put your faith in your feelings."

Now that the fact of the love between Sophia and Molchalin has convinced my feelings that it has a justifiable basis, it comes to life for me and is quite acceptable. I believe in the truth of its existence. My emotional analysis has accomplished its first mission, it has created important inner circumstances for the play, and for my role as Chatski. Besides, the fact of the sincere affection between Sophia and Molchalin immediately throws light on many other scenes. It explains the whole line of the love between Sophia and Molchalin and the circumstances that interfere with that love. In addition it is like a live wire, sending out currents to all the other parts of the play which have any relation to it.

Now suddenly Famusov enters and finds the lovers at their meeting. Sophia's position becomes much more difficult, and I cannot refrain from emotional excitement at the thought of being in her place.

Coming suddenly face to face with a despotic character like Famusov, when one is in such compromising circumstances, makes one feel that some bold and unexpected step is called for so that one's adversary will be thrown off balance. At such a moment one must know the adversary well, know his individual peculiarities. But I do not know Famusov except for some hints about him which I recall from the first reading of the play. Neither the director nor the actor playing Famusov gives me any help, for they are as ignorant about him as I am. I have no recourse except to define his character for myself, his individual peculiarities, the inner shape of this old and wilful creature. Who is he?

"He is a bureaucrat, an owner of serfs," is the information quickly supplied by my mind, which recalls my literature lessons in school.

"Splendid!" my imagination is already on fire. "That means Sophia is a heroine!"

"Why that?" queries my bewildered mind.

"Because only a heroine can twist a tyrant around her little finger with such calm and self-assurance," says my excited imagination. "Here is a clash between old customs and new! The freedom to love! It's a modern theme!"

"But what if Famusov is only imposing in appearance, in order to maintain the customs of the family, the traditions of his class, in order to curry favor with Princess Maria Alexeyevna?" This is a new phantasy. "What if Famusov is a good-natured old body, hospitable, irascible, but easily placated? What if he is the kind of a father who is led around by his nose by his daughter?"

"In that case—things would be altogether different! Then the escape from the situation which has been created is perfectly clear! It's not difficult to deal with a father like that, especially since Sophia is shrewd, like her late mother," so my mind informs me.

Having realized how to deal with Famusov it is possible to find inner approaches for the basis of many other scenes related to him, and conversations with him.

The same kind of appraisal must be made of the return of Chatski, one who is almost a brother to Sophia, almost a fiancé, once the beloved; one who is always bold, tempestuous, free, and in love. His arrival from abroad after years of absence is a far from usual thing for those times when there were no railroads, when people traveled in heavy coaches, when a journey might well take months to accomplish. As ill-luck would have it Chatski arrives unexpectedly, and just at the wrong time. This makes Sophia's embarrassment all the more understandable, also her feeling that she must put up some pretense and screen her embarrassment, her prick of conscience; finally it explains Sophia's attacks on Chatski. When one considers Chatski's position, his childhood friendship with Sophia, and compares it with her present cold attitude toward her former friend, one can understand what the change is and how astonished Chatski feels. On the other hand, if one looks at the things from Sophia's angle one is inclined to forgive her irritable attitude and realize that the unfortunate impression Chatski's aspersions and sharp wit make on her is because of the nocturnal lovers' meeting followed by her down-to-earth scene with her father, and because Chatski's conduct is such a contrast to Molchalin's unresisting gentleness.

If one puts oneself in the place of other characters, relatives of Sophia, one can understand them too. Would they ever stand for the free speech and ways of Westernized Chatski? Would they not, living in a country where serfdom still existed, be alarmed at his speeches aimed at undermining the foundations of their society? Only an insane man would dare to talk and act as Chatski does. Against this background Sophia's revenge, then, is all the cleverer and more remorseless when she makes others believe that her erstwhile friend and fiancé is not sane. And again, standing in Sophia's stead one realizes the weight of the blow of Molchalin's insulting duplicity to her over-indulged self-esteem. One must have lived in one's imagination amid serf-owners and known their habits, customs, tenor of life, to understand—hence to feel—the power of the infinite indignation of Famusov's daughter and her pain at the shameful discharge of Molchalin, as if he were a hired footman. And one must put oneself also in the place of Famusov to understand the depth of his anger, his animosity, the sense of retribution and horror summed up in his final phrase: "Oh, good God, what will Princess Maria Alexeyevna say!"

As a result, after testing all the separate facts, all the external and internal circumstances, by your own experience you can comprehend (therefore sense) how exciting, how full of unexpected happenings, is this day in the life of the Famusov household which Griboyedov chose for his play. It is only now that you will be aware of one special quality of this comedy, something often overlooked by producers of *Woe from Wit:* the pace, the temperament, the tempo. Indeed, to squeeze in and account for the abundance of facts, deeply significant as they are, which develop through the four acts of the play, which means several hours in performance, it is necessary to set a rapid pace; the actors must be on the alert in their attitude toward everything that happens on the stage. It is, moreover, necessary to estimate the inner tempo of the underlying human spirit in the Famusov household —this is obligatory for all the characters in the play.

The more an actor has observed and known, the greater his experience, his accumulation of live impressions and memories, the more subtly will he think and feel, and the broader, more varied, and substantial will be the life of his imagination, the deeper his comprehension of facts and events, the clearer his perception of the inner and outer circumstances of the life in the play and in his part. With daily, systematic practice of the imagination on one and the same theme everything that has to do with the proposed circumstances of the play will become habitual in his imaginary life. In turn these habits will become second nature.

Actually what difference is there now between the dry catalogue of facts, as read to me when I first became acquainted with the play, and the present appraisal of those same facts? At first they all seemed theatrical, external, mere accessories of the plot and the structure of the play; but now they are living events in an infinitely exciting day, impregnated with life, indeed my own.

In the beginning the simple, dry item read "enter Famusov"; now those same words contain a serious threat to the discovered lovers: Sophia stands in danger of being exiled "to the deep country," and Molchalin is threatened with discharge.

In the beginning what was a simple stage cue, "enter Chatski," now becomes the return of the prodigal son to the bosom of his family and the reunion, for which he has waited for years, with his beloved. How much imagination, how many inner and external circumstances—how many individual bits of inner life, suppositions, images, yearnings, actions—are now included in that dry stage instruction and in every word the playwright set down!

Now that I have tested the facts of the play through my own personal experiment, all the life and the inner and outer circumstances of my role seem no longer alien, as they did earlier, but actual and real. All the circumstances of life in the Famusov house have acquired significance and meaning. I accept them not piecemeal but as an indivisible part of the whole complicated chain of circumstances of the play. My attitude toward them becomes a reality.

In transmitting the facts and plot of a play the actor involuntarily transmits its inner content, whatever is included in it; he conveys that living spirit which like a subterranean river flows under the external facts. On the stage all one needs are facts of inner content, facts which represent the end result of inner feelings, or facts which act as motive forces to set emotions in action. A fact as a fact, by itself and of itself, a fact which is no more than an entertaining episode, is not worth anything; indeed, it is harmful because it takes away from true inner life.

The significance of the appraisal of facts lies in its forcing

41

people to come into contact, mentally, with each other, making them take action, struggle, overcome, or give in to fate or to other people. It uncovers their aims, their personal lives, the mutual attitudes of the actor himself, as a living organism in a role, with other characters in the play. In other words it clarifies the circumstances of the inner life of the play and that is what we are looking for.

What else does this appraisal of facts and events signify? It means that we have to dig down under the external events and in the depths find that other, more important, inner event which perhaps gave rise to the external facts. It means also that we must follow out the line of development of that inner event and sense both the degree and nature of its effect, the direction and the line of effort of each character, discern the pattern of the many inner lines of the characters, their crisscrossing and diverging as each aims toward his particular goal in life.

In brief, to appraise the facts means to comprehend (therefore feel) the inner pattern of the life of a human being. To appraise the facts is to take all the alien life created by the playwright and make it one's own. To appraise the facts is to find the key to the riddle of the inner life of a character which lies hidden under the text of the play.

It would be a mistake to fix the appraisal of facts and events in a play once and for all. As work progresses it is necessary to come back all the time to fresh re-estimates, which add to the inner substance. Moreover the facts should be newly evaluated every time you repeat your creation of a part. Man is not a machine. He cannot feel a part the same way every time he plays it; he cannot be stirred each time by the same creative stimuli. Yesterday's estimate is not quite the same as today's. There will be infinitesimal, scarcely perceptible changes in the approach, and that is often the main stimulus to today's creativeness. The power of such stimulus lies in its novelty, its unexpectedness.

All the innumerable complexities of accident through the influence of weather, temperature, light, food, the combination of outer and inner circumstances, in one degree or another affect the inner state of an actor. In turn an actor's inner state affects his relation to the facts. His capacity to take advantage all the time of these changing complexities, his ability to refresh his stimulation through new approaches—all this is an important part of an actor's inner technique. Without this faculty an actor can lose interest in his part after a few performances, he can lose touch with the facts and living events, and be deprived of his sense of their significance.

CHAPTER TWO

The Period of Emotional Experience

WHEREAS THE FIRST period of work on a role was only one of preparation, this second period is one of creation. If the first period could be compared to the early courtship between two lovers, the second represents the consummation of their love, the conception and the formation of the fruit of their union.

Nemirovich-Danchenko illustrated this moment of creation by a comparison: In order to produce a plant you must sow the seed in the ground; that seed must decompose and from it emerge the roots of the plant to be. In exactly the same way the seed of the author's creation must be planted in the soul of the actor, it must go through the stage of decomposition and then put forth its roots from which a new creation will be forthcoming; it will belong to the actor, but in spirit it will be the progeny of the playwright.

If the preparatory period produced the given circumstances, then this second period will create the sincerity of emotions, the heart of a role, its inner image, its spiritual life. *This emotional experience of a role is the basic, most important phase in our creativeness.*

The creative process of living and experiencing a part is an *organic* one, founded on the physical and spiritual laws governing the nature of man, on the truthfulness of his emotions, and on natural beauty. How does this organic process originate and develop, of what does the creative work of the actor here consist?

Inner Impulses and Inner Action

Having learned in my early preparation of *Woe from Wit* how to "be," to exist, amid the circumstances of life in the Famusov

44

household, having thanks to my imagination found a personal human basis for living there, having come face to face with certain facts and events, having met the inmates of the household, come to know them, felt what their emotions are, established direct communication with them, I have, unbeknown to myself, begun to harbor certain desires, impulses toward a certain goal which has asserted itself of its own accord.

For example, I recall my morning visit to Famusov, when he was singing, and now I not only feel myself there with him, in his room; I not only feel the presence of a live object and sense his emotions; I also begin to be aware of certain desires, impulses toward some nearby objective. For the time being these desires are extremely simple: I wish Famusov would pay some attention to me. I seek appropriate words and actions to bring this about; for instance, I am tempted to tease the old man because I believe he must be funny when his dander is up.

These creative impulses are naturally followed by impulses leading to action. But impulse is not yet action. The impulse is an inner urge, a desire not yet satisfied, whereas the action itself is either an external or internal satisfaction of the desire. An impulse calls for inner action, and inner action eventually calls for external action. It is, however, as yet too soon to speak of this.

At present, being aware of my impulses to action, the imagined emotional experience of some scene in the life of the Famusov household, I begin to take aim at some subject of my observation, to search for means of carrying out an objective. Thus when I recall the love scene between Sophia and Molchalin as interrupted by Famusov, I cast about as Sophia to find a way out of the situation. First of all I must hide my embarrassment by the appearance of calm, I must summon all my self-control, I must think of a plan of action, I must find some way to adapt myself to Famusov, to approach him in his present state of mind. I choose him as my objective. The more he rages, the calmer I strive to be. As soon as he cools off I try to disconcert him by my innocent, compliant, reproachful looks. Meantime, all sorts of subtle inner adjustments spring up in me: the slyness of a resourceful heart, a complexity of emotions, unexpected inner impulses to action, which only nature can supply, only intuition knows how to foster.

As soon as I feel these stirrings I can go into action, not physically as yet, only inwardly, in my imagination. . . .

"What would you do," my imagination asks my feelings, "if you were in Sophia's situation?"

"I would tell my face to put on an angelic expression," answer my feelings without hesitation.

"And then what?" my imagination continues.

"I would say to keep stubbornly silent," my feelings reply. "Let my father say as many harsh and stupid things as he likes. This is all to the advantage of his daughter who is usually so spoiled. Then when the old man has poured out all his venom, is hoarse with his shouting, and exhausted with emotion, when there is nothing left in the bottom of his soul except his customary good nature, indolence, love of tranquillity, when he has sat down in a comfortable armchair to catch his breath and wipe away his perspiration, I would order more silence, a more angelic expression such as only a righteous person can muster."

"And then?" urges my imagination.

"I would order Sophia surreptitiously to wipe away a tear, but do it so that her father notices it, and I would stand as immovable as before, until the old man would get worried and ask me, rather guiltily: 'Why are you so silent, Sophia?' But I would not reply. 'Don't you hear me?' the old gentleman would now beg. 'What is the matter with you? Tell me.'

" 'I hear,' the daughter would answer in a humble, defenseless, childlike voice, in a way to render him helpless."

"What would happen next?" my imagination asks rather insistently.

"Next I would order her still to remain silent, and stand there humbly, until her father begins to get angry, but now not because he caught her with Molchalin but because she is silent and puts him in an awkward position. This is an excellent method of distracting a person's attention, of moving the conversation from one topic to another."

Finally taking pity on her father she would ask, with extraordinary calm, that he be shown the flute which Molchalin is awkwardly and stupidly trying to hide behind his back.

"Look, father," I have her say in a humble voice.

"What's that?" asks her father.

"A flute," she replies, "that's why Molchalin came."

"I see, I see how he is trying to hide it in his coat tails. But how did it get here, into your room?" asks the old gentleman with fresh emotion.

"Where should it be? We were practicing a duet together yesterday. You know very well, father, that he and I were practicing a duet for the party this evening."

"Well! . . . Yes, I know," her father agrees cautiously, although he is still indignant over his daughter's composure, which would seem to proclaim her innocence.

"To be sure, we worked longer than propriety allows. And for that I ask your forgiveness, Father." Here Sophia kisses her father's hand, he kisses her lightly on the forehead and says to himself: "What a clever girl!"

"We absolutely had to finish learning the duet because otherwise you would have been annoyed if your daughter had disgraced herself in front of all your relatives by playing the duet badly. Wouldn't you have been annoyed?"

"Well, . . . it would have been annoying," the old gentleman agrees almost guiltily, feeling that the shoe is already being put on the other foot. "But why here?" he suddenly explodes, as if trying to extricate himself.

"Where then?" Sophia, with her angelic expression, asks the old gentleman. "You forbade me to go into the reception room where the piano is. You said it was not proper to be alone with a young man way off there. Besides it is very cold, as those rooms were not heated yesterday. Where should we practice our duet if not here, on the clavichord, in my room? There is no other instrument. Of course, I ordered Liza to remain here all the time so as not to be alone with a young man. And for that, Father, you . . . Of course, I have no mother to take my side! I haven't anyone to counsel me. I am an orphan. . . . Poor me! Dear God! If death would only take me!" If Sophia is lucky and tears come to her eyes, the whole matter will be solved by her receiving the present of a new hat. . . .

* * *

Thus out of desires, inclinations, impulses to act I am naturally moved to that important thing: inner action.

Life is action; that is why our lively art, which stems from life, is preponderantly active.

It is not without reason that our word "drama" is derived from the Greek word which means "I do." In Greek this is related to literature, to playwriting, to poetry, and not to the actor or his art; nonetheless it can be to a large degree pre-empted by us. Incidentally our art used to be called "actors' action" or "facial action," to wit, miming. In most theatres action on the stage is taken incorrectly to mean external action. It is commonly thought that plays are rich in action if people are arriving or departing, getting married or being separated, killing or saving one another; in brief, that a play rich in action is one with a cleverly woven and interesting external plot. But this is an error.

Scenic action does not mean walking, moving about, gesticulating on the stage. The point does not lie in the movement of arms, legs, or body but in inner movements and impulses. So let us learn once and for all that the word "action" is not the same as "miming," it is not anything the actor is pretending to present, not something external, but rather something internal, nonphysical, a *spiritual activity.* It derives from an unbroken succession of inde‑ pendent processes; and each of these in turn is compounded of desires or impulses aimed at the accomplishment of some objec‑ tive.

Scenic action is the movement from the soul to the body, from the center to the periphery, from the internal to the external, from the thing an actor feels to its physical form. External action on the stage when not inspired, not justified, not called forth by inner activity, is entertaining only for the eyes and ears; it does not penetrate the heart, it has no significance in the life of a human spirit in a role.

Thus inner impulses—the urge to action and the inner actions themselves—acquire an exceptional meaning in our work. They are our motive power in moments of creation, and only that crea‑ tiveness which is predicated on inner action is scenic. By "scenic" in the theatre we mean action in the spiritual sense of the word.

By contrast, a passive state kills all scenic action, it produces feelings for the sake of feelings, technique for the sake of tech‑ nique. That kind of feeling is not scenic.

Sometimes an actor practically luxuriates in inaction, wallows in his own emotions. Blinded by the feeling that he is at home in his part, he thinks that he is creating something, that he is truly living the part. But no matter how sincere that passive feeling may be, it is not creative, and it cannot reach the heart of the spectator, so long as it lacks activity and does not promote the inner life of the play. When an actor feels his part passively his emotion re‑ mains inside him, there is no challenge to either inner or outer action.

Even in order to project a passive state in theatrical terms one must do it actively. Escaping from active participation (in any matter or event) is in itself action. Indolent, sluggish action is still action, typical of a passive state. . . .

Real life, like life on the stage, is made up of continuously arising desires, aspirations, inner challenges to action and their consummation in internal and external actions. Just as the separate, constantly repeated explosions of a motor result in the smooth motion of an automobile, so this unbroken series of outbursts of human desires develops the continuous movement of our creative will, it establishes the flow of inner life, it helps an actor to experience the living organism of his part.

In order to invoke this creative experience on the stage an actor must keep up a continuous fire of artistic desires all through his part so that they in turn will arouse the corresponding inner aspirations, which then will engender corresponding inner challenges to act, and finally these inner calls to action will find their outlet in corresponding external, physical action.

Need one point out that while the actor is on the stage all these desires, aspirations, and actions must belong to him as the creative artist, and not to the inert paper words printed in the text of his part; not to the playwright, who is absent from the performance; nor yet to the director of the play, who remains in the wings? Need one emphasize that an actor can experience or live his part only with his own, genuine feelings? Can one live in ordinary life or on the stage with the feelings of others unless one has been absorbed by them body and spirit as an actor and human being? Can one borrow the feelings or the sensations, the body and soul, of another person and use them as one would one's own?

An actor can subject himself to the wishes and indications of a playwright or a director and execute them mechanically, but to experience his role he must use his own living desires, engendered and worked over by himself, and he must exercise his own will, not that of another. The director and the playwright can suggest their wishes to the actor, but these wishes must then be reincarnated in the actor's own nature so that he becomes completely possessed by them. For these desires to become living, creative desires on the stage, embodied in the actions of the actor, they must have become a part of his very self.

Creative Objectives

How does one evoke the desires of one's creative will on the stage? One cannot simply say: "Desire! Create! Act!" Our creative emotions are not subject to command and do not tolerate force. They can only be coaxed. Once coaxed, they begin to wish, and wishing they begin to yearn for action.

There is only one thing that can lure our creative will and draw it to us and that is an attractive aim, a creative objective. *The objective is the whetter of creativeness, its motive force. The objective is the lure for our emotions.* This objective engenders outbursts of desires for the purpose of creative aspiration. It sends inner messages which naturally and logically are expressed in action. The objective gives a pulse to the living being of a role.

Life on the stage, as well as off it, consists of an uninterrupted series of objectives and their attainment. They are signals set all along the way of an actor's creative aspirations; they show him the true direction. Objectives are like the notes in music, they form the measures, which in turn produce the melody, or rather the emotions—a state of sorrow, joy, and so forth. The melody goes on to form an opera or a symphony, that is to say the life of a human spirit in a role, and that is what the soul of the actor sings.

Such objectives may be reasoned, conscious, pointed out by our mind, or they may be emotional, unconscious, arising of their own free will, intuitively.

A conscious objective can be carried out on the stage with almost no feeling or will; but it will be dry, unattractive, lacking in scenic quality and therefore unadaptable to creative purposes. An objective which is not warmed or infused with life by emotions or will cannot put any living quality into the inert concepts of words. It can do no more than recite dry thoughts. If an actor achieves his objective purely through his mind he cannot live or experience his part, he can only give a report on it. Therefore he will not be a creator but a reporter of his role. A conscious objective can be good and scenically effective only when it is attractive to the living feelings and will of the actor and sets them to working.

The best creative objective is the unconscious one which immediately, emotionally, takes possession of an actor's feelings, and carries him intuitively along to the basic goal of the play. The power of this type of objective lies in its immediacy (the Hindus call such objectives the highest kind of superconsciousness), which acts as a magnet to creative will and arouses irresistible aspirations. In such cases all the mind does is to note and evaluate the results. Often such objectives are destined to remain, if not entirely, then at least half in the realm of the unconscious. All we can do is to learn how not to interfere with the creativeness of nature, or work to prepare the ground, seek out motives and means whereby even obliquely we can catch hold of these emotional, superconscious objectives.

Unconscious objectives are engendered by the emotion and will of the actors themselves. They come into being intuitively; they are then weighed and determined consciously. Thus the emotions, will, and mind of the actor all participate in creativeness.

The ability to find or create such objectives as will arouse the activity of an actor, and the ability to handle such objectives, are the crucial concerns of our whole inner technique. There are many approaches. One must find among them the one which is most congenial with the nature of the actor in a part, the way to stir him to greatest creative action. How is this accomplished? Here is an example.

Let us suppose that Chatski is anxious to convince Sophia that neither Molchalin nor Skalozub is a proper match for her. Unless this conviction is backed up by warmth of feeling it will be external, merely verbal, dry and unsatisfying. The actor would not be convinced, he would simply go through the physical external motions that cannot possibly make him believe in the sincerity and truth of his feelings. Yet without this faith an actor cannot feel his part, just as without truly feeling his part he will not have faith in his emotions.

What is it that will give me, as Chatski, such faith in my objective that I shall have the strong wish to go into action? Is it the sight of charming, helpless, inexperienced Sophia at the side of that pitiable nonentity Molchalin or coarse-grained Skalozub? But these people do not as yet exist, at least I do not as yet see them either in actuality or in my imagination. I do not know them. Yet I do know of my own experience the feeling of pity, humiliation, aesthetic outrage at the thought of any fine young girl (whoever she may be) sacrificing herself in a marriage with a coarse fool, like Skalozub, or with a shallow opportunist, like Molchalin. The prospect of such an unnatural and unaesthetic union would arouse one's instinct; the desire to stop an inexperienced girl from taking a wrong step would be alive in any one of us. For the sake of such a desire it would never be difficult to stir one's impulses, which in turn would enkindle genuine desire, and action itself.

Of what do these impulses consist? One senses the need to affect the feelings of someone else with one's own feeling of offense because a fine young life is being destroyed. Something urges one to go to Sophia, or any young girl like her, and try to open her eyes to life, convince her not to destroy herself through an unsuitable marriage that would inevitably bring her sorrow. One searches for means to make her believe in the sincerity of one's kindly interest in her. In the name of that sincerity one wants to ask permission of her to talk on intimate subjects, matters concerning her heart.

First of all I would try to convince Sophia of my own good feelings toward her in order to gain her preliminary confidence in me. Then I would attempt to paint the most vivid picture possible of the difference between her and the coarse nature of Skalozub, between her and the shallow, mean little soul of Molchalin. What I said about Molchalin would require extreme tact, because Sophia is determined at all costs to see him through rosy spectacles. Sophia must realize all the more vividly how my heart contracts at the thought of what is in store for her. Let my fears for her, which I want her to feel, frighten her and make her stop and think. Each method of convincing her, each approach to her heart must be softened by radiations of tender feeling, a caressing look, and so forth. Can one even count all the inner and physical actions, all the inner impulses, that would well up of their own accord in the heart of a person touched by his own efforts to save an inexperienced girl intent on destroying herself?

*　　*　　*

Conscious or unconscious objectives are carried out both inwardly and outwardly, by both body and soul. Therefore they can be both *physical* and *psychological*.

For example, going back to the imaginary scene when I made my morning call on Famusov, I recall an infinite number of physical objectives which I had to execute in my imagination. I had to go along a corridor, knock at a door, take hold of and turn the doorknob, open the door, enter, greet the master of the house and anyone else present, and so forth. In order to preserve the truthfulness of the occasion I could not simply fly into his room in one movement.

All these necessary physical objectives are so habitual that we execute them mechanically, with our muscles. In our inner realm, too, we find an infinite number of necessary, simple psychological objectives.

I recall now, as an example, another imaginary scene in the life of the Famusov household—the interrupted meeting between Sophia and Molchalin. How many simple psychological objectives Sophia had to execute with her emotions in order to soften her father's anger and escape punishment. She had to mask her embarrassment, she had to throw her father off balance by her calm, embarrass and move him to pity by the angelic expression on her face, disarm him with her humility, undermine his position, and so forth. She could not, without destroying the truthfulness and living quality of her action, by one sweep of emotions, one inner movement, one psychological objective have brought about the miraculous transformation in the heart of the angry man.

Physical and simple psychological objectives are to some degree necessary to all human beings. When a person has been drowned, for example, he is forced to breathe by mechanical means. As a result, his other organs begin to function; his heart begins to beat, his blood begins to circulate, and finally by the sheer momentum of living organisms his spirit is revived. This is the inborn habitual and mutual bond among the physical organs.

It is this sort of organic habit, a part of our nature, this sort of consecutiveness and logic in our actions and feelings, that we make use of in our art when we give birth to the process of living a part. This common necessity of the actor-human-being and the human-being-part is what brings the actor and his part close together for the first time.

Both physical and psychological objectives must be bound together by a certain inner tie, by consecutiveness, gradualness, and logic of feeling. It sometimes happens that in the logic of human feelings one will find something illogical; after all in the harmony of music there are occasional dissonances. But on the stage it is necessary to be consecutive and logical. You cannot step from the first floor in a house to the tenth. It is impossible with one inner movement or one physical movement to do away with all obstacles and immediately persuade another person to do something, or to fly from one house to another. You must go through and carry out a whole series of consecutive and logical physical and simple psychological objectives. You must go out of the house, take a cab, enter the other house, go through several rooms, find the person you are looking for, and so forth, before you reach the point of meeting that other person.

Similarly, to reach the point of convincing the other person you must fulfill a series of objectives: You must attract the person's attention, you must try to sense what is in his heart, to comprehend his inner state, then adapt yourself to it, trying out several ways of conveying your own feelings and thoughts. In short you must carry out a series of psychological objectives and inner actions in order to convince your companion of your thoughts and influence him by your feelings.

It is not easy to maintain with exactitude all the physical and simple psychological objectives on the stage so that they correspond to the aspirations and actions of the character portrayed. The trouble is that the actor tends to identify himself with the inner life of his character only when he is saying his lines. As soon as he stops talking and gives the stage to the person playing opposite him, the inner thread of his role breaks; the actor lapses back into his own life and feelings as if he were merely awaiting his cue to renew the interrupted life of his role. When this happens, when the actor breaks the logical chain of physical and psychological objectives and replaces it with other things, he is crippling life. All moments in a role that are not filled out with creative objectives and feelings are a temptation to actors' clichés, theatrical conventionality. When violence to our spiritual and physical natures is present, when our emotions are in chaos, when we lack the logic and consecutiveness of objectives, we do not genuinely live a part.

The Score of a Role

I shall put myself in the place of the actor playing Chatski in *Woe from Wit*, and attempt to find out what physical and simple psychological objectives naturally form themselves in me when I begin, in imagination, to exist in the center of circumstances, to "be" in the vortex of life in the Famusov house in Moscow in the 1820's.

Here I am—for the time being I am myself without any of the feelings or emotions of Chatski. I have just returned from abroad; without going home I have driven up in a heavy traveling coach, drawn by four horses, to the gates of the house which is almost another home to me. Now my coach has stopped and the coachman has called the yardman to open the gates to the courtyard.

What do I desire in this moment?

A. *I desire to hasten the moment of my meeting with Sophia, something I have dreamed of for so long.*

But I am powerless to do anything about it, so I sit helplessly in my carriage and wait for the gates to be opened. Out of impatience I pull thoughtlessly on the window cord which has annoyed me all during my journey.

Now the yardman has come, he has recognized me and is hurrying. The hinges on the gates creak; now they are open and the coach can roll in; but the yardman holds it back, comes up to the window and greets me with tears of joy in his eyes.

a. *I must speak to him, be agreeable, exchange greetings.*

I patiently go through all these motions so as not to offend the old man, who has known me since I was a child. I even have to listen while he goes over the familiar memories of my own childhood.

Now finally the great coach with creaking and crunching of snow moves into the court and pulls up at the porte-cochère.

I jump out of the coach.

What is the first thing I must do?

b. *I must quickly rouse the sleepy doorman.*

Now I take hold of the bellcord, yank it, wait, ring again. Meantime, a pet mongrel is whimpering and fawning on my legs.

As I wait for the doorman:

c. *I desire to greet the dog, and pet this old friend of mine.*

Now the front door is opened and I rush into the vestibule. The familiar atmosphere of the house immediately envelops me. The feelings and memories I left behind me now crowd into my heart and fill it to overflowing. I stand still, full of tender emotion.

Now the doorman greets me with something like the whinny of a horse.

57

d. *I must say how do you do to him, be nice to him, exchange greetings.*

I patiently carry out this objective, if only I can get to Sophia without further delay.

Now I am on my way up the front stairs. I reach the first landing. Here I run into the steward and the housekeeper. They are speechless with surprise at the unexpected meeting.

e. *I must greet them too, I must ask about Sophia. Where is she? Is she well? Is she up?*

Now I come to the array of reception rooms.

The steward trots on ahead of me.

I wait in the corridor. Now Liza dashes out with a little scream. Now she takes me by the coat sleeve.

What do I desire at this moment?

f. *I want to get to my main goal quickly, see Sophia, the dear friend of my childhood, almost my sister.*

And now at last I lay eyes on her.

Here my first objective—A—has been fulfilled with the aid of a whole series of small, almost exclusively *physical* objectives (getting out of the carriage, ringing the door bell, running up the stairs, and so forth.)

A new and large objective now emerges naturally before me: B. *I wish to greet the dear friend of my childhood, one who is almost a sister to me; I want to embrace her and exchange pent-up feelings with her.*

However this cannot be done at once, with one inner gesture. There must be a whole series of small, inner objectives which altogether will add up to the main, large objective.

a. *First of all I want to look at Sophia carefully, to see her familiar and dear features, to appraise the changes that have taken place in my absence.*

A girl can change between the ages of fourteen and seventeen so you hardly recognize her. And this wonderful change has taken place in her. I thought to meet a girl and now I see her grown into young womanhood.

Through my own memories of the past and my personal experience I know the feeling of bewilderment which overcomes one at such a time. I remember the awkwardness, embarrassment, when faced with the unexpected. If I can but trace one familiar feature, the flash of the eyes, the movement of lips or eyebrows, shoulders or fingers, a familiar smile, then I would recognize instantly my own dear Sophia. The transient shyness disappears. The former easy fraternal relationship is restored and a new objective is formed.

b. *I want to convey my feelings in a brotherly kiss.*

I rush forward to embrace my friend and sister. I hug her, and do it so hard that it hurts a little, this on purpose to let her feel the strength of my friendship.

But that is not enough, I must find other ways to express to her the feelings I have restrained.

c. *I must caress Sophia by look and by word.*

And again, as if taking my aim, while searching for endearing, friendly words I turn on her the radiation of my own warm feelings.

But what do I see? A cold expression, embarrassment, a shade of displeasure. What is this? Is it my imagination? Is it the result of the unexpectedness of my greetings?

A new objective naturally develops out of this.

C. *I must understand the reason for this cold reception.*

In turn this objective is made up, in the course of its execution, of a lot of independent small objectives.

a. *I must get Sophia to confess what is the matter.*

b. *I must shake her up with interrogation, reproaches, cleverly put questions.*

c. *I must draw her attention to me, and so forth.*

But Sophia is clever. She knows how to hide behind an angelic expression. I feel that it would not be difficult for her to convince me, if only temporarily, that she is glad to see me. It would be all the easier for her since that is what I wish to believe, so that I can move more quickly to a new, large, and more interesting objective.

And this large objective, D, *To cross-examine Sophia about herself, her relatives, acquaintances, and all the life of this house and of Moscow,* is then carried out by a series of small objectives.

But now Famusov himself enters and interrupts our friendly tête à tête. Here objective E appears with the concomitant small objectives, up to the point at the end of the play when I reach my final objective:

Z. *"Away from Moscow! No longer to this place*
I'll come. No turning back, but out into
The world I go, to find a place where
I can lick my wounds!"

To carry out this last large objective I have to:

a. *Give an order to the footman:*
"My carriage, quick, my carriage!"
b. *Leave the Famusov house rapidly.*

As I was mentally choosing and carrying out all these objectives I felt the internal and external circumstances of their own accord stirring my *will* and *desires.* In turn they evoked creative *aspirations* which were capped by inner impulses to action. They all combined to lead me to the creative moment of putting life into my part.

Out of them all a whole series of *units* was formed, around each large objective. For example if you look at the inner meaning of all the component objectives Aa to Af, consider all the desires of Chatski from the moment when he drove into the courtyard of the Famusov house to the moment of his meeting with Sophia, we see that he was carrying out one large objective—A—one unit in the life of his role which we can formulate as: *hastening his meeting with Sophia.*

Then all the minor objectives Ba-Bc combine to make another

large objective, another unit in his role—B—and this can be called: *desiring to greet and embrace Sophia and exchange feelings with her*.

Out of the small objectives Ca-Cc we form a third large objective and unit—C—the meaning of which is: *searching for the reason for the cool reception given him by his childhood friend*.

And so it continues through the whole play.

The first four units create a whole scene which we may call: *The first meeting between Chatski and Sophia*. The next four units go to make up another scene: *The interrupted meeting*. The grouping of other units and objectives form a third and fourth scene, and so forth. In turn this series of large scenes merges to form the acts. The acts make a whole play, which is to say a large and important section of the life of a human spirit.

Let us agree to call this long catalogue of minor and major objectives, units, scenes, acts, the *score of a role*. It is made up, for the time being, of physical and simple psychological objectives. The score of Chatski's role would be (with minor deviations and changes) the same for anyone living in circumstances analogous to those in the play, just as it would be for any actor who is going through the experience of this role. Anyone arriving home from a journey, or reliving in his emotion memory his return to his native country, would either in reality or mentally get out of his conveyance, enter the house, greet people, orient himself, and so forth. These are physical necessities.

And anyone returning from a journey would be obliged to go through a whole series of simple psychological objectives: to exchange emotions, greetings, be interested in what he saw and heard about his dear friends, and so forth. Not everything one's heart is full of can be conveyed at once; one goes through with greetings, embracing, looking at each other, understanding each other, in consecutive order.

None of the listed objectives of the score, let us note, is profound; they can affect only the periphery of the actor's body, the external manifestations of his psychic life, and only slightly affect his feelings. Nevertheless they were the creations of live feelings and not the product of dry reason. They were prompted by artistic instincts, creative sensitivity, the actor's own life experiences, habits, the human qualities of his own nature. And each objective contained its own consecutiveness, gradual development, logic. One can call them natural objectives. There can be no doubt that such a score, based on such objectives, will draw the actor as a human being—physically speaking—closer to the real life of his character or role.

With time and frequent repetition, in rehearsal and performance, this score becomes habitual. An actor becomes so accustomed to all his objectives and their sequence that he cannot conceive of approaching his role otherwise than along the line of the steps fixed in the score. Habit plays a great part in creativeness: it establishes in a firm way the accomplishments of creativeness. In the familiar words of Volkonski it makes what is difficult habitual, what is habitual easy, and what is easy beautiful. Habit creates second nature, which is a second reality.

The score automatically stirs the actor to physical action.

The Inner Tone

The physical and simple psychological score has now been prepared. Does it respond to all of the needs of an actor's creative nature? The first requirement is that the score should have the power to *attract*, because creative enthusiasm, an exciting objective, is the only means of affecting the capricious emotions and will of an actor.

There can be no doubt that the score so far does not possess all the necessary qualifications to warm an actor's enthusiasm and arouse his emotions each and every time he creates it. Even when I was searching for and choosing my objectives as Chatski they did not excite me very much. Nor is this surprising. All the objectives chosen were external. They affected only the periphery of my body, touched my feelings and the life of my part only superficially. Nor can this be otherwise since the line of my creative endeavor consisted of external facts and events on the plane of the physical and simple psychological life of my part and only occasionally touched the deeper levels of my inner life.

This kind of a score and the experiences that go with it do not reflect the more important aspects of a living human spirit in which we find the essence of a theatre creation, the inner individuality of the life of the role. Any person would have done what the score of objectives proposed. The objectives are typical for any person and therefore do not characterize the particular role in its own peculiar individuality. The score can show the way but it cannot arouse true creativeness. It does not produce life and it is soon outworn.

Deeply passionate emotions are necessary to carry away feelings, will, mind, and all of an actor's being. These can only be aroused by objectives with a deeper inner content. The secret of inner technique and its essence are concealed in them. Therefore the next concern of an actor should be to find objectives that constantly move his feelings and thus put life into his physical score. This creative score must excite the actor not only by its external physical truth but above all by its inner beauty, buoyancy. Creative objectives must call up not simple interest but passionate excitement, desires, aspirations, and action. Any objective lacking these magnetic qualities is not fulfilling its mission. One cannot, of course, say that every stirring objective is good and suitable for the creative score of a part, yet one can say surely that any objective that is dry is of no use at all.

The fact of Chatski's arrival, demonstrated by the major and minor objectives with which it is accompanied, is interesting only because of its inner content, emotions, psychologic motives. They are the factors that affect his inner being. Without them there would be no heart to the role. Without them the objectives would be insubstantial, empty.

Let us now add depth to the score of Chatski's role, leading him along what might be called its submarine current, closer to the source of his inner life, his own nature as an actor, closer to that mysterious and intimate center which is the "I" in a role. What must we do to accomplish this? Should we change the objectives and the whole physical and simple psychological score that provide the external life of his role? Yet are they not indispensable, and do they cease to exist if depth is added? No! They continue to exist but they gain in substance. The difference will lie in the inner life, the general state of the actor, the moods in which each objective is carried out. His new inner state will refresh and add color to his objectives, will add a depth of meaning, a new basis and inner motivation to them. This changed inner state or mood I shall call the *inner tone*. In actor's jargon it is called the *germ of feeling*.

When depth is added to the score of a part, the facts and the objectives are altered only in the sense that inner impulses, psychological intimations, an inner point of departure—all the things that constitute the inner tone of the score and give it a firm basis of justification—have been added.

The same thing occurs in music: Melodies and symphonies may be played in varying keys, major or minor, they can be played in varying tempi, while the melody itself does not change, only the tone in which it is played. In a major key and lively tempo the melody will have a triumphant, bravura character; in a minor key and slow tempo it will acquire a sad, lyrical character. Thus we actors can experience varying emotions when playing a score with the same objectives but in different keys. You can live through all the emotions of a homecoming, go through all the physical and simple psychological objectives connected with it; in a quiet or a joyful key, in a sad or a disturbed or an excited key, or in the key of a lover who says of himself:

>   . . . beside myself,
> Two days and nights on end, and never closing eye
> I traveled fast over the many hundred miles, through wind and storm,
> In turmoil, many times I fell. . . .

So now let us set a new objective: take the score as it has been constituted so far and add to it in depth.

I must first of all ask myself: What would be changed in the score if I came home from abroad, as Chatski did, given the circumstances of his life, yet not in the state of a returning friend, but rather inflamed with an ardent love for Sophia? In other words, I shall try to feel the same score but in a different key.

In this new key of a lover's passion the score is illuminated to its depths. It acquires an entirely different color, a greater inner content. These changes must be adapted to Chatski's role. For that purpose I must introduce new given circumstances. Let us suppose Chatski has come back from abroad not only as Sophia's friend but as one who idolizes her, a fiancé desperately in love. What is changed in the score and what remains as it was?

Whatever state of passion a man may be in on his return home, physical circumstances would oblige him to wait until the yardman opens the gates into the courtyard, he must rouse the sleepy doorman, he must greet various members of the household, and so forth. In short Chatski must to all intents and purposes carry out almost the same physical and simple psychological objectives of the score as before. The essential difference introduced by his state of being violently in love is not so much in the objectives themselves but in how he executes them. If he is calm, unruffled by deep inner emotions, he will carry out his objectives patiently and scrupulously. If, however, he is on fire, if he gives himself up to the force of his feelings, he will have quite a different attitude toward his objectives. Some of them will be slurred over, fusing and merging with one another, being swallowed up in the one over-riding objective; others will acquire more edge because of the lover's nervousness and impatience.

When a man is completely dominated by passion, involved in it with his whole being, he forgets his physical objectives, he executes them mechanically, oblivious to them. In real life we are often oblivious of what we are doing—walking, ringing a bell, opening a door, greeting someone or other. All this is done largely in an unconscious way. The body lives its own habitual, motor existence and the soul lives its deeper psychological life. This apparent division does not, however, destroy the bond between body and soul. The appearance derives from the fact that the center of attention moves from one's external to one's internal life.

Thus the physical score, which the actor has perfected to the point of mechanical execution, goes deeper now and is rounded out with new feeling and has become, one might say, psycho-physical in quality. The way this is accomplished is through indirect means, through preliminary work to make it possible: One has to sense the *nature* of the passion that is to be portrayed, in this case the passion of love.

First one must plot a line along which the passion will develop; one must comprehend, feel the component parts the passion; one must prepare a whole scheme which will be like a canvas on which creative emotions will embroider consciously or unconsciously their inscrutable and complex patterns. How can one comprehend this passion of love, by what can one be guided in making a scheme of it?

To define love from the scientific point of view is a job for the psychologists. Art is not science; although I as an artist must constantly draw creative materials and knowledge from life and science, still, in moments of creativeness, I am accustomed to using my own emotions, susceptibilities, impressions.

Besides, I am not at present concerned with a detailed study of the passion of love; what I need is a general, brief, sensitive outline, the basis for which I shall find not in my brain but in my heart. Let this outline lead me and direct my creative nature in my forthcoming work of preparing a subtler inner, psycho-physical score for the role of Chatski.

This is how I feel the nature of love: I feel that this passion, like a plant, has a seed from which it springs, has roots from which its stem emerges, has a stem, leaves, flowers which crown its development. It is not without reason that they speak of the "roots of passion" or say that a "passion grows," that love "blossoms," and so forth. In short, I feel that in love, as in any other passion, there is a whole series of processes—the first seed, the conception, growth, development, flowering, and so forth. I feel that the development of a passion proceeds along a line laid down by nature itself and that here, as in the physical realm, there is a certain sequence, logic, law, which cannot be contravened with impunity. Let an actor exercise compulsion on his own nature, let him substitute one feeling for another, destroy the logic of his emotions, the consecutiveness of the changing periods as they succeed each other step by step, let him cripple the natural structure of a human passion—and the result will be emotional distortion.

Every passion is a complex of things experienced emotionally, it is the sum total of a variety of different feelings, experiences, states. All these component parts are not only numerous and varied but they are also often contradictory. In love there is often hatred and scorn, and adoration, and indifference, and ecstasy, and prostration, and embarrassment, and brazenness.

In this sense, human passions can be compared to a pile of beads. The general tone is achieved through the colorful combination of an innumerable quantity of individual beads of the most varied hues (red, blue, white, black). Put together and mixed they give the general tone to the pile of beads (gray, pale blue, yellowish). So it is in the realm of feelings: The combination of many individual and most varied, even contradictory, feelings forms entire passions. A mother brutally beats her beloved child because it was nearly run over. Why is she so angry at the child while she is beating it? Just because she loves it so and fears to lose it. She beats the child so that in the future it will never again play such a dangerous trick. The transient hatred exists alongside her constant love. And the more a mother loves her child, the more she hates it and beats it at such times. . . .

Not only the passions themselves but also their component parts are mutually contradictory. For instance one of De Maupassant's heroes kills himself because he is afraid of a duel he is facing. His bold, decisive act, the suicide itself, is brought about through his cowardice in trying to evade the duel.

Each role is composed of the same sort of individual ingredients, producing whole passions, which in turn give us the inner, spiritual image of the character to be portrayed. Let us then take the role of Chatski.

This role, and in particular the love of Chatski for Sophia, is not made up exclusively of love scenes but of a variety of other moments, containing conflicting emotions and actions which in their sum total add up to love. And indeed, what is Chatski doing all through the play? Of what actions is his role composed? In what way does he manifest his love for Sophia? First of all he hastens to see Sophia as soon as he arrives; he studies her carefully when they meet, and tries to discover the reason for her cool reception of him; he reproaches her, then jokes, pokes fun at relatives and acquaintances. At times he makes stinging remarks to Sophia; he thinks a great deal about her, is tortured and baffled; he eavesdrops, catches her at a rendezvous when she is preparing to betray him, listens to her, and finally flees from his beloved. Among all these varied actions and objectives only a few lines of the text are devoted to words and confessions of love. Nevertheless the total of individual moments and objectives, taken all together, establish the passion, the love of Chatski for Sophia.

One's emotional palette, one's score which is to portray human passions, must be rich, colorful, and varied. In portraying any of the human passions an actor should not think about the passion itself but of the feelings which go into its make-up, and the greater the sweep he wishes to give to the passion the more variegated and contradictory are the emotions he must search out. Extremes extend the gamut of human passions and enlarge the palette of the actor. Therefore when he is playing a good man, he should seek out what there is of evil in him; if he is playing an intelligent character, find his mentally weak spot; if he is playing a jolly person, find his serious side. That is one of the ways to enlarge a human passion: If you do not at once find the color you want, you must look for it.

Human passions do not usually have their inception, develop, and reach their climax at once, but gradually and over a long period. Dark feelings imperceptibly and slowly change into brighter ones, and vice versa. So, for example, Othello's heart is radiantly full of all joyous, bright, loving emotions, like burnished metal reflecting the rays of the sun. Then here and there dark spots are suddenly discernible; these are the first moments of doubt. The number of the dark spots increases, and the shining heart of loving Othello is mottled over with evil emotions. These shadows lengthen, grow, and finally his shining heart becomes darkened, almost blackened. In the beginning there were brief hints of growing jealousy, now only a few moments recall his tender, confident love. Finally these moments are gone and his whole soul is enveloped in complete darkness.

To be sure there are instances when a man is suddenly and completely overwhelmed by a passion: Romeo was suddenly seized by his love for Juliet. Yet who knows whether Romeo, had he survived, might not have experienced the general destiny of man and lived through the many difficult times, the many dark emotions, which are the inevitable concomitants of love?

Too often on the stage everything happens in sharp contrast to the nature of human passions. Actors fall in love at once, are jealous at the first possible opportunity. Many of them are innocent enough to believe that human passions, whether love, jealousy, miserliness, are like cartridges or bombs which an actor can plant in his heart. There are actors who even specialize in quite primitive ways in one or another of the human passions. Call to mind the operatic tenor, so prettified, effeminate, with his hair curled to make him look like an angel. His specialty is love, only love, which is to pose on the stage, pretend to be thoughtful, dreamy, constantly pressing one hand to the heart, rushing around portraying passion, embracing and kissing the heroine, dying with a sentimental smile, sending her a last plea for forgiveness. And if by chance the role contains portions unrelated to love, simple bits of human life, then the tenor either does not act at all or tries to use those portions as part of his specialty, theatrical love, pretending to meditate after striking a becoming pose. Actors who play heroic parts in dramas do this same sort of thing; so do the so-called moralists, the noble fathers in dramas, or the bassi in the opera, whose usual function is to play hatred on the stage. These actors are forever intriguing or hating or protecting their children for all they are worth.

The attitude of such actors toward human psychology and passions is naïvely one-sided and single-tracked: Love is portrayed by love, jealousy by jealousy, hatred by hatred, grief by grief, joy by joy. There are no contrasts, no mutual relationships between inner nuances; all is flat and monotone. Everything is done in one color. The villains are all black, the benefactors all white. For each passion the actor has his own special color, the way painters paint a fence or children paint pictures. The result is acting "in general." Such actors love "in general," they are jealous "in general," they hate "in general." They portray the complex components of human passion by means of elementary and mostly external signs. Too often one actor asks another:

"What are you playing such and such a scene on?"

"On tears," or "on laughs," "on joy," or "on alarm," replies the other, never even suspecting that they are not talking about inner action but about its external results.

An actor must know the nature of a passion, know the pattern by which he must be guided. The better the actor knows the psychology of the human soul and nature, the more he studies them in his free time, the deeper he will be able to penetrate the spiritual essence of human passion and therefore the more detailed, complex, and varied will be the score of any part he plays.

You wish to observe the development of a passion more closely, so I return to the work we interrupted on the Chatski score when we recast it in the key of his love for Sophia.

Using the scheme we drew up, I shall try to find in it all the degrees necessary to the development of the passion of love in accordance with the period, just as it strikes Chatski on his return from abroad.

I recall the state of a man in love and put myself in the center of the circumstances, that is to say in Chatski's position. This time I shall work back from the larger objectives to the minor ones.

Here I am, newly arrived from abroad, I have not even gone home but have driven straight to the gates of the Famusov residence.

My desire to see Sophia is so strong that I should really revise my first large objective to:

2A. *See my passionately beloved Sophia as soon as possible.*

What must I do to that end?

Now my coach has stopped; my coachman is calling the yardman to open the gates.

I cannot sit still in the coach. I must do something. My overflowing energy makes me act with greater vigor, my buoyancy is increased tenfold, it drives me on.

2a. *I wish to hasten the moment of our meeting, about which I dreamed so ardently when I was abroad.*

Now I jump out of my coach, I rush to the gate, pound it with the chain hanging on it; I wait for the yardman to open it and meantime I stamp vigorously up and down out of excess of energy. The gates creak on their hinges. As soon as they are slightly ajar I slip through; but the yardman bars my way, he wants to show his joy at seeing me.

2b. *I must exchange greetings with him, be nice to him.*

I would be glad to do this especially as he is *her* yardman. But an inner force is driving me on so that I am almost mechanical in my greeting and run on before the words are really out of my mouth.

Thus the need of hastening the meeting with Sophia merges my small objective 2b with the previous 2a and it becomes a mechanical action.

Now I run across the large courtyard to the front door.

2c. *I must quickly arouse the sleepy doorman.*

Now I grab the bell and pull it with all my might. I wait. I ring again.

I cannot keep my hands from moving although I know I run the risk of breaking the bellcord.

Now the family mongrel whimpers and fawns around my feet. He is her dog.

2d. *I want to caress the dog, who is an old friend of mine, and also because it is* HER *dog.*

But I have no time. I must ring the bell. So this objective merges with 2c.

Finally the door is opened and I rush into the vestibule. The familiar atmosphere envelops me and makes me feel giddy. An inner force drives me on harder than ever, it does not let me even stop to look around. But there is a new delay. The doorman greets me with his whinnying voice.

2e. *I must greet him, be nice to him, exchange a few words with him.*

But this objective merges in my larger over-all objective, and through my desire to hasten my meeting with Sophia my greetings are perfunctory.

I rush on, quickly muttering something. I jump up the stairs four steps at a time. Then halfway up, on the landing, I run into the steward and the housekeeper. They are alarmed by my head-long speed and are transfixed by the unexpectedness of seeing me.

2f. *I must exchange greetings with them, I must ask about Sophia; where is she? is she well? is she up?*

The nearer I come to the end of my striving, the stronger the pull in her direction. I almost forget to greet them first but immediately exclaim:

"Is Mademoiselle up? May I go in?"

And, without waiting for a reply, I run through the familiar rooms, along the corridor. Someone calls after me; someone runs after me.

Then I stop and begin to come to.

"I may not go in? She is dressing?"

It takes all my will to contain my excitement and begin to catch my breath.

To give vent to my painful impatience I stamp my feet. Someone comes running up to me with a little scream.

"Ah! Liza!"

Now she takes me by the coatsleeve and I follow her.

Now something occurs. I lose my head, I don't know, I don't remember anything. Is it a dream? My childhood returned? A vision? Or is it some joy I once knew in this or some other life? It must be she! Yet I cannot say anything about her. I only know that Sophia stands before me. There *she* is. No, it is something better. It is another Sophia.

Then of its own accord, a new objective takes shape.

2B. *I want to greet, to speak with this vision!*

But how? For such a blossoming young woman I must find new words, a new relationship.

In order to find them:

2a. *I must examine Sophia carefully, look at her familiar and loved features, weigh the change in her since we have been separated.*

73

I gaze at her, I want not only to look at her but to see into her very soul.

At this moment in my dream I see a charming young girl in the dress of the 1820's. Who is it? The face is familiar! Where did it come from? From some engraving? Could it be from a portrait or some memory which I have mentally transposed and dressed in the costume of the period?

I gaze at this imaginary Sophia, I feel the *truth* in my look. Probably Chatski himself looked at Sophia with this same sense of concentrated attention. To this is then added a familiar sensation, perhaps of bewilderment, perhaps of awkwardness.

What is this feeling? What does it remind me of? Where did it come from?

I make a guess. It goes back a long way. When I was still almost a child I met a little girl. The people around us joked about us, said that we were a couple, a betrothed pair; I was embarrassed and afterwards I used to think a great deal about her; we wrote to one another. Many years passed. I grew up, but in my imagination she remained a little girl. Finally we met and we were both embarrassed because we hadn't expected to look the way we did to each other. I couldn't imagine how to talk with a grown girl such as she had become. I had to talk with her in a different way; I did not know exactly how, but it could not be the way I used to. . . .

All the awkwardness, the perplexity, the search for a new relationship come out of my memory now by analogy with the present. A lively memory adds the warmth of lively feeling to my present dream, it makes my heart beat, and I feel the actual truth of my situation. I feel inside myself something which is aiming at, looking for an approach to, trying to establish, new mutual relationships with someone who is a new object yet a familiar one. These attempts have the feel of truth about them, they warm my emotions, they put life into this moment of meeting which I have imagined.

74

At this second a moment from my childhood recurs in memory. At some time or other I stood before my small friend just like this, overwhelmed with unspeakable joy, and all around lay toys in disorderly array. I do not know anything more about this moment in my life, yet it is deep and important. Now as then, in my thoughts I kneel to her, not knowing why, but realizing it is very effective! At the same time I remember a picture in a child's book of fairy tales. There on the flying carpet kneels, as I am doing now, a handsome young creature and before him, as before me, stands a lovely maiden.

At this point as Chatski what I wish to do is:

2b. *To convey in a kiss all my pent-up feelings.*

But how? The girl I used to know I would have hugged and lifted off her feet. But this one? I lose my head, timidly approach Sophia, and kiss her somehow in a different way.

2c. *I must caress Sophia with look and words.*

Now that I have come to feel the real truth of these moments in my role, I ask myself: What would I do if, like Chatski, I noticed the embarrassment, the coldness of Sophia, and had felt the sting of her unfriendly look?

As if in answer to this question, I feel an inner shrinking from the hurt, bitterness from my offended feelings fills my heart, and my disillusionment chills my energy. I want as quickly as possible to escape from this state. . . .

The score as formed and gone through in the key of a lover will only convey Chatski's love for Sophia when it actually becomes his own score, when it has been tested against the text of the play and made to fit it; that is to say, when it flows in accordance with the events of the play, parallel with the passion of love in it, and when all the words of the play acquire a corresponding basis in the score. Now, as we establish and try out the physical and simple psychological score, we must return to the text of the play in order to choose from it the objectives and units in consecutive logical sequence that serve to develop the passion of Chatski.

In doing this work you must know how to dissect the text of your part. You must know how to cull from it all the component units, objectives, moments, which in their sum total add up to a human passion. You must know how to study these units, objectives, and moments in connection with the established pattern of a passion which you use as a guide. You must also know how to provide these moments, drawn from the text of the playwright, with a lively basis and inner motivation. In brief you must subordinate the text of your part not to the external but the internal pattern of the development of the given passion, you must find the right place in the chain of passions for each moment of your role. . . .

Let us now draw a comparison between the two scores for the role of Chatski, the score set in the key of a friend, and in the key of a lover.

What changes and what remains constant in these two scores? I shall explain in an example.

Submerged in his desire to see Sophia as quickly as possible, amorous Chatski greets all the people along the way—the yardman, the doorman, the steward, the housekeeper—fleetingly, mechanically, only half aware of what he is doing. Whereas when he was playing this in the key of a friend he executed each one of these bits with careful attention. Later on as a lover, he has no time to look around at the familiar rooms. He rushes toward the goal of his longing, he jumps up the staircase four steps at a time. In the key of a friend it was quite the contrary; his meeting with the yardman and doorman, the viewing of the familiar apartments, was given much more time and attention. Here the inner tone not only broadens but also deepens because it embraces both the tone of a friend and the tone of the man in love.*

* In the original manuscript, Stanislavski indicated but did not carry through his intention of developing further the layers of Chatski's role. He would have

In this way the deeper the tone, the nearer it is to the heart of the actor, the more powerful, passionate, and penetrating it becomes, the more it conveys, diffuses, combines in itself the individual objectives which merge with one another until they form the substantive parts of the role. Meantime the number of objectives and units decreases in the score, but their quality and substance are enhanced.

This example of work on the part of Chatski illustrates vividly that the same physical and simple psychological score of a part, experienced emotionally in varying and increasingly deeper tones, grows closer to the heart of an actor at all creative points.

The combination of these inner elements of a role, when added to its varied internal and external circumstances, results in infinite variety. Together they create a long scale of emotional experience; of their own accord and unconsciously they take on the most varied rainbow shadings of feeling. As a result the simple objectives in the score acquire deep and important meanings for the actor as well as inner justification. The score saturates every particle of an actor's inner being, it enthralls him and acquires a deeper and deeper hold over him.

By degrees we reach the innermost depths which we define as the core, the mysterious "I." That is where human emotions exist in their pristine stage; there in the fiery furnace of human passions all that is trivial, shallow, is consumed, only the fundamental, organic elements of an actor's creative nature remain.

The Superobjective and Through Action

In this innermost center, this core of the role, all the remaining objectives of the score converge, as it were, into one *superobjective*.

---

explored it in the keys not only of the friend and the lover, as he did here, but also of the free man and the patriot. Thus in the end the score would have "as it were, three linings." (See also his reference to the role in *An Actor Prepares,* p. 257.)—EDITOR

That is the inner essence, the all-embracing goal, the objective of all objectives, the concentration of the entire score of the role, of all of its major and minor units. The superobjective contains the meaning, the inner sense, of all the subordinate objectives of the play. In carrying out this one superobjective you have arrived at something even more important, superconscious, ineffable, which is the spirit of Griboyedov himself, the thing that inspired him to write, and which inspires an actor to act.

In Dostoyevski's novel *The Brothers Karamazov* the super-objective is the author's search for God and Devil in the soul of man. In Shakespeare's tragedy of *Hamlet* such a superobjective would be the *comprehending* of the *secrets of being*. With Chekhov's *The Three Sisters* it is the *aspiration for a better life* ("to Moscow, to Moscow"). With Leo Tolstoy it was his unending search for "self-perfection," and so forth.

Only artists of genius are capable of the emotional experience of a superobjective, the complete absorption into themselves of the soul of the play, and the synthesis of themselves with the playwright. Actors of lesser talents, who lack the marks of genius, must be satisfied with less.

The great objectives comprise in themselves a quantity of live emotions and concepts, filled with profound content, spiritual insight, and vital force. One superobjective planted in the spiritual core of an actor, naturally and of its own accord, creates and manifests thousands of separate small objectives on the external plane of a part. This superobjective is the main foundation of an actor's life and part, and all the minor objectives are corollaries to it, the inevitable consequence and reflection of the basic one.

Nevertheless a creative superobjective is still not creativeness itself. In an actor it consists of constant striving toward the superobjective and the expression of that striving in action. This striving, which expresses the essence of creativeness, is the *through action of the role or play*. If for the writer this through action is expressed by the progression of his superobjective, then for the actor the through action is the *active attainment of the super-objective.*

Thus the superobjective and the through action represent creative goal and creative action, which contain in themselves all the thousands of separate, fragmentary objectives, units, actions in a role.

The superobjective is the quintessence of the play. The through line of action is the leitmotif which runs through the entire work. Together they guide the creativeness and strivings of the actor.

The superobjective and through action are the inborn vital purpose and aspiration rooted in our being, in our mysterious "I." Every play, every role, has concealed in it a superobjective and a line of through action which constitute the essential life of the individual roles and of the whole work. The roots of the through action are to be looked for in natural passions, in religious, social, political, aesthetic, mystical, and other feelings, in innate qualities or vices, in good or evil origins, whatever is most developed in the nature of man and which mysteriously governs him. Whatever occurs in our inner life or in the outer life which surrounds us, it all has significance in relation to the mysterious, often unconscious, bond with some main idea, with our innate aspirations, and with a line of through action which is our human spirit.

Thus a miser seeks in everything that occurs to him the secret bond with his aspiration to enrich himself, an ambitious man with his thirst for honors, an aesthete with his artistic ideals. Often, in life and also on the stage, the through line will manifest itself unconsciously. It will become defined only after the fact, and its ultimate goal, the superobjective, will have been secretly, unconsciously, exercising a pull, drawing to itself our human aspirations.

If we deviate from this main line we fall into error. For example, years ago we planned the last act of Gorki's *Lower Depths* as a party in the flop-house. We did not know how to feel and to convey the philosophy of the play, we merely went through the external motions of drunken carousing. This false representation of feelings was always repellent to me, but by force of habit I went through the action in a perfunctory, mechanical way. I made this same mistake for eighteen years; but recently, before the beginning of the act, finding myself loath to play it, I began to search for some new stimulation, a new approach. What did the carousing have to do with my feelings in the role of Satin? It was just part of the external circumstances, unimportant in itself, whereas the essence of the scene was entirely different. Luka has left behind an impress—love of one's neighbor. Satin is affected by this. He is not drunk, he is concentrated on his new feeling of pride. I tried to cast aside my false acting; I relaxed my muscles and concentrated my attention. My physical objectives and thoughts took on new shapes. I played well.

The actor must learn how to compose a score of lively physical and psychological objectives; to shape his whole score into one all-embracing supreme objective; to strive toward its attainment. Taken all together the superobjective (desire), through action (striving), and attainment (action) add up to the creative process of living a part emotionally. Thus the process of *living your part consists of composing a score for your role, of a superobjective, and of its active attainment by means of the through line of action.*

Yet no movement, striving, action is carried out on the stage, any more than in real life, without obstacles. One runs inevitably into the counter-movements and strivings of other people, or into conflicting events, or into obstacles caused by the elements, or other hindrances. Life is an unremitting *struggle*, one overcomes or one is defeated. Likewise on the stage, side-by-side with the through action there will be a series of *counter-through actions* on the part of other characters, other circumstances. The collision and conflict of these two opposing through actions constitute the dramatic situation.

Every objective must be within the powers of an actor; otherwise it will not lead him on, indeed it will frighten him, paralyze his feelings, and instead of emerging itself it will send in its stead mere clichés, craft acting. How often we see this happen! As long as a creative objective maintains itself on the level of affective feelings, an actor will truly live his part. But as soon as he sets himself a complicated objective beyond the powers of his own creative nature, drawn from some lesser-known level of human emotions, his natural feeling of his part stops short; it is replaced by physical tension, false feeling, and cliché acting.

The same thing occurs when an objective raises doubts, uncertainty, weakening or even destroying the striving of one's creative will. Doubt is the enemy of creativeness. It holds back the process of living one's part. Therefore the actor must watch over his objectives, keep them free of anything that distracts the will from the essence of creativeness or weakens the aspirations of the will.

The Superconscious

When he has exhausted all avenues and methods of creativeness an actor reaches a limit beyond which human consciousness cannot extend. Here begins the realm of the unconscious, of intuition, which is not accessible to mind but is to feelings, not to thought but to creative emotions. An actor's unpolished technique cannot reach it; it is accessible only to his artist-nature.

Unfortunately, the realm of the unconscious is often ignored in our art because most actors limit themselves to superficial feelings, and the spectators are satisfied with purely external impressions. Yet the essence of art and the main source of creativeness are hidden deep in man's soul; there, in the center of our spiritual being, in the realm of our inaccessible superconsciousness, our mysterious "I" has its being, and inspiration itself. That is the storehouse of our most important spiritual material.

It is intangible and not subject to our consciousness; it cannot be defined in words, seen, heard, known through any senses. Indeed how could one attain, by conscious means, all the subtleties of a living soul, for instance a soul as complex as that of Hamlet?

Many of its shadings, ghost phantoms, hints of emotions, are accessible only to unconscious creative intuition.

How to reach it then? How to plumb the depths of a role, an actor, or an audience? It can only be done with the aid of nature. The keys to the secret places of the creative superconscious are given over to the nature of the actor as a human being. The secrets of inspiration and the inscrutable ways to approach it are known only to nature. Only nature can perform the miracle without which the text of a role remains lifeless and inert. In short, nature is the only creator in the world that has the capacity to bring forth life.

The more subtle the feeling, the closer it comes to the superconscious, the closer to nature, and the farther it is removed from the conscious. *The superconscious begins where reality, or rather, the ultranatural, ends,* where nature becomes exempt from the tutelage of the mind, exempt from conventions, prejudices, force. Thus the natural approach to the unconscious is through the conscious. The only approach to the superconscious, to the unreal, is through the real, the ultranatural, that is to say through nature and its *normal, unforced, creative life.*

The yogis of India, who can work miracles in the realm of the subconscious and the superconscious, have much practical advice to offer. They also proceed toward the unconscious through conscious preparatory means, from the physical to the spiritual, from the real to the unreal, from naturalism to the abstract. Take a handful of thoughts, they suggest, and throw them into your subconscious sack, saying: I have no time to bother with them so you (my subconscious) attend to them. Then go to sleep. When you wake up, you ask: Is it ready? The answer is: Not yet. Take another handful of thoughts and again throw it into the sack, and go for a walk. When you return, ask: Is it ready? The answer is still: No! And so on. But in the end your subconscious will say: It is ready. And then it will return to you what you gave it to do.

How often, when we are going to sleep or taking a walk and

struggling to remember a melody or thought or name or address, we say to ourselves: "The morning is wiser than the evening"; and when we wake up in the morning we find that we have somehow recalled what we sought. The work of our subconscious and superconscious does not end either day or night, either when the body and all of our being is resting or when our thoughts and feelings are distracted by the cares of everyday life. But we are not aware of the work constantly in progress because it goes on beyond the reach of our consciousness.

In order to establish some sort of communion with his superconscious, an actor must know how to "take some handfuls of thoughts and throw them into the sack of his subconscious." The food for his superconscious, the material for creativeness, lies in those "handfuls of thoughts." Of what do these consist and where are they to be had? They are made up of knowledge, information, experience—all the material accumulated and stored in our memories. That is why an actor must be constantly filling the storehouse of his memory by studying, reading, observing, traveling, keeping in touch with current social, religious, political, and other forms of life. And when he turns over these handfuls of thought to his subconscious he must not be in a hurry; he must know how to wait patiently. Otherwise, so say the yogis, he will be like the stupid child who planted a seed in the ground and then dug it up every half hour to see if it was putting down roots.

All the work we do on ourselves and our roles is aimed at preparing the ground for the inception and growth of living passions and for inspiration which lies dormant in the realm of the superconscious. Some believe that inspiration comes of its own accord, regardless of what the actor does, and provides its own creative inner state. But inspiration is a spoiled creature. It will appear only in prepared circumstances, and any deviation from them will frighten it away to hide itself in the recesses of the superconscious.

Before he even thinks about the superconscious and inspiration, an actor must concern himself with establishing a proper internal state so firmly that he cannot tolerate any other, so that it becomes second nature to him. More than that he must learn to accept the given circumstances of his part as his own. Only then will his fastidious inspiration open its hidden doors, step out freely, and take into its masterful hands the entire initiative of his creativeness.

*   *   *

We have now come to the end of our second large period in the preparation of a role. What have we accomplished? If the first period was one of analysis to prepare the inner ground for the inception of creative desire, then this second period of emotional experience has developed that creative desire, it has called forth aspiration, an inner impulse to creative action, and thus prepared us for the external, physical action, the actual embodiment of the role.

CHAPTER THREE

The Period of Physical Embodiment

THE THIRD PERIOD of creativeness is *the embodiment of the role*.

If the first period was compared to the first acquaintance of two beings who are to become lovers, and the second to their marriage and pregnancy, the third is comparable to the birth and growth of a young being. Now that we have prepared our desires, objectives, aspirations, we can put them into action, not only inwardly but outwardly, using words and movements to convey our thoughts and feelings or simply carrying out our objectives in physical form.

Let us say that having been assigned the role of Chatski, I am on my way to the theatre for our first rehearsal, which has been set after a whole series of preparatory sessions such as those already described. I am excited about the impending rehearsal. I want to prepare myself for it. What shall I begin with? Shall I assure myself that I am not myself but Alexander Chatski? That would be wasted effort. Neither my body nor my soul would be taken in by any such obvious deception. It would only kill any faith I have, mislead me, and cool my ardor. I cannot exchange myself for anyone else. A miraculous metamorphosis is out of the question.

An actor can alter the circumstances of the life portrayed on the stage, he can find it in himself to believe in a new superobjective, he can give himself up to the main line of action which goes through a play, he can combine his recalled emotions in one way or another, he can put them in this or that sequence, he can develop habits in his role which are not native to him, and methods of physical portrayal as well, and he can change his mannerisms, his exterior. All this will make the actor seem different in every role to the audience. But he will always remain himself too. He acts on the stage in his own right, even though spiritually and physically he may transform himself to be more akin to the role he is playing.

Now, while I am sitting in my cab, I want to begin to transform myself physically into Chatski, while still being first and foremost myself. I shall not even attempt to get away from reality; it is much more to the purpose to use reality for my creative ends. For if you take an imaginary but lifelike circumstance and inject it into actual life it acquires a kind of vitality, often more attractive and artistic than reality.

How can I find a bond between the imaginary circumstances of my role and my present surroundings, sitting in a cab? How shall I begin my work, begin to be, to exist, amid everyday reality? How can I relate it to the life of my part? First of all I must establish the state of "I am." This time I am not doing it in my imagination but in real life; not in the imaginary home of Famusov, but in a cab.

It would be fruitless to try to convince myself that I have, only today, returned from abroad after a long absence. I would not believe that invention. I must seek some other approach, without forcing myself or my imagination, and yet putting myself in the desired state. I try to weigh the meaning of the fact of returning home from abroad. To this end I ask myself: Do I understand (really feel) what it means to come back to one's own country after a prolonged absence? To answer that question I must first re-evaluate, as deeply and broadly as I can, the very fact of the return; I must compare it to analogous facts in my own life, familiar to me through my own experience. I have often returned to Moscow from abroad, after a long absence, and then as now taken a cab to the theatre. I recall distinctly how happy I was at the prospect of seeing my colleagues, the theatre, Russians in general, of hearing my own language spoken, seeing the Kremlin, talking to the uncouth cab driver—I was happy to inhale "the vapors of our fatherland," which are to us "so sweet and congenial." Just as a man is happy to exchange his closely fitting evening clothes and patent leather shoes for a comfortable dressing gown and soft slippers, so one is delighted to return to hospitable Moscow after the hurly-burly of foreign cities.

This sense of serenity, rest, of arriving at one's own hearth is something one feels even more deeply when the journey has not been made in a comfortable sleeping car but in a bouncing coach and with relays of horses. I remember such a journey! The gaping public, the post horses, the drivers, the waits, the shaking, one's bruised sides, back, hips, the sleepless nights, the marvelous sunrises, the unbearable daytime heat or wintry frosts—in brief, all that was both wonderful and terrible and went with traveling by coach! If it was hard to travel for one week, as I did, imagine what it would have been to travel for months as Chatski did!

And how great was the joy of the return! I can feel it now as I sit in my cab and drive to the theatre. And involuntarily Chatski's own lines come to my mind:

> . . . beside myself,
> Two days and nights on end, and never closing eye,
> I traveled fast over the many hundred miles through wind and storm. . . .

I realize now the emotional impact of these words. I understand, I feel, what Griboyedov must have felt when he wrote them. I realize that they were larded with the quivering, live emotions of a man who had traveled widely, had often left and returned to his fatherland. That is why the words are so warm, deep, and full of meaning.

Warmed by the ardent feelings of the patriot, I try to put to myself another question, namely: What would Alexander Chatski feel if he were driving to see Famusov and Sophia? Putting myself in his stead, I already feel a certain awkwardness, a sense of somewhat losing my balance. How can one guess the feelings of another? How can one get inside his skin, put oneself in his place? I hastily withdraw the proposed question and replace it with another, namely: What do men in love do when, after an absence of years, they are driving to see the lady of their dreams?

Put in that form the question does not alarm me; yet it seems a bit dry, vague, generalized, and therefore I hasten to give it a more concrete formulation: What would I do if I, as now, were riding in a cab, but not going to the theatre, going to see *her*, and never mind whether she is called Sophia or something else?

I want to underscore the difference between these two versions of the question. In the first version I ask what the *other man* would do, whereas in the second *my own feelings* are involved. Such a question strikes closer to home; therefore it has more vitality, is warmer in feeling. In order now to decide what I would be doing if I were on my way to her, I must put myself in the state of feeling the magnetism of her charms.

For every man a *she* exists, sometimes a blonde, sometimes a brunette; sometimes she is kind, sometimes fierce, but always wonderful, fascinating, the kind of a she with whom one could at any moment fall in love again. I, like anyone else, think of my ideal she and rather easily find in myself the familiarly aroused emotions and inner impulses.

Now I shall try to transplant her into the surroundings of the Famusov home in the 1820's in Moscow. Why indeed should she not be Sophia Famusov and at the same time the kind of girl Chatski imagined her? Who can check on this? Therefore let it be as I choose. I begin to think about the Famusovs, about the atmosphere into which I now project the lady of my heart. My memory easily recreates the great mass of material previously collected in my work on the emotional pattern of my role. The familiar external and internal circumstances of life in the Famusov household are again reconstructed in order and envelop me on all sides. I already feel myself to be at their core, I begin to be, to exist, in them. Now I can already determine hour by hour what the whole of today will be, I can provide meaning and justification for driving to the Famusovs.

Nevertheless, while I am doing this work I am aware of a certain awkwardness; something keeps me from seeing *her* in the Famusov house and believing in my imagination. What is this? What is the reason for it? On the one hand, here am I, and here she is, a modern man and woman, a modern cab, modern streets; and on the other hand, there are the 1820's, the Famusovs, their vivid representatives. Yet is the life of the times and the epoch so important in the eyes of the eternal emotion of love? For the life of a human spirit, is it so important that in other days the carriages had other springs under them, that the streets were not so well paved, that the people going by wore clothes of another cut, that the sentries carried halberds? Is it important that their architecture was better, and that futurism and cubism did not exist? Yet the quiet lane, flanked with old private houses, down which I am now driving can scarcely have changed at all since those days; there is the same sad, poetic atmosphere, the same lack of bustle, the same serenity now as then. As for the feelings of a man in love, it has in all centuries been composed of the same elements without regard for streets or the clothing of the passersby.

Searching for a further answer to the question of what I would do if I were on my way to *her* if she were living in the circumstances of the Famusov household, I look into myself to find the answer in my own incipient impulses. They remind me of the familiar excitement and impatience of a man in love. I feel that if this excitement and impatience were increased in degree I would find it difficult to sit still, I would find my feet pushing against the partition of the cab in an effort to make the driver hurry. I would have the physical sensation of a surge of energy. I would feel that I must direct it, harness it to some action. I now feel that the principal motive powers of my inner life have gone to work to provide the reply to the questions: How shall I meet her? What shall I say and do to make this meeting memorable?

Buy her a bouquet? Candies? How trivial! Is she a cocotte to whom one takes flowers and sweets on a first assignation! What can I think of? Some present from abroad? That's even worse! I am no salesman to heap presents on her the first time I see her, as though she were my mistress. I blush at such low thoughts and prosaic impulses. Yet when I see her, how can I greet her in worthy fashion? I shall bring her my heart, lay myself at her feet. "The day is scarcely on its feet, and I am at yours!" Chatski's own words burst from me. I could not have found a better way to greet her.

These first words in the part of Chatski, which used to be distasteful to me, suddenly are a necessity, I like them, and even the kneeling, with which they are usually accompanied on the stage, no longer seems theatrical but perfectly natural. In this instant I have realized the emotional impact, the inner impulses, which led Griboyedov to write those lines.

However, if I am to lay myself at her lovely feet, I would like to feel that I am worthy of her. Am I good enough to give myself to her? My love, my loyalty, my constant worship of my ideal, all these are pure and worthy of her, but what about me myself? I am not handsome and poetic enough! I wish I were better, more refined. Here I involuntarily straighten up, try to put on a better face, to find a graceful pose; I console myself with the thought that I am not worse than others, and to check this I compare myself to the passersby. Luckily for me deformed people are the only ones to be seen.

By turning my attention to the people in the street I, without noticing it, move slightly away from my former purpose; I begin to observe the familiar scene from the point of view of a person accustomed to Western countries. That's not a man, over there at the gate, it's a pile of fur. A metal plate gleams on his head like the single eye of a cyclops. He is a Moscow yardman. Good God, what barbarism! He must be an Eskimo!

There's a Moscow policeman! With the end of his scabbard he

is pushing against the ribs of a poor old foundering jade, as if he would break her in two because she cannot haul an overburdened cart full of wood. There are yells and curses, the waving of a whip. Just like Asia, just like Turkey! And we ourselves—are we not vulgar, rough-hewn country bumpkins, even if we are all dressed up in foreign clothing? I blush again at the thought of comparison with the West and my heart sinks. How must foreigners look at all this when they come here. . . .

To all of Chatski's words I find an emotional response inside myself, the same sort of thing Griboyedov had when he wrote them. When you begin to examine familiar phenomena closely, then the old things which you were tired of and had ceased to look at suddenly make more of an impression on you than new and unexpected ones. So it is now with me. The more I observe the things I meet with along the way to the theatre, the more I seem to filter these reviewed impressions through the prism of a person just returned from abroad, the more strongly my feelings as a patriot are enhanced. I realize that it was not bitterness but anguish of soul, a great love for Russia, a deep understanding of what was precious and what was lacking in her, that made Chatski excoriate those who ruin our lives and obstruct her development. . . .

"Ah, good day to you," I call out in a perfunctory way, and bow to someone without taking time to think what I am doing.

Who was that? Oh, yes. He is a famous aviator and automobile racer.

That might seem quite an anachronism. My illusion should be blown right away by it. Not at all! I repeat: It is not a question of time, of way of life, it is only a question of the emotions of a man in love and the feelings of a patriot on returning home. Could not a man in love have an aviator cousin? Could a patriot returning home not meet an automobile racer? One thing is, however, strange. I do not seem to recognize my own manner in the way I greeted him. It is somehow different. Could it be the way that Chatski would have done it?

Another strange thing: Why do I feel a certain artistic satisfaction in the way I greeted that man so spontaneously? How did it happen? My arm unconsciously made a kind of movement which was evidently just right. Or was it perhaps right because I did not have time to think about my gesture and was impelled to make it by an inner direct impulse? It would be useless to remember such an unconscious gesture and attempt to fix it in my memory. It will either never recur or it will recur of its own accord, unconsciously; and if it recurs frequently it will eventually become habitual and be permanently a part of my role. In other words, to bring this about I must try to recall not the gesture itself but the general state I was in and which evoked, if only for a second, an external image, which may already be forming itself inside me and seeking an outer shape.

That is what happens when you remember a forgotten thought or melody. The harder you search for it the more stubbornly it hides from you. But if you are able to recall clearly the place, the circumstances, your general frame of mind, when you first had the thought, it will of its own accord be resurrected in your memory.

Here my inner work is interrupted as my cab draws up at the theatre and stops at the stage door. I get out and enter the theatre with the feeling that I am already warmed up and ready for the rehearsal. My part has been weighed and I feel that "I am."

Inside the theatre we sit at a large table in the rehearsal room. The reading begins. The first act is read. The director knits his eyebrows, all sit around with their eyes glued on their books. Bewilderment, embarrassment, perplexity, disillusionment! You do not want to read any more. The book only bothers you, there is no vital reason for sitting there with your nose in it. Now we feel as if we had been ducked in water, and we wonder what has become of all that we searched for so long, what we created with such effort in the quiet of our studies or sleepless nights? In my own case, I felt an inner image, emotionally and physically, of the man I am to portray, I knew the whole inner life of my part. What has become of all those feelings? It is as though they had been broken up into tiny fragments and it would be impossible to find and reassemble them inside myself. Worse than that, I feel that in the place of my stored-up creative riches I have been given cheap actor's tricks, habits, worn-out routines, a strained voice, forced intonations. Instead of the harmonious order I was aware of when I was working at home, I am now subjected to muscular anarchy which I am unable to control. I feel I have lost the score it took me so long to compose, and that I shall have to begin all over again. The first time the play was ever read I felt I was a trained master and now I feel like a helpless apprentice. Then I could confidently go through cliché acting and I felt like a virtuoso in my craft. Now I am diffidently trying to put my role into physical form and I feel like a student. What has happened to it all?

The answer to these harrowing questions is clear and simple. No matter how long an actor has been on the stage, such moments of helplessness, like labor pains, are inevitable at the moment when he brings forth his role. No matter how many roles he has created, no matter how many years he has worked in the theatre, no matter what experience he has acquired—he will never get away from these creative doubts and tortures that we are now experiencing. And no matter how many times this state is repeated it will always seem terrifying, hopeless, irreparable while this mood is on him.

No experience, no persuasion will convince actors that the creative work of emotionally experiencing a part and then putting it into physical form must not be done suddenly, all at once, but gradually in slow stages. At first, as we have seen, you experience your role mentally, and then it is embodied in an imaginative image during those sleepless nights, then in a more conscious way but still in the quiet of your study, then in intimate rehearsals, then in the presence of a few spectators, then in a whole series of dress rehearsals, and finally in a numberless quantity of performances. And each time you do the same work over from the beginning.

The question now posed is how we can recreate in an intimate rehearsal the role we have prepared at home. The director has already quietly and cheerfully announced that we are not yet ready for the pure text of Griboyedov. It is not right to muddle and wear out the words of a play ahead of time. Therefore he proposes that we abandon further reading.

The verbal text of a play, especially one by a genius, is the manifestation of the clarity, the subtlety, the concrete power to express invisible thoughts and feelings of the author himself. Inside each and every word there is an emotion, a thought, that produced the word and justifies its being there. Empty words are like nutshells without meat, concepts without content; they are no use, indeed they are harmful. They weigh down a role, blur its design; they must be thrown out like so much trash. Until the actor is able to fill out each word of the text with live emotions, the text of his role will remain dead.

In a work by a genius there is not one superfluous moment or feeling, and therefore, in the score of his part as composed by an actor, there should be only those feelings absolutely necessary to carry out the superobjective and the through action. It is only when an actor prepares such a score and inner image that the text will turn out to be the exact measure of the actor's creation. A play by a genius requires a score to match. Until that is created, there are too many or too few words, too many or too few emotions.

If many of the words in the text of *Woe from Wit* seem superfluous that only means that the actor's score is not yet perfected, and requires trying out on the stage in actual creative action. It is not enough to discover the secret of a play, its thought and feelings—the actor must be able to convert them into living terms. A truly great text is condensed, yet that does not prevent it from being profound and full of meaning. The external form and its ways must match it; the score itself must be solid, the form in which it is conveyed must be packed solidly, and the physical image must be vivid, incisive, and full of substance.

When the actor in his creativeness measures up to a remarkable text, the words of his part prove the best, the most indispensable, the easiest form of verbal embodiment with which he can make manifest his own creative emotions through his inner score. Then the words of another, the playwright, become an actor's own words, and the whole text becomes the best score for the actor. Then the unusual verse forms and rhythms of Griboyedov will be necessary not only for audible enjoyment but also for the sake of keenness and finish in conveying emotions and all that is in an actor's score.

Generally, the lines of the play become indispensable to the actor only in the last phase of his creative preparations, when all the inner material he has accumulated is crystallized in a series of definite moments, and the physical embodiment of his role is working out methods of expressing characteristic emotions.

This time has not yet been reached by us. In our present phase, the unadorned text of the play is only a deterrent. The actor is not yet capable of making a full or deep or exhaustive estimate of it. His role is still in the period of searching for a physical embodiment, and his score has not yet been tested on the stage—superfluous feelings and ways of expressing them are still inevitable. The pure text of the playwright seems too brief and actors fill it out with words of their own, interpolations of "well," and "now," and so forth.

In the beginning of the process of physical embodiment an actor is immoderate and extravagant in using anything and everything to convey his creative emotions—words, voice, gesture, movement, action, facial expression. At this point the actor spares no means if only he can somehow externalize all that he feels inside him. It seems to him that the more ways and means he uses in putting each individual moment into physical form, the greater the choice, the more substantial and stuffed out will be the physical embodiment itself. But in this period of search, not only the alien words of the author but even one's own words are too concrete to express the young, scarcely full-blown emotions of the score.

* * *

The director was right in breaking off the reading. We are invited instead to go on with some improvisations on themes of our choice. These are preparatory exercises in finding physical expression for feelings, thoughts, actions, and images analogous to those of our parts. With their aid and by means of adding ever new circumstances we feel out the nature of each emotion, its component parts, its logic and sequence.

When we begin our improvisations, the point is to put into action all casual desires and objectives that well up inside us. These desires and objectives should be derived, at first, not from make-believe facts drawn from the play, but from the actual circumstances that surround the actor at rehearsal. Let his inner impulses as they spontaneously shape themselves in him prompt the most immediate objectives and also the superobjective of the improvisation. However, while he is doing this work the actor should not forget the circumstances proposed by the playwright, which are those the actor has already been through, and which, in any case, he would unwillingly part with since he has grown so close to them in the previous period of experiencing his part emotionally.

The actor now begins to exist amid his actual surroundings, which this time are not imaginary but real, while at the same time they are under the influence of the past, present, and future of his role and are filled with inner impulses congenial to the character he is portraying.

96

How is this done? I must make a bond between my actual surroundings—a rehearsal in the foyer of the Moscow Art Theatre—and the circumstances of the Famusov house in Moscow in the 1820's, and with the life of Chatski, which is to say my own life as set inside the conditions of the life of the hero of the play, together with his past, present, and the prospect of his future life. It was not difficult before to feel my way into the imaginary circumstances of his life, mentally and emotionally. But how can I do it here amid contemporary life and today's realities? How can I put sense into my presence in the Moscow Art Theatre? How can I find a basis for the circumstances which surround me in this rehearsal? How can I justify my being here in this room and not break the close bond with a life analogous to that of Chatski?

This new creative objective first of all brings into action the motive forces of my inner life—my will, mind, and feelings—and arouses my imagination. It is already beginning to work.

"Why could not I, even in the circumstances of the life of Chatski, have friends among the actors of the Moscow Art Theatre?" suggests my imagination.

"It would be strange if I did not," asserts my mind. "People like Chatski could not but be interested in art. Chatski himself if he had lived in the 1820's and 1830's could have been in the group of Slavophiles, the patriots, among whom were actors and even Mikhail Shchepkin himself. If Chatski were alive now he would undoubtedly be a frequent visitor to our theatres and would have friends among the actors."

"Who are all these people?" my feelings now ask.

"The same as they are in real life, they are actors of the Moscow Art Theatre," explains my imagination.

"No, I think that man sitting over there opposite me is not an actor but 'that swarthy man on crane's legs,' "* decide my feelings, not without a touch of acid.

---

* Chatski's taunting description of an ubiquitous guest at Moscow parties.

"All the better. As a matter of fact, he is very like 'that swarthy man,' " say my feelings, agreeing with themselves.

Discovering the resemblance to the "swarthy man" gives me great pleasure because, I fear, the actor sitting opposite me does not have much attraction for me. Chatski himself would look at that "swarthy man" just as I am looking now at my partner in our improvisation.

Taking hold of this incipient feeling, which relates me to Chatski, I hasten to greet the "swarthy man" in the way that Chatski, the elegant man dexterous in the ways of foreign salons, would do.

But I am rudely punished for my haste and impatience. All the cliché forms of polite manners and good taste are lying in wait to jump out and take me unawares. My elbow sticks way out at one side when I shake hands, my arm is as bowed as an ox-yoke, I slur all my words; in my affectedly casual manner I distort my way of walking, theatrical triviality invades my being from all sides and takes me over.

Numb with shame, I hate my partner and I hate myself. I sit motionless for a long time, and keep soothing myself with: "Never mind, this is normal. I should have known what the result of haste would be. Until the thousand thousands of cobweblike creative desires have been bound together to form a heavy cable I shall not be able to cope with cramped muscles. I must wait until my creative will is stronger and able to subject my entire body to its initiative."

While I am reasoning in this fashion my "swarthy man" companion, overacting like mad as if on purpose, demonstrates to me the horrible results of uncontrolled muscles.

As if to reproach me, he acts with great gusto, self-assurance, brilliance, cheap elegance, and does everything I have done. It seems as though we have suddenly landed on the stage of some third-rate provincial theatre. I freeze up with embarrassment, shame, and fear. I dare not raise my eyes; I do not know how to extricate myself from him, how to get away from his self-satisfied actor's aplomb. And he, to make matters worse, goes on cavorting cheerfully in front of me, dragging his "crane's legs" around, playing with his make-believe monocle, and rolling his r's like the worst kind of provincial actor in a society part.

The longer it goes on the stupider becomes his incessant chatter. The "swarthy man" is more repulsive to me than ever, and I long to pour out my feelings of antipathy to him.

But how to do it? With words? He would be offended. With my hands, gestures, actions? I could not get into a scuffle with him. Only my eyes and my face remain. It is not without reason that they say the eyes are the mirror of the soul. Our eyes are the most responsive organ of our body. They are the first to react to the manifestations of internal or external life. The speech of the eyes is most eloquent, subtle, direct, and at the same time least concrete. Besides it is very convenient. You can say far more, say it with greater force, with your eyes than with words. Yet what you say gives no cause for offense, for it conveys only a general mood, the general character of feelings, and not concrete thoughts and words to which objection can be taken.

In my need, I now turn to my eyes for help, realizing that in the beginning one must as far as possible avoid action, movements, words, in order not to provoke the destructive anarchy of muscles. When I thus find an outlet for my feelings without being obliged to put them into physical form, to act them out, I feel relieved of my muscular tension, I become quite calm, and from having the sense of being a machine to represent something I return to being just human. Then everything around me goes back to its normal and natural state. Here I am sitting quietly, observing the antics of the "swarthy man," laughing at him inwardly; and not wishing to hide my feelings, I give them free rein.

Just at this point the rehearsal is broken off. I hurry after the "swarthy man" who is moving toward the exit. Like Chatski I want to laugh at him. But along the way I am overtaken by another of my comrades, one who likes to propound deep philosophy on stupid themes.

"Do you know," his bass voice booms impressively in my ear, "it just occurred to me that there was a reason why the playwright named the character I play Skalozub [show-your-teeth]. Evidently he must have a habit, don't you know, of . . ."

". . . showing his teeth," I suggest.

I cannot tolerate slow wits in the field of art. An irritated, almost sharp remark is on the tip of my tongue, but again I recall the Chatski improvisation and it seems to me that he would have looked at this odd creature differently. So I restrain myself.

"It had not occurred to me," I reply lightly. "It must be so. Griboyedov characterizes people by their names, not just Skalozub but others too. For instance Khlyostova [stinger] is called that because she makes stinging sallies. Tugoukhov [slow ears] because he is hard of hearing. Zagoretzski [hot head] probably because he gets hot so easily. Repetilov [repeater]? Surely because his part calls for many rehearsals. Tell the man who plays it, because he is lazy. And by the way, don't forget me. Think about why Griboyedov called my character Chatski."

I have the impression that when I leave him my slow-witted friend is preparing to take deep thought on the subject. No doubt Chatski would have expressed himself with more wit than I was able to do; nevertheless it seems to me that his interchange with my odd comrade would have been analogous to the one I had.

At the same time, I think to myself: Although I scarcely realized it I was speaking in Chatski's stead and in a quite simple, unforced way. Yet a half hour ago the real words of my part were of no use to me. Why is this so? The secret of it is that between our own words and those of another "the distance is of most unmeasurable size." Our own words are the direct expression of our feelings, whereas the words of another are alien until we have made them our own, are nothing more than signs of future emotions which have not yet come to life inside us. Our own words are needed in the first phase of the physical embodiment of a part because they are best able to extract from within us live feelings which have not yet found their outward expression.

*   *   *

It is with the help of the eyes, face, mimetics that a role most easily finds physical expression. Then what the eyes cannot spell out the voice takes up and expresses by words, intonations, speech. To reinforce and explain one's feeling and thought, gestures and movements add vivid illustration. This physical action is finally crowned and is converted into fact by the effort of one's creative will.

The speech of the eyes and face is so subtle that it conveys emotions, thoughts, feelings with scarcely perceptible muscular movements. The muscles must be fully and directly subordinated to feeling. Any arbitrary, mechanical tightening of the muscles of the eyes and face—whether it comes from indignation, excitement, a nervous tic, or other forms of force—destroys this subtle, scarcely perceptible "speech."

Therefore an actor's first concern must be to protect his delicate visual and facial apparatus from all lawlessness on the part of his muscles by means of counterhabits ingrained as the result of systematic exercise. It is impossible to root out a bad habit unless one puts in its stead something better, more true and natural.

After the eyes the next centers of action to express feelings are the face and its mimetics. The face is less subtle than the eyes, but more concrete, and sufficiently eloquent to convey the messages of the subconscious and the superconscious. The mimetics of the face are also more in danger of lack of control. Facial tension and artificiality can distort an emotion beyond all recognition. It is necessary to fight against this danger so that facial expression will remain in direct relationship with inner emotions and convey them with precision and immediacy.

When you have made as much use as you can of the subtle means of expression of your eyes and face, you can then begin to use your voice, sounds, words, intonations, and speech. To be sure, from under the words and between the words there is much that can be conveyed with the aid of facial expression, eyes, and psychological pauses. Yet in expressing all that is concrete, definite, conscious, personal—words are a necessity. They are indispensable when one is obliged to convey thoughts and ideas in particular form. Yet the danger of tension and clichés is also inherent in the realm of voice and speech. Tension in the voice ruins its sound, pronunciation, intonation, making it inflexible, coarse; and vocal clichés are unusually stubborn. They must be combatted so that voice and speech remain in complete dependence on inner feelings and are their direct, exact, and subservient expression.

As separate objectives, units, and finally the whole score become clarified, there follows the natural urge to put desires and aspirations into effect. Without his knowing it, the actor begins to act. Action naturally calls for the movement of the whole body, and the same demands are made of the body as were first made of the eyes and face: It must respond to the subtlest, most imperceptible inner feelings and convey them with eloquence. The body too must be protected from arbitrary force, from muscular tension. This is one reason why the physical incarnation of a role has to be held back until the final phase of our work, when the inner facets of the role are perfected and strong enough to control not only the eyes, the facial expression, and the voice, but also the body. When this last is under the direct management of inner feelings then the deadening power of cliché acting is less baneful.

Let the body go into action when it can no longer be held back, when it feels the deep inner essence of experienced emotions, inner objectives which it has prompted. Then of its own volition there will emerge an instinctive, natural urge to carry out the aspirations of creative will in the form of physical action.

In the battle of the body with artificialities and tensions an actor must remember that nothing is accomplished by prohibitions. You cannot forbid your body to do certain things, but you can persuade it to work along the line of beautiful external expression. If you try prohibitions, instead of one stencil type of action and one kind of tension you will have ten. It is a kind of law that a cliché will fill any empty space much as weeds will do out of doors. A gesture which is made for its own sake is a piece of force perpetrated on one's inner feelings and their natural manifestation.

The mechanical habits of an exercised body and its muscles are very strong and stubborn. They are like a willing but stupid slave, often more dangerous than an enemy. External methods and mechanical artificialities are acquired with extraordinary speed, and are retained for a long time; after all, the muscular memory of a human being, especially of an actor, is extremely well developed. Whereas on the contrary his emotion memory, the memory of sensations, emotional experiences, are extremely fragile.

Alas for the actor if there is a slippage between his body and his soul, between his inner action and his outward movements. Alas for him if his bodily instrument falsifies his feelings, puts them off the right key. It is what happens to a melody played on an instrument out of tune. And the truer the feeling, the more painful the discordance.

The bodily incarnation of a part, of a passion, should be not only exact but also beautiful, graceful, sonorous, colorful, harmonious. How can one manifest what is exalting by trivial means, or what is noble by vulgar means, what is beautiful by what is deformed? A street player, a bad fiddler, does not need a Stradivarius; a simple violin suffices to convey his feelings. But for a Paganini, a Stradivarius is a necessity. The more substantial the inner creativeness of an actor, the more beautiful his voice should be, the more perfect should be his diction, the more expressive should be his facial movements, the more graceful his body, the more flexible his entire physical equipment. Embodiment on the stage, like any other artistic form, is only good when it is true and at the same time executes in artistic form the inner substance of the work. The shape must conform to the inner substance. If the shape is a failure, the fault lies with the inner creative feeling that engendered it.

Up to now we have been speaking of finding a physical form for the inner score of the part, the image that contains its essence. But every living organism has an outer form as well, a physical body which uses make-up, has a typical voice as to manner of speech and intonation, typical way of walking, manners, gestures, and so forth.

The conscious means of embodying a part begins with the intellectual creation of an outer image, with the aid of the imagination, the inner eye, ear, and so forth. An actor strives with his inner eye to see the exterior, the costume, gait, movements, and so forth, of the character he is to play. Mentally he searches for samples in his memory. He recalls the appearance of people he knows. From some he borrows certain qualities and from others he borrows certain others. He makes his own combination and composes the external image he has in his mind.

If, however, he does not find either in himself or his memory the material he needs, then he must search for it. Like a painter or sculptor he must seek a live model by looking everywhere, in the street, in the theatre, at home, or in the places where he can find groups of people in certain categories—military, bureaucratic, merchants, aristocrats, peasants, and so forth—depending on his needs.

Every actor should constantly collect materials to help enlarge his imagination for use in creating the external appearance of roles, materials for make-up, whole figures, carriage, and so forth. For this purpose he should amass a collection of all kinds of photographs, engravings, sketches for make-up, typical faces, as seen in reproductions or described in literature. At times when his imagination runs dry this material will rouse it, make creative suggestions, remind him of things that perhaps have been familiar but have slipped out of his memory.

If this material is of no avail then the actor must try other means to stir up his dormant imagination. Let him attempt to make a careful sketch of the face or figure he is searching for, draw the features, the mouth, eyebrows, wrinkles, the outline of the body, the cut of the clothes. Such a sketch, prepared with a few strokes, will supply a combination of lines rather like a caricature to suggest the more typical aspects of his external image.

Having plotted the design the actor then has to transfer it with all its typical lines to his own face and body.

Often the actor looks for this image on himself. He tries all kinds of ways of dressing his hair, of using his eyebrows; he contracts various muscles of his face and body, tries out various ways of using his eyes, of walking, gesticulating, bowing, shaking hands, moving about. This experiment is carried further with make-up. He will put on a whole series of wigs, paste on all sorts of beards, mustaches, use colored creams to try to find the exact shade of complexion, lines of wrinkles, shadows, highlights, until he stumbles on the thing he is looking for—something which, by the way, often quite surprises him. When the outer image comes to life, the inner image recognizes its body, gait, manner of movement. The same work has to be repeated in choosing a costume. First the actor searches in his affective, visual memory, then in drawings, photographs, pictures, then in his own life. He makes sketches, tries on clothing, in a variety of cuts, pins them up, alters their aspect, until he accidentally or consciously finds what he is looking for, or what he did not at all expect to find.

*   *   *

The ability to keep one's body completely at the service of one's feelings is a principal concern of the external technique of incarnating a role. Still, even the most perfect physical equipment cannot transmit many incommunicable, superconscious, invisible feelings. They are conveyed directly from soul to soul. People commune with one another by means of invisible inner currents, radiations of their spirit, compulsions of their will. These have a direct, immediate, powerful effect on the stage, and they convey things which neither words nor gestures are capable of doing. You experience an emotional state and you can make others, with whom you are in communion, do the same.

A great and inveterate mistake made by actors is to believe that only what is visible and audible to the public, in the wide expanse of the theatre building, is of scenic quality. But does the theatre exist only to cater to the eyes and ears of the public? Does everything that passes through our soul lend itself only to words, sounds, gestures, and movements?

The irresistibility, contagiousness, and power of direct communion by means of invisible radiations of the human will and feelings are great. It is used to hypnotize people, to tame wild animals or a raging mob; the fakirs put people to death and resuscitate them; and actors can fill whole auditoriums with the invisible radiations of their emotions.

Some think that the conditions of having to create in public are a deterrent. On the contrary, they encourage this kind of communion, because the atmosphere of a performance, heavily impregnated with the nervous excitement of the crowd, serves as the most effective channel for an actor's creativeness. The mass feeling enhances his feeling of being electrified, it intensifies the atmosphere in the auditorium, and it increase the flow of inner currents. Let the actor pour out the radiations of his emotions, when he is silent or motionless, in the dark or in the light, consciously and unconsciously. Let the actor believe that these are the most effective, irresistible, subtle, powerful means to convey the most important, superconscious, invisible things which cannot be put into words by the playwright.

Part II

Shakespeare's *Othello*

Between 1930 and 1933, when Stanislavski was preparing the following study based on *Othello*, he devised the form of presentation that he was to use in *An Actor Prepares* and *Building a Character*. The familiar cast of characters—including Stanislavski-as-teacher-Tortsov and Stanislavski-as-student-Kostya—appear here, as well as in the study of *The Inspector General* that follows. As the chapter titles indicate, the basic concepts developed in connection with *Woe from Wit* are carried forward here, but with a shift of emphasis to the "new and unexpected method" for releasing the inner life of a role by first creating its physical life.—EDITOR

CHAPTER FOUR

First Acquaintance

TORTSOV began by saying: "You now know what a working creative state is on the stage. This makes it possible for you to enter the next phase of our program on the preparation of a part. For this we must have a specific role to work on. It would be even better to have a whole play for that purpose so that each of you would have appropriate work to do in it. So it is with the choice of a play that we shall begin. Let us decide what we shall act, or rather what we shall use to put into effect all that we have learned so far."

The entire lesson was given up to choosing parts, separate scenes, and a whole play on which we would work.

To my great joy, Tortsov fixed his choice on *Othello*. I shall not go into the details, the long arguments that are inevitable in this sort of a decision. We all know of similar scenes connected with amateur groups and performances. It will be better for me to put down the motives which impelled Tortsov to confirm as the choice for our further activities the very play he had considered too difficult and dangerous for young beginners.

These were his reasons:

"We need a play that will interest you all and in which we can find suitable parts for all or nearly all of you. *Othello* is absorbing to everyone and the roles are excellently distributed: Brabantio— Leo; Othello—Kostya; Iago—Grisha; Desdemona—Maria; Roderigo—Vanya; Cassio—Paul; Emilia—Dasha; the Doge—Nicholas. Only Vasya remains without a part.

"*Othello* is an appropriate choice also because it contains many small parts; there are crowd scenes too. These I shall distribute among a group of apprentices in the theatre with whom we shall work as we have in the past in elaborating our method.

"This tragedy of Shakespeare's is, as I have said before, too difficult for beginners. Moreover, it is too complicated to put on our stage. This will prevent you from indulging in efforts at a 'half-baked' production and performances which could undermine your none-too-secure powers. You see I am not going to oblige you to *act* the tragedy. We need it only as material we can use for study. For that we could not find a better play. There is no question of its first-rate quality from the artistic point of view. Besides, this tragedy is well defined in the pattern and construction of its individual sections, in the consecutiveness and logical development of its tragedy of emotions, in its through line of action, and in its superobjective.

"There is still another practical consideration. You, as beginners, are above all drawn to tragedy. In most cases this desire derives from the fact that you are not yet fully aware of its problems and demands. So learn about them as soon and as intimately as possible so that in the future you will not thoughtlessly let yourselves be carried away by dangerous temptations.

"Every director has his individual approach to the preparation of a part and his own program for carrying out this work. This is something for which no fixed rules can be set. Yet the fundamental stages, the psychophysiological methods of doing this work, must be rigorously observed. You have to know them, and I must demonstrate them to you in practice; I must make you feel them and test them in your own persons. That is, so to speak, the prototype of the whole process of preparing a part.

"Besides, you must know, understand, and learn to control all possible approaches to this work, because the director will make variations in keeping with the necessities, the development of the work, its conditions, the individual peculiarities of the actors. I must also demonstrate these approaches to you. That is why I shall do the many scenes of *Othello* in different ways. Whereas the first one I shall do in accordance with a fundamental, classic plan, the others will have new variations on their composition introduced into them constantly. As I introduce these variations I shall give notice of them in advance."

* * *

"Let us read *Othello*," proposed Tortsov at the beginning of our class.

"We know it already! We've read it!" exclaimed several students.

"All the better. In that case take away all the copies of the play and do not return them until I say so. And you must promise not to get any others. Since you know the play, tell me its contents."

We were silent.

"It is difficult to tell the contents of a complex, psychological play; so to begin with, let us be satisfied with the simple external plot, the line of events."

No one responded to that request either.

"Well, you begin," Tortsov urged Grisha.

"To do that, you see, you have to know the play well," he replied evasively.

"But you said you knew it."

"Excuse me, if you please. I know by heart the whole role of Othello himself, because, you see, I'm his type; but I just glanced through the other parts," confessed our tragedian.

"So that is how you made your first acquaintance with *Othello*!" ejaculated Tortsov. "That's very sad. Perhaps you will tell us the contents of the play," said Tortsov, now turning to Vanya who was sitting next to Grisha.

"I couldn't do it, not for anything. I read it, but not all. There were a lot of pages missing."

"What about you?" Tortsov asked Paul.

"I don't recall the play as a whole; I saw some foreign stars in it. They cut it a lot, as you know, especially the parts not directly connected with their roles," replied Paul.

Tortsov shook his head

Nicholas had seen the play in a small town and so badly done it would have been better if he had never seen it at all.

Vasya read the play on a train and was all mixed up about it. He recalled only the principal scenes.

Leo was familiar with all the literary criticism concerning *Othello*, from Hervinus* on down, but he was unable to state any facts concerning the actions or their sequence.

"This is very bad. As important an event as your first acquaintance with the work of a poet, and it takes place just anywhere, in a train, in a cab, or a streetcar! The worst of it is that you read it not for the sake of coming to know the play but in order to flatter yourselves by picking out advantageous roles.

"So this is how actors first meet the best classics which they in due course are supposed to incarnate! This is how they approach a part with which sooner or later they are to identify themselves, in which they are to find their alter ego!

"Why, this moment of your first meeting with a part should be unforgettable.

"As you know, I attribute decisive significance to these first impressions. If the impressions of a first reading are properly received, that is a great gauge of future success. The loss of this moment is irreparable because a second reading no longer contains the element of surprise so potent in the realm of intuitive creativeness. To correct a spoiled impression is more difficult than to create a proper one in the first place. *One must be extraordinarily attentive to one's first acquaintance with a part because this is the first stage of creativeness.*

---

* The German specialist on Shakespeare.

"It is dangerous to ruin that moment by the wrong approach to the work of a poet, because it may give you a false conception of the play and part or, what is worse, a *prejudice* about it."

On being questioned by the students Tortsov explained what he meant.

"Prejudice has many aspects. Let me begin with the fact that it can be in favor of something as well as against," he said. "Take, for example, the cases of Grisha and Vanya. They acquired a partial acquaintance with *Othello*. One read only the role of Othello himself, the other is unaware of the contents of the parts missing from his copy.

"Not knowing the whole play but just the one role, which is magnificent, Grisha is delighted and judges the rest on faith. That's all very well if one is dealing with a masterpiece like *Othello*. But there are many poor plays with magnificent parts in them—*Keene, Louis the Eleventh, Ingomar, Don César de Bazan.** Vanya could insert anything he chose into the pages torn out of his copy. If he believed his own imagined contents, that could be the basis of a prejudice that did not correspond to Shakespeare's ideas. Leo filled his head with criticism and commentary. Can that be infallible? Much of it is untalented nonsense and if you take stock in it, it will build a prejudice which will bar a direct approach to the play. Vasya, by reading the play in a train, jumbled his impressions of it with those of his travel. There again is fertile soil for prejudice. Nicholas, not without reason, fears to recall the small-town performance he saw of *Othello*. I am not at all surprised to find that he has a negative impression of the play.

"Imagine that you cut a beautifully drawn figure out of a canvas or that someone shows you bits snipped from a fine painting. Could you judge or come to know the whole picture from that?

* *Keene* by Alex. Dumas père, *Louis XI* by Casimir Delavigne, *Ingomar* by Fr. Halma, *Don César de Bazan* by Dumanoir and Dennery.

It is lucky that *Othello* in all its component parts is such a perfect work of art. But if it were otherwise, if the title role were the only successfully written one and the others were not worth doing, the actor who judged the whole play by the one part would be prejudiced favorably but wrongly by it. One could call that a positive prejudice. And if things were the other way round, and the author had been successful with all parts except that of the hero, then the incorrect impressions and the prejudice would be negative.

"Let me tell you of such an instance.

"A well-known actress had never seen performances of *Woe from Wit* or *The Inspector General* when she was young; she knew the plays only from her lessons in literature. The things that remained in her memory were not the plays themselves but the critical dissection to which they were subjected by her not-too-gifted instructor. Her classroom impression remained that these two classical plays were fine works but—very boring.

"Fortunately for that actress she eventually performed in both plays; but it was only years later, when she had firmly grown into her parts, that she was able to tear out at last the thorns of prejudice planted in her and see the plays not through the eyes of others but with her own. Now there is no more ardent admirer of these two classic comedies. And you should hear what she thinks of her teacher!

"Just see to it that this does not happen to you because of a wrong approach to *Othello*!"

We defended ourselves by saying that we had not read the play in school and no one had instilled foreign notions about it in our minds.

"Prejudices can be formed outside school as well," replied Tortsov. "Suppose, for example, before you ever read the play you heard all sorts of true and false comments about it, good and bad criticism, you would then begin to criticize it yourselves. Many of us really believe that to evaluate and understand a work of art we should be able to discover flaws in it. Actually it is far more important to know how to look for and find what is fine, to discover the merits of a piece of work.

"Unless you are unfettered in your own attitude toward a work you will not be able to withstand the generally accepted estimate of a classic which has tradition to back it up. This will force you to accept *Othello* exactly as 'public opinion' says you must.

"The reading of a new play is often turned over to the first person who comes along and whose only attribute is a loud voice and clear diction. Moreover, the text is handed to him only a few minutes before he is to begin the reading. Is it surprising that this accidental reader presents the play in hit-or-miss manner without any conception of its inner essence?

"I have known an instance when such a reader rendered the principal role in a play in the quavering voice of an old man, not realizing that the hero, who was nicknamed 'old man,' was still quite young but had acquired the epithet because he was disillusioned with life. Such a mistake can mutilate a whole play.

"A model reading which is too talented, too good, too vivid, which gives the reader's own interpretation too imaginatively, can produce prejudices of another kind. For example, the conception of the reader may differ from that of the author and still be so talented and entrancing that the actor is carried away by it. In this case the prejudice is favorable, but the struggle with it is hard. At such times the actor is in an impossible position: On the one hand, he is unable to break away from what fascinated him in the reader's interpretation, and on the other hand, this does not jibe with the play.

"Here is yet another instance. Many playwrights are excellent readers of their own works, and these readings often create great popularity for their plays. After the ovation given to the author the play is ceremoniously handed over to the theatre, and the electrified company is all set to undertake an interesting piece of work. How great is their disillusion when a second reading proves that they have been tricked, that the talented part of the play, the thing that aroused their enthusiasm, was an attribute of the reader and disappeared with him, while the lesser or worse part belonged to the writer and is left behind in the form of the play. How is one to get rid of what was fascinating and talented, and how reconcile oneself to the ungifted, disillusioning aspect of the play?

"In this case, prejudice is all the more powerful and inescapable because the playwright appears in full panoply before a disarmed auditorium. The reader is far more powerful than his listeners, for he has finished his creative work, they have not yet begun theirs. It is not surprising that the former conquers the latter, that they surrender unconditionally to his effect on them.

"Even when one is alone in one's room at home one has to know how to approach a new play and not allow any kind of pre-conception to enter. How could it do so, you may ask; where would it come from? From unpleasant personal impressions, personal difficulties which have nothing at all to do with the play, a bad humor, a state in which everything seems wrong, or a lazy, apathetic, undemonstrative mood, or any other personal or private reasons.

"Then there are a number of plays which have to be studied at length, read and re-read, in order to enter into their spirit, because they are elusive, complicated, or confused in inner content. Such are the plays of Ibsen, Maeterlinck, and many other authors who tend away from realism in the direction of generalization, stylization, synthesis, the grotesque, or all sorts of conventions with which modern art is filled. Such works have to be decoded. You approach them as you would a riddle; they require great intellectual effort. Yet it is important not to burden them with too much sheer intellectual process on first acquaintance, as this could easily create a dangerous prejudice that they are boring.

"Be afraid to approach such plays brains first. Brain-cudgeling processes can often provide the worst preconceptions of all.

"The more intricate the reasoning the farther it leads you away from creative experience and toward purely intellectual acting or over-acting. Any plays which call for symbols and stylization call for especial caution when you first become acquainted with them. They are difficult because in them a major share is left to intuition and the subconscious. You cannot over-act symbolism, stylization, or the grotesque; the approach must be through sensing the essentials of the play and their artistic shape. Reason counts least of all, while most important of all is artistic intuition, which is, as you know, extraordinarily timorous.

"Do not frighten it further with prejudices."

"And yet," I protested, "there are cases that I have read about when an actor achieves a role immediately, in all its smallest details, when it carries him away the very first time he sees it. These bursts of inspiration are what attract me most about creative stage work; genius shines through them so vividly, with such fascination!"

"I should think so! That's what people like to write about in fiction," was Tortsov's ironic rejoinder.

"You mean it doesn't happen?"

"On the contrary, it's absolutely possible, but it is far from being the rule," explained Tortsov. "In art as in love an attraction can flare up in an instant. More than that it can have not only an instantaneous genesis but also instantaneous fulfillment.

"In *My Life in Art* there is an example of two actors to whom the leading roles in a new play had just been assigned, and when they left the room where the first reading had taken place they were already walking in their new characters. They not only felt their parts at once but they also reacted to them physically. Evidently dozens of accidental coincidences in real life had prepared the creative material for their ready use; it almost seemed as though nature had predestined these two men to play those two parts.

"It is a joy when the merging of the actor with his part happens immediately, through unfathomable means. This is an example of the direct, intuitive approach in which there is no room for preconceptions. In such cases it is better to ignore technique and give oneself up wholly to one's creative nature.

"Unfortunately, however, such occurrences are extraordinarily rare—they happen to an actor once in a lifetime. You cannot take them as a rule.

"Accident plays a great part in our work. How, for example, can you explain why a certain play or a certain part will cause revulsion in an actor, make it impossible for him to function in it even though his qualities would have suggested that he was made for the part? Or the reverse: How can you explain why another part seemingly completely unsuited to an actor draws him, and he is excellent in it? Evidently in these cases there is some beneficent or malign, accidental, unconscious prejudice at work which affects the actor in some incomprehensible way for better or for worse.

"Yet there are times when an actor has preconceptions against a play and still is not impeded from sensing its innermost essentials and expressing them on the stage."

Here again Tortsov referred us to *My Life in Art* and a description of a director who wrote a splendid production plan for a new type of play which he not only did not understand but did not even like. In this the artistic subconscious of that director came through, and expressed itself by awakened creative impulses. Despite the director's conscious feelings, the new tendency of the play came alive in him and was carried over into the atmosphere of the theatre.

"All my examples show that the process of first acquaintance with a part deserves far greater attention than is usually accorded to it. Unfortunately this simple truth is far from being recognized by actors, including you. You have come to know *Othello* under the most unfavorable circumstances; it is probable that you have already received a most incorrect impression of the tragedy, one which has formed preconceptions in you."

"But according to what you say, don't you see," interrupted

Grisha, "an actor shouldn't read classical or any other plays for fear of spoiling his first acquaintance with them and because he might possibly get a part in one of them sooner or later. Nor should an actor, you know, read criticisms or commentaries, even good ones, or else he may be infected with false, preconceived opinions. But, excuse me please, you can't protect yourself against other people's views, you can't put cotton in your ears when they talk about old or new plays, you can't tell what play who will sooner or later be acting in!"

"I quite agree with you," Tortsov replied calmly, "and it is just because it is so difficult to protect oneself from prejudices that it is necessary to learn how either to avoid them or to counter their effects."

"How do you accomplish that?" I asked.

"What can we do and how do we go about becoming acquainted with a play for the first time?" asked the other students.

"I shall tell you," Tortsov explained. "First of all you should read and listen to everything, as many plays as possible, criticism, commentaries, opinions. This supplies and extends your creative material. But at the same time you must learn to protect your independence and ward off preconceptions. You must form your own opinions and not recklessly accept those of others. You must know how to be free. This is a difficult art which you will achieve only through knowledge and experience. These, in turn, will be gained not by some kind of law but by a whole complex of theoretical knowledge and practical work on the technique of art, and especially by personal reflection, by entering into essentials, by long years of practice.

"Use your time in school to amplify your scientific knowledge, and to apply the theory you learn to practice as you come to know plays and parts.

"Gradually you will become adept in sorting out your impressions of a new play. You will learn how to reject what is untrue, excessive, unimportant, how to discover what is fundamental, how to listen to others and to yourself, and how to find your own way amid the opinions of others.

"The study of world literature will be of tremendous help to you in these processes. In every play, as in every living creature, there is a bony structure, members: hands, feet, head, heart, brain. A person of literary training will, like an anatomist, study the structure and form of each bone and joint, and recognize its components. He will dissect the work, evaluate its literary or social import, search out its mistakes, where it blocks, or deviates from, the development of the main theme. He can sense new and original departures in a play, its inner and outer characteristics, the interweaving of lines, the interrelationship of characters, the facts, the events. All this knowledge, ability, and experience is extraordinarily important in evaluating a piece of work. Remember all this and use your lessons as zealously, as deeply and fully as you can to study the language, the words, the literature taught you in this school.

"But remember too that the literary experts are not always competent in questions related specifically to our problems as actors and directors. Not every play, fine as it may be as a piece of literature, is stageworthy. The demands of the stage, although they can be studied, are not fixed in any canon. There is no stage grammar. So your first estimate of a new work should be made without benefit of aid from scholarly colleagues, on the basis of the practical methods taught here. In this area, what can I add now to what you already know or will know shortly? I can only say that you should read every new play remembering, during your first acquaintance with it, to guard against acquiring a wrong or prejudiced attitude about it."

*　　*　　*

"Regardless of how unfortunate your first contact with *Othello* has been, we are obliged to reckon with it and make use of it to the extent that it will influence your further work.

"Try to recall accurately what has remained in your memory from your first reading of the play. In constructing a part you will have to adapt yourselves to whatever sank deeply into you that first time. Who can tell, perhaps among your feelings there will be some that contain elements of your future role, the germs of real life. Kostya, I want you to tell me all that you remember about the play and the various parts, what affected your memory most, what created the greatest impression on you, what your mind's eye sees most clearly, what your inner ear hears."

"As for the beginning of the tragedy," said I, as I began to analyze my recollections, "I have forgotten . . . yet right now I have the feeling that there were interesting moods: an abduction, gatherings, a chase. No, that's not it. I am conscious of this through my mind rather than with my feelings. I have intimations concerning them but do not see them with my inner vision. Othello himself is not clear to me either in this part of the play. His appearance, his being sent for by the Senate, his departure, the Senate itself—all this is clouded for me. The first vivid moment is Othello's speech to the Senate, but after that it is all dark again. The arrival in Cyprus, then the drinking scene and quarrel with Cassio I have quite forgotten. Nor do I recall the next scenes, Cassio's request, the arrival of the general, and the love scene with Desdemona. After that comes a bright patch, in fact a whole series of them that grow and broaden. Later there is a blank right up to the end. All I can hear is a sad little song about a willow, and my feelings are touched by the deaths of Desdemona and Othello. I think that is all that has stuck with me."

"We must be thankful for even that much," said Tortsov. "Since you do feel individual moments you must use and strengthen them."

"What do you mean by strengthening them?" I asked.

"Listen," Tortsov explained, "there is a little corner of your soul that still contains glimmerings of the feelings that were ignited when you became acquainted with the play—this is like an unlighted room with closed windows. If it were not for some chinks, holes, cracks, complete darkness would reign.

"Yet separate gleams, broad or narrow, bright or dull, cut through this darkness making light spots of the most varied shapes. These glimmerings modify the dark. Although you are unable to see any objects in the dark you can guess they are there from certain suggestions of outline.

"If you could only enlarge the chinks in the shutters then the spots of light would grow bigger and bigger and the gleams would get stronger. Finally light would fill the entire space and banish all darkness. There would be nothing left but shadows here and there in the corners.

"That is the picture I have of an actor's inner state after his first reading of a play and then after his further acquaintance with it.

"The same thing is happening with you after your first acquaintance with *Othello*. Only separate moments in different places have stuck in your feelings and memory; all the rest is wrapped in darkness and remote from the area of your emotions. Only here and there are hints which you try vainly to recover. These random impressions and bits of feeling are scattered through the play like the gleams in the dark.

"Later on when you come to know the play more closely these moments will grow, broaden, will make contact with one another, and finally will fill out the entire role and play.

"Such a creative beginning, growing out of separate flashes and moments of feelings, exists in other forms of art as well.

"In *My Life in Art* there is a description of just this happening to Anton Chekhov before he sat down to write *The Cherry Orchard*. First he saw someone fishing and nearby in a pool someone was bathing, then along came a rather helpless gentleman who loved to play billiards. Next he felt a wide-open window through which a branch of a flowering cherry tree pushed its way into the room. From that grew a whole cherry orchard . . . which suggested to Chekhov the beautiful but useless luxury that was slipping away from Russian life. Where do you find any logic, any bond between the helpless billiard player, the flowering branch of a cherry tree, and—the coming Russian Revolution?

"Indeed the paths of creation are not to be made known."

After me, Vanya described his memory of the play and showed how dangerous it is to read a work incompletely. His memory was filled by a nonexistent duel between Othello and Cassio.

Paul, who knew the play from seeing it performed by visiting foreign stars, had a visual recollection of the more vivid acting highlights—of the different ways Othello strangled first Iago and then Desdemona, of how he tore off the handkerchief she bound on him and almost with revulsion turned away from his beloved. He remembered in sequence one pose after another, one gesture after another; how Othello worked up his jealousy in the principal scene, how in the end he rolled around on the floor in an epileptic fit, and how he finally stabbed himself and died. I had the impression all this was visually fixed in his mind with some kind of reflected light, yet without any real sequence of development in the events or emotions of the part. In the end it appeared that Paul knew the visiting actors' playing of *Othello* very well but did not know the play itself. Fortunately he did not remember at all the role of Cassio, which he is to play and which is usually badly performed by third-rate actors.

The same investigation of impressive moments was made with other students and it turned out that many moments in the play —like, for example, Othello's speech in the Senate, his big scene with Iago, his death—affected nearly everyone in the same degree. This discovery gave rise to many questions: Why did some places in the play excite feeling while others, which were logically bound up with them, did not; why did some spots vividly and instantly evoke emotions, affect our emotion memory, while others touched us only coldly, in a conscious, intellectual sort of way? Tortsov explained the affinity of emotion and of thought: Some experiences touch us closely by nature, others are alien to us. But here he pointed out that creativeness is sometimes born as well of sources which at first appearance have nothing at all in common with the spiritual essence of a work.

"A true poet scatters the pearls of his talent with an open hand throughout a play. This is the best material for excitement, the hot, explosive stuff with which to ignite inspiration.

"The beauties of a work of genius are inherent throughout—in its external forms as well as in its hidden depths. If the stimuli to creative fervor have been strewn by the author only over the surface of the play then the work itself, the actors' interest and feelings, will prove merely superficial. If, however, the emotional wealth lies deeply embedded or hidden in the region of the subconscious, then the play, the creative enthusiasm and living responses to it, will be profound; and the further down they penetrate, the nearer they will be to the genuine human nature of the characters portrayed and of the actors themselves.

"This *enthusiasm* deriving from one's first contact with a play is the earliest intimation of an inner bond between an actor and various parts of his role. This bond is precious because it is formed directly, intuitively, naturally."

* * *

"Your first acquaintance with *Othello* left certain impressions and patches in your memory. We must now undertake a series of measures to enlarge and deepen them.

"First of all we must read the whole play carefully. But in so doing let us avoid the mistakes you made during your first contact with it.

"Let us try, during this reading, to observe all the rules which should prevail during any study of an author's works.

"Let this second reading be undertaken as if it were the first. Of course, much of the direct and affecting impact has already been lost and cannot be regained. Yet, who knows, perhaps some feelings will still be stirred in you. Only this time our reading must proceed according to rules."

"What do they consist of?" I asked.

"First we must decide where and when the reading shall take place," explained Tortsov. "Each one of us knows by experience where and how he receives impressions best. One person likes to read a play in the quiet of his room; others prefer to hear someone else read it aloud in the presence of the whole company.

"Wherever you decide to make this second acquaintance, it is important to prepare an atmosphere favorable to opening your emotions to the joyful reception of artistic impressions. Nothing should impede your intuition, the flow of lively feelings. The reader should lead the actors along the fundamental line of the author's creative impulse, along the main line of the unfolding of the life of a human spirit, of a living organism, in each part and in the whole play. He must help the actor to find at once in the soul of his part a fragment of himself, of his own soul. To teach this is to teach you to understand and feel the actor's art.

"When, however, this identification with the play is only partial, or there is a lack of general emotional contact between an actor and his part, then it is necessary to undertake the arduous task of preparing that *enthusiasm* without which there can be no creativeness.

"Artistic enthusiasm is a motive power in creativeness. Excited fascination which accompanies enthusiasm is a subtle critic, an incisive inquirer, and the best guide into the depths of feeling which are unattainable to a conscious approach.

"After this first acquaintance with a play, actors should give freer and freer rein to their artistic enthusiasm. Let them infect each other with it; let them be carried away by the play and read and re-read it as a whole or piecemeal; let them brood over the places they particularly like; let them show one another each freshly discovered gem and beauty; let them argue, shout, be wrought up; let them dream about their own parts and those of other actors, about the whole production. Enthusiasm—being swept away by the play and by one's part—that is the best way to come close to it, to understand and really know it. The creative emotions of an actor thus aroused will unconsciously probe throughout a role into depths of feeling not seen by his eyes or heard by his ears or noticed by his reason, but only unconsciously guessed at by his ardent artistic emotions.

"The ability to fire his feelings, his will, and his mind—that is one of the qualities of an actor's talent, one of the principal objectives of his inner technique."

After we had heard Tortsov, the question was raised: Was *Othello*, since everyone knew it, a proper play to demonstrate the process of first acquaintance? For it to be a *first* acquaintance it should not be *universally known*. Based on this consideration the students, headed by Grisha, concluded to my disappointment that *Othello* was not a proper choice.

But Tortsov took a different view. While he believed that a renewed acquaintance with the play because of the spoiled first impressions would be more complicated, at the same time the technical solution of the problem would be more subtle. For this reason he concluded that it would be both practical and instructive to study this technique under such circumstances—in other words by using not an unknown new play but the universally familiar *Othello*.

* * *

What can I call, how can I define, Tortsov's reading of *Othello* today? He set himself no artistic objectives. On the contrary he eschewed them in order to avoid imposing his personal interpretation, his individuality, on his hearers or evoking in them any preconceptions favorable (but not theirs) or unfavorable. I could not call his reading "reporting," because one usually associates dryness with that word. Perhaps he gave us a clarification of the play. Yes, in places he set out this or that line that he considered of importance for the whole work and interrupted his reading to explain it. It seemed to me that above all Tortsov did his best to present the plot and structure of the play. And indeed many scenes and places which formerly had passed unnoticed now came to life and received both their real position and significance. He was not moved himself by what he read, yet he hinted at places that require the participation of emotions.

He was careful to point out the literary beauties of the text. In certain places he even stopped and repeated phrases or expressions, comparisons or separate words. Yet he did not accomplish all that he hoped for. For example he did not succeed in revealing the point of departure of the playwright—I did not understand what impelled Shakespeare to sit down and write *Othello*. Tortsov did not help me find myself in the title role. Yet I seemed to feel something of the drift, the line, that one should follow.

He also rather vividly marked out the main phases of the play. I had never before sensed the significance of the opening scene; but now, thanks to his reading and various comments he let drop, I appreciated the skill with which it was constructed. Indeed, instead of the usual dreary butler and maid exposition which less skillful playwrights indulge in, or an artificially contrived meeting between two country yokels, Shakespeare created a whole scene full of an interesting event important to the action of the play. The point is that Iago is preparing to raise an uproar but Roderigo is balking. He has to be convinced, and the motive used for that purpose is what leads you right into the play. Thus two birds are killed with one stone—boredom is avoided and the dramatic action is set in motion as soon as the curtain goes up.

Later, simultaneously with the development of the plot, the exposition was artfully filled out with the departure for and arrival in the Senate. The end of that scene, the concoction of Iago's diabolical plot, was also clear to me now. Further along I now discovered a similar scene, a continuation in the development of

Iago's plan, when he talks with Cassio during the revelry on Cyprus. The uproar, carried to its ultimate limits, enlarges the guilt of Cassio at the dangerous moment of heightened excitement among the conquered peoples. In Tortsov's reading one felt, not just a row between two drunken men, but something far greater, the hint of mutiny on the part of the natives. All this greatly enhanced the significance of what was occurring on the stage; it enlarged the dimensions of the scene and excited me in places which earlier had not affected me at all.

The most important result of the reading, I felt, was the revelation of the two principal protagonists, the conflicting lines of Othello and Iago. Before this I had only felt a single line—that of love and jealousy. Without the vivid counteraction, which was now defined in Iago, my former line for the play had not had nearly the significance it now gained from the countering impact. I sensed the powerful tightening of the tragic knot.

And here was another important result from today's reading: It made me feel the sweep of space in the play, room enough for great action. I still did not feel it all, probably because I was not yet aware of the author's ultimate inner goal which lay hidden beneath his words and would eventually draw me to itself. Nevertheless I knew that the play boiled with inner activity and movement toward an as yet undesignated, universal objective.

Tortsov was pleased with the results of the reading.

"It is not necessary that all the program I laid down be carried out, but we have accomplished something in addition to what you received from your first reading. The spots of light have been somewhat enlarged.

"Now, after this reading, I am going to ask very little of you. Tell me, but in order, the factual sequence of the tragedy, or, as they call it, the plot, and you," here Tortsov turned to me, "as our perennial scribe, make a note of what each one says.

"First you must sort it all out so that you get the line of the play; this is necessary for all of you because without it there is no play. Each play has its skeleton—any distortion of it is crippling. This skeleton must now first of all hold you together, as it does the flesh of a body. How do you find the skeleton of a play? I propose this method: Answer the question, 'Without what thing, what circumstances, events, experiences, would there be no play?' "

"Without Othello's love for Desdemona."

"What else?"

"Without the cleavage between two races."

"Of course, but that is not the main thing."

"Without Iago's wicked intrigue."

"What else?"

"Without his diabolical slyness, vengeance, ambition, and resentment."

"What else?"

"Without the trustfulness of the barbarian. . . ."

"Now let us examine your answers separately. For instance: Without what would there be no love between Othello and Desdemona?"

I was unable to give an answer.

Tortsov replied in my stead: "Without the romantic ecstasy of a beautiful young woman; without the Moor's fascinating, legendary stories about his military exploits; without the innumerable obstacles to their unequal marriage, which arouse the emotions of a visionary young girl-revolutionary; without the sudden war, which forces the recognition of the marriage of an aristocratic girl with the Moor in order to save the country.

"And without what would there be no cleavage between the two races? Without the snobbery of the Venetians, the honor of the aristocracy; without their scorn of conquered peoples, to one of which Othello himself belongs; without a sincere belief in the disgrace of mixing black and white blood. . . .

"Now tell me, do you consider that everything without which there would be no play, no framework, is necessary to each one of the characters?"

129

"We do believe that," we were compelled to admit.

"In that case you now have a whole series of firmly grounded conditions in accordance with which you must be guided, and which will lead you along like signals on your path. All these proposed circumstances of the author affect every one of you and from the very beginning must be registered in the score of your roles. So keep them firmly in mind."

CHAPTER FIVE

Creating the Physical Life of a Role

"AS WE CONTINUE our search for a direct, material, intuitive inner approach to a play and a part," said Tortsov today, "we come across a new and unexpected method which I commend to your attention. My system is based on the close relationship of inner with outer qualities; it is designed to help you to feel your part by creating a *physical life for it*. I shall explain it by means of a practical example that will be demonstrated in the course of several lessons. To begin with, let Grisha and Vanya go up onto the stage and play for us the first scene in *Othello*, between Roderigo and Iago in front of Brabantio's palace."

"How can they play without script or preparation?" was the bewildered reaction of the students.

"They cannot play all of it, but they can do some of it. For instance, the scene begins with the entrance of Roderigo and Iago. Make an entrance. Then the two Venetians proceed to raise an alarm. They can do that too."

"But that is not acting the play."

"You are mistaken to think that; they would be acting in accordance with the play. To be sure it would be only on its most superficial level. Yet this is difficult enough; perhaps the most difficult thing to do is to execute the simplest physical objectives like a real human being."

Grisha and Vanya walked rather uncertainly into the wings and soon emerged downstage, stopping hesitantly near the prompter's booth.

"Is that the way you walk along a street?" was Tortsov's critical comment. "That is only the way actors 'tread the boards.' But Iago and Roderigo are not actors. They did not come here to 'represent' anything or to 'entertain' the public, especially since there is no one else around. The street is empty because everyone is asleep."

Grisha and Vanya repeated their entrance and again came to a full stop down stage.

"Now you see how right I was when I said that with every single part you have to learn everything from the beginning: how to walk, stand, sit. Let's get on with it! Now do you know where you are?" asked Tortsov. "Where is Brabantio's palace? Draw some kind of plan, whatever occurs to you."

"The palace is . . . there, and the street . . . over there," said Vanya, making an outline with some chairs.

"Now go out and make your entrance again!" ordered Tortsov.

They carried out his instruction; yet from making more effort they were even more unnatural.

"I don't understand why you again made a procession down-stage and stopped with your backs to the palace and facing us," Tortsov said.

"Otherwise, don't you see, we'd be standing with our backs to the public," explained Grisha.

"You simply can't do that," said Vanya with great emphasis.

"Who told you to put the palace upstage?" asked Tortsov.

"Where else?"

"On the right or on the left, as far downstage as possible. Then you would be facing the building and turning your profiles to us, or if you moved upstage even a little we would see three-quarters of your face," explained Tortsov. "You must know how to handle and master the conventions of the stage. These require that at the high point of his part the actor should stand as much as possible in a place where the public can see his face. This is a condition you have to accept once and for all. And so, since the actor has to be turned as much as possible toward the spectators and his position cannot be altered, nothing remains but to change the position of the scenery and plan it in accordance with that fact."

"That's right!" said Tortsov approvingly when the chairs were moved over to the right side of the stage. "Remember that I have told you more than once that every actor must be his own director. This instance confirms my words.

"Now why are you standing and staring at the chairs? After all they represent the palace of Brabantio. This is the objective for the sake of which you have come to this place. Is it only there for you to stare at? You must know how to become interested in the object of your attention, how to invent an objective connected with it, arouse some action. What you have to do is to ask yourself: 'What would I do if these chairs were the walls of the palace and if I came here to raise the alarm?' "

"You would be obliged," suggested Vanya, "to look at all the windows. Is there any light anywhere? If you see one you know that someone is awake. That means I'll call up to that window."

"That's logical," said Tortsov to Vanya encouragingly. "But if that window is dark, what will you do?"

"Look for another. Throw a stone, make a noise to waken people. Listen, bang on the door."

"You see how much action you have rolled up, how many *simple physical objectives?*" teased Tortsov. "Thus you have," said he in confirmation, "a logical sequence for the score of your roles:

"One. You enter, you look around, convince yourselves that no one sees or is listening to you.

"Two. You examine all the windows of the palace. Is there no light in any of them, no sign of any of the inhabitants of the house? If you get even the merest hint of anyone standing by a window you try to call attention to yourself. In order to do this you do not merely shout; you move about, wave your arms. Repeat this search in different places, in front of different windows.

Do this in the simplest, most realistic, natural terms so that you will be obliged physically to feel the genuineness of what you are doing and accept it physically. When, after a variety of tests, you are convinced that no one hears you, invent stronger, more decisive measures.

"Three. Get more little stones and throw them at the windows. Of course, few of them are well aimed, but if any do reach their goal, watch carefully to see if anyone comes to the window. After all you need rouse only one person and he will rouse the rest of the household. You will not succeed at first so you will have to try other windows. If your efforts are still in vain you must have recourse to even stronger means and action.

"Four. Try increasing the noise, knocking to reinforce your voice and yells. Use your hands, clap them, stamp your feet on the stone doorstep. Or go over to the door where you will find a small hammer hanging in the place of the doorbell of modern times. Bang with this hammer on a metal disk or make a noise with the heavy door handle. Or pick up a stick and strike whatever you can find. This will also intensify the racket.

"Five. Use your eyes: Peek in the windows or squint through the lock on the door. Use your ears: Lay one to the door or the crack of a window and listen attentively.

"Six. Don't forget one more factor which will offer the basis for even more activity: The point is that Roderigo should be the principal person in this nocturnal alarm. But he is angry at Iago, he pouts and balks, so Grisha has the job of convincing this reluctant man to take the most active part in the invented provocation. This is no longer a physical objective but a simple *psychological* one.

"In these small and large objectives and actions seek out the small and large *physical truths*. It is only when you have sensed them that your small or large *faith* in the actuality of your physical acts will follow of its own accord. And faith, in our kind of work, is one of the most powerful magnets to attract feelings and help you experience them intuitively. When you believe, you feel that your objectives and actions have become something real, living, purposeful. Out of such objectives and actions an unbroken line is formed. But the main thing is to believe to the end in a few objectives and acts no matter how small.

"If you are only going to stand beside those chairs and stare at them you are bound to fall into the worst kind of falseness.

"Go out and enter again and do the best you can to execute the series of objectives and actions we have laid out. Repeat them, correct them until this little bit of your roles is something you really feel, something true that you can believe and have faith in."

Grisha and Vanya went off and after a minute or so they entered and bustled up and down in front of the chairs, raising their hands to their eyes, walking on tiptoe as if to look in the upper storey. All this was done with extreme bustle and in a theatrical manner. Tortsov stopped them.

"In all your movements you have not created even a tiny piece of truth. It was sheer falseness that led you to all the usual stage conventions, the clichés, the illogical and incoherent actions.

"The first false note was the excessive bustling. It derived from your great anxiety to entertain us and not from any intention to carry out specific objectives. In real life, rapid tempo is entirely different from the way actors on the stage portray it. The action itself is unhurried; it takes exactly the space of time needed for its execution. Yet not a single second is wasted on thrashing about after the execution of each small act and before the transition to the next small objective. You bustled around both during and after your action. The result was purely theatrical activity and not vital action.

"Why is it that, in real life, energy makes us move with precision, whereas on the stage, the more an actor 'acts' in a purely theatrical way the more he blurs his objective and confuses his action? Because the representational type of actor does not feel the need of any objective. All he is interested in is pleasing the public; since the author and director of the play require him to carry out certain actions, he does them merely for the sake of doing, without any regard for the results. Yet for Iago and Roderigo what results from their plan is far from a matter of indifference. On the contrary, it is a question of life and death. So look for a light in the windows, call out, not for the sake of fussing around those chairs but in order to achieve a genuine, living, close contact with the people inside. Knock and yell not to rouse us, the audience, or even yourselves, but to wake Brabantio—Leo. You must take as your target those who are sleeping behind the thick walls of the palace. You must radiate your will to penetrate those walls."

When they played in accordance with Tortsov's instructions we, the onlookers, really believed in their activity. But this did not last for long because the magnetic power of an audience again distracted the attention of Grisha and Vanya. Tortsov tried in every way to anchor their attention on the stage.

"The second false note is that you are over-exerting yourselves. I have told you more than once that on the stage it is easy for an actor to lose his sense of measure so that it seems to him as though he is doing too little, that with a big audience he should do a lot more. So he turns himself inside out. Actually he should proceed in exactly the opposite way. Knowing this peculiarity of the stage, an actor should always remember not to increase his activity, but rather to cut three-fourths of it. You make a gesture or carry out some action—well then, next time cut it down from seventy-five to ninety percent. During your earlier studies you learned the process of relaxing your muscles and you were astonished to find so much extra tension.

"The third thing you do wrong is that you have no logic or sequence in your actions. This results in a lack of finish and control. . . ."

Grisha and Vanya played the scene over from the beginning, and Tortsov watched them carefully to see that they carried through their physical actions to the point where they themselves believed in them. He stopped and corrected them each time they swerved in the wrong direction.

"Vanya," he warned, "your point of attention is not on the stage but in the auditorium! Grisha, you are thinking about yourself. You must not do that. Don't be admiring yourself. Don't be in such a hurry. That's false. You cannot see or hear what is going on inside the palace as quickly as that. You need more time and concentration. The way you walk is affected and does not ring true. It is too actory. Make it simpler and freer. Walk with a purpose. Do it for Leo—for Brabantio—not for yourself or for me. Relax your muscles! Not so much effort. No need for grace and poses! Don't mix rubber-stamp movements with true actions. Do everything in consonance with your objective!"

Tortsov was intent on hammering in habits, on training us to work out, as he said, the right stencils for the score of our parts. When we expressed astonishment at his using the word "stencils" and urging us to acquire them, he replied:

"There can be good stencils or clichés as well as bad ones. A good, ingrained habit which helps to hold the true direction in a part—that is a helpful thing. As a matter of fact if you will form the fixed habit of doing all the things you should on arrival in the theatre for your performance—do the exercises of going over and freshening up all your objectives throughout the score of your role, the through line of action, the superobjective—I see nothing bad in that.

"If you school yourselves to a mathematically exact execution of the score of your parts and carry this to the point of its being a stencil, I shall not protest. I do not object to a stencil which reproduces true and genuine feeling in a part."

After a great deal of work over a long time it seemed to us that the scene of raising the alarm was at last in order. But Tortsov was still not satisfied. He tried to get more truthfulness in it, greater natural simplicity in each action and movement. Most of all he struggled with the way Grisha walked, which was still pompous and false. Tortsov said to him:

"To walk on the stage and especially to make an entrance is difficult. Nevertheless this is not a reason to be reconciled to theatricality and conventionality, because they are false and as long as they persist you cannot achieve any faith in your own actions. Our physical nature will not accept even the slightest imposition of force. Muscles will do what they are told, but that will not insure the necessary creative state. Indeed one small untruth will destroy and contaminate all the rest. If in all the genuine action there is 'a single blot . . . by chance brought in, that spells catastrophe,'* and the whole purport of the action is perverted into theatrical falseness.

"There is an example of this in *My Life in Art*: Take a chemical retort and put some organic substance into it, then pour in any other organic substance. They combine. But put in no more than a single drop of some artificial chemical substance and the whole is ruined. It gets opaque, sediment, flakes, and other signs of disintegration appear. An artificial manner or movement is similar to that drop of synthetic chemical, it spoils and disintegrates all the other movements of the actor. He ceases to believe in the truthfulness of what he is doing and this loss of faith breeds other elements detrimental to his inner creative state, turning him into a mood of rubber-stamp conventional acting."

Tortsov was unable to rid Grisha of the spasms in his legs, and this cramping of his physical being induced a number of other false theatrical habits which kept Grisha from believing in what he was doing.

"There is nothing left for me to do but to take this way of walking away from you," Tortsov decided.

"What do you mean? You'll have to excuse me, please, but I

* Pushkin, *Boris Godunov*.

simply cannot stand in one place, you know, like a stone statue," protested our artificial Grisha.

"Do you mean to say all Venetians are made of stone? Yet most of them ride in gondolas rather than walk, especially a rich young man like Roderigo. So now you, instead of strutting around the stage, ride up the canal in a gondola; then you will not have time to be a stone statue."

This idea was grasped with enthusiasm by Vanya.

"I'm not going another step on foot," he declared, pulling some chairs together to form a gondola, the way children do when they play games.

Inside the gondola our two actors felt much more at ease, enclosed, as it were, in a small circle. Besides, they found a lot of things to do there, a number of small physical objectives which took their attention away from the auditorium and fixed it on the stage. Grisha took up the station of the gondolier. A long piece of wood took the place of an oar. Vanya seated himself at the tiller. They floated along, stopped, moored the boat, then untied it again. At first they did all this for the sake of the actions themselves, because they were emotionally involved in them. But soon, with the help of Tortsov, they were able to transfer what they were doing in the boat to something more closely connected with the plot, which was to raise an alarm in the night.

Tortsov had them go over and over the pattern of physical actions in order to "nail it down." Then he began to extend the line of action in the scene. But the moment Leo appeared at the make-believe window, Grisha and Vanya instantly fell silent, not knowing what to do next.

"What's happened?" Tortsov inquired.

"Well, you see, we haven't anything to say. We haven't any text," explained Grisha.

"But you have thoughts and feelings which you can put into your own words. The point is not the words. The line of a role is taken from the subtext, not from the text itself. But actors are lazy about digging down to the subtext, they prefer to skim along the surface, using the fixed words which they can pronounce mechanically, without wasting any energy in searching out their inner essence."

"Excuse me, but I cannot remember in what order the thoughts are expressed in a role I am not familiar with."

"What do you mean you cannot remember them? I have only just read you the whole play!" exclaimed Tortsov. "Have you already had time to forget it?"

"I remember it only in general outline, you see. I recall that Iago announces the abduction of Desdemona by the Moor and offers to organize a chase after the fugitives," Grisha explained.

"Well then, go ahead and do your announcing and make your offer! Nothing else is needed," said Tortsov.

When they repeated the scene it appeared that Grisha and Vanya remembered the sequence of thought very well. They even threw in some of the actual words that they recalled from the text. They gave the import of the scene correctly, even though not quite in the sequence fixed by the author.

In this connection Tortsov gave some interesting explanations. He said:

"You yourselves have uncovered the secret of my method and expounded it by your playing. The point is that if I had not taken the text away from you, you would have worked too hard over the printed words and would have rendered them without thought, formally, before you had penetrated to the underlying meaning which shapes the line of your role. Had you done that you would have suffered the inevitable consequence of that unnatural method. The words would have lost their active, vital meaning, they would have become mechanical, gymnastic exercises for your tongue, making noises to which it was trained. But I was too forehanded to let that happen. Instead I have deprived you of the text for the time being, until the line of your role is fixed; I have saved up for you the author's magnificent words until such time as they will have better use, so that they will not be just rattled off but employed to carry out some fundamental objective.

"Keep my command strictly and, until I allow you to do so, do not open the book of the play. Take the time necessary to fix the habit of the subtext firmly and shape the line of your role. Let the words themselves become for you only the weapons with which to go into action, one of the external means to embody the inner essence of your role. Wait until the words are necessary to you for the better accomplishment of your objective: to convince Brabantio. When this time comes, the author's words will be a prime necessity to you. You will soon come to understand, when you have identified yourselves with the real objectives of your part, that there are no better means of achieving them than through the words written with the genius of Shakespeare. Then you will snatch at them with enthusiasm, they will come to you freshly, not tarnished and threadbare from being dragged around during all the rough work of preparation.

"Treasure the words of a text for two important reasons: first, not to wear the sheen off them, and second, not to introduce a lot of mechanical patter, learned by rote and bereft of soul, into the subtext of the play."

In order to "nail down" firmly the line of the subtext they had just created, Tortsov made Grisha and Vanya play through the whole scene according to the sequence of physical and simple psychological objectives and actions.

Some things were still not successful, and Tortsov explained why.

"You still do not grasp the nature of the process of convincing a person. You must understand feelings when you are showing them. If the news brought is unpleasant, the recipient will instinctively set up as many buffers inside himself as he can in order to ward off the impending misfortune. So it is with Brabantio—he does not want to believe what they are telling him. Out of a sense of self-preservation he chooses to ascribe this nocturnal disturbance to drunken revelers. He scolds them and drives them away. This complicates matters for those who would convince him. How can they gain his confidence and dispel his mistaken notion of them? How can they make the abduction become an actuality in the eyes of the unhappy father? It is terrifying to him to face reality. The dreadful news, which will upset his whole life, is something he cannot accept at once, the way an actor in the theatre does. The actor would show him gay and serene while he is unaware of anything; then when he has scarcely heard the news, he would already be dashing around, tearing his collar off to keep from stifling. But in real life this crisis takes place during a series of logical steps, a whole psychological sequence leading up to the consciousness of the dreadful misfortune which has occurred."

This descent Tortsov divided into coherent objectives each one flowing out of the preceding one:

1. First Brabantio is merely angry and scolds at the drunken revelers who have disturbed his pleasant slumbers.

2. He is made indignant by having these vagrants bandy about the good name of his family.

3. The closer he comes to taking in the terrible news, the more forcibly he struggles not to believe it.

4. Even so, several words have pierced to his heart and sorely wounded his feelings. Still he rebuffs even more fiercely the on-coming misfortune.

5. More convincing proof is offered. He must find new ground to stand on, a new position to take up. How can he live? Where shall he turn? Something must be done! Inaction is the most painful of all in such a situation.

6. At last he decides what to do. To hurry, to overtake them, avenge himself, rouse the whole city! Save his treasured daughter!

Leo is a person with literary flair. He can follow the line of the subtext, though it will be out of reasoned thought, not out of feelings. Therefore it was not necessary to argue with him about the words. He easily found his own words to express his thoughts

nd he kept right to the main intent of the scene since he under-
tood its inner meaning. Tortsov was satisfied that there was no
iscrepancy between him and the text in the matter of logical
equence, apart from some rather inexact or unhappy choices of
vords. Grisha and Vanya found it easier to follow along the firm
erbal line laid down by Leo.

So the scene went along rather well. Yet Grisha had to spoil it.
Ie jumped out of the gondola and began again to strut around.
3ut Tortsov soon tamed him by reminding him that it would not
lo for Iago to be too much in evidence. On the contrary, it was
)est for him to remain under cover, calling from a hiding place
o that he would not be recognized. Where should he hide? In
his connection there was a lengthy discussion about the architec-
ure of the pier, the platform, and the main entrance to the palace.
The actors wanted corners, or columns, behind which they could
iide. In addition, because Grisha was strutting again, they rehearsed at length Iago's inconspicuous exit.

*   *   *

Today there was a rehearsal of the crowd scene. A number of
apprentices in the theatre, who had been quietly watching the
previous rehearsals from the back rows of the auditorium, were
moved up into the front rows. From the beginning they had
caused surprise by their discipline, and now we were not only
astonished but also humbled by their attitude toward their work.
It was obvious that Tortsov found it easy and agreeable to work
with them—quite rightly, because they understood what was to be
done. All the director or teacher had to do was to point out mistakes and clichés which were to be got rid of, or good parts which
were to be retained and fixed. These apprentices do their work at
home and bring it in to class for checking and approval.

"Do you know the play?" Tortsov asked them.

"We do!" came the reply, spoken with military precision and
resonantly through the auditorium.

"What are you to show and experience in the first scene?"

"Alarm and pursuit."

"Do you know the nature of these actions and experiences?"

"Yes."

"We shall see." Here Tortsov turned to one of the apprentices. "What are the physical and simple psychological objectives and actions which go to make up this scene of nocturnal alarm and pursuit?"

"To understand while still half asleep what has happened. To clarify something no one can make head or tail of. To question each other, argue back and forth; if answers do not satisfy, to voice one's own ideas, to come to agreement, to test or prove whatever is not well founded.

"Having heard cries outside, to look out of the windows to understand what's going on. At first you can't find room. At last you succeed. You look out and listen to what these noisemakers are yelling. Who are they? Arguments follow, some take them for entirely different persons. Roderigo is recognized. You listen to him and try to understand what he is yelling. At first it is impossible to believe that Desdemona would do such a thing. You try to make the others believe this is a trick or a drunken dream; scold the noisemakers for keeping you from sleeping; threaten them and chase them off. Gradually you believe the truth of what they are saying. You exchange first impressions with the neighbors; express reproaches or regret for what has happened; hurl hatred, curses on the Moor and threats against him, clarify what to do and how to go about it. Think of all sorts of solutions for the situation. Defend your plan, criticize that of the others. Try to find out the opinion of the leaders. Support Brabantio in his talk with the noisemakers. Egg him on to revenge. Listen to orders concerning the pursuit. Rush to fulfill them promptly.

"Further objectives and actions," the apprentice continued, "will conform to the roles of the characters and also to the duties of the people in the palace. Some will bring out arms, others will fetch lanterns and light up the rooms, will dress themselves in coats of mail and cuirasses, will pick out helmets and side arms. They will help each other. The women will weep as though they were sending their menfolk off to war. The gondoliers will ready their gondolas, oars, all their equipment. Leaders will form groups, explain plans of action, send them in different directions after the fugitives. It is explained where to go and where to meet again. The leaders confer with their subordinates and urge them on against the enemies. They disperse. If the scene needs to be lengthened, pretexts must be invented to have them return, carry out the new objectives they came back to accomplish.

"Since there are too few people for such a fighting scene it will be necessary to organize a 'walk around' and a 'variegation,'" the spokesman warned.

Tortsov hurried to explain to us the meaning of those special terms. A "walk around" meant a continual movement of various groups to one side. To one group Tortsov assigned coming out of the palace, conversations, the forming of a squad of men and their exit on the right. Another group was to do the same but exit on the left. Both groups on arriving back stage were immediately to repeat the maneuver not as the same characters but as others of newly formed squads. In order to mask the change there would be dressers and propmen stationed backstage who would remove the more noticeable or typical parts of their costumes and arms (helmets, capes, hats, halberds, spears) and in exchange give them different parts of costumes or arms not resembling those just removed.

As for "variegation," Tortsov explained it this way: If there is a mass movement in one direction, the impression is created of a definite push toward a given place, it looks like an organized movement. But if you send two groups in different directions in order to have them meet, clash, exchange words, separate, and keep going off the stage—then you have the impression of bustle, chaos, haste. Brabantio has no organized force. It is formed for the occasion out of his servants. So they cannot have any military discipline; everything happens on the spur of the moment, without sense, all in confused movement. "Variegation" helps to create such a mood.

"Who prepared you for today's rehearsal?" inquired Tortsov after he had finished the questioning.

"Petrunin," came the reply, "and Rakhmanov checked us."

Tortsov thanked them both and congratulated the spokesman, accepted the proposed plan without alteration, and then invited the apprentices to execute it in conjunction with us, the actors.

The apprentices stood up as one man and went onto the stage without hesitation and in most orderly fashion.

"Not the way we do!" I whispered to Paul who was sitting beside me.

"How do you like that? Watch out! This is being done to edify us!" answered Paul.

"Gee, but they work well! Tongue and groove!" exclaimed Vanya approvingly.

When the apprentices arrived on the stage they took some time at first to concentrate on how best to accomplish their objectives. With great intentness they moved from one place to another both in front of the chairs defining the palace and in back of them, that is to say inside the palace. When they could not get the action they wanted they stopped, thought it out, made some changes, and repeated what had not been successful before. In his turn Tortsov who, as he expressed it, played the part of a mirror and reflected what he saw, gave his conclusions:

"Bespalov—I don't believe you! Dondych—that's fine! Vern— you're exaggerating."

I was struck by the fact that although the apprentices played without props, I understood what they were doing, what things they were supposedly putting on or picking up. And they did not handle a single thing without paying due attention to it. Each thing was "used" to the full.

A kind of solemn, almost churchlike atmosphere filled the stage and the auditorium. Those on the stage spoke in low tones, the audience sat motionless, silent.

During a short pause, Tortsov asked to have explained to him what role each person was playing. Each one of the participants came forward to the footlights in turn and explained who he was.

"The brother of Brabantio!" explained one handsome, imposing-looking man, no longer in his first youth. "He organizes the pursuit and acts, as it were, in capacity of commander-in-chief of the expedition. He is an energetic, austere person."

"Four gondoliers," announced two good-looking young men, and two others not so good-looking.

"Desdemona's nurse," said a stout elderly woman.

"Two maids who helped in the abduction. They were in a plot with Cassio who arranged the elopement. . . ."

"Now play the physical actions of the first scene for me. Let us see how it turns out."

We played it. Not counting a few mistakes it seemed to us the scene went well, especially what the apprentices did.

Tortsov said:

"If you will always follow this line in your parts and sincerely believe in each physical action you will soon create what we call the score, the physical life of your parts. I talked to you about this before. Now you are seeing in your own experience how it is put together. If you will compress, concentrate, make a synthesis of the essence of each of these principal fundamental objectives and actions, then you will have the score for the first scene of *Othello*.

"I shall name for you the main divisions out of which that score is made:

"The first fundamental objective and action is: *Convince Roderigo to help Iago.*

"The second is: *Rouse the entire household of Brabantio* (the alarm).

"The third: *Set them on the pursuit.*

"The fourth: *Organize the squads and the pursuit proper.*

"Now when you come onto the stage to play this first scene do not think of anything except the best possible execution of these *fundamental objectives and actions.* Each one of them has been checked, discussed, studied from the point of view of its physical and simple psychological nature as well as from that of its logic and coherence. So that now when I mention to you any one of the phases of the score—as, for instance, 'Rouse the entire household of Brabantio'—you know how that would be done in real life and how it is done on the stage. Concern yourselves with seeing that it is done as fruitfully as possible for the main characters and for the main goal of the play. That is all you need to do for the present. Only do not let up on the work we have begun; come every day and go over, if not the whole scene, at least its basic outline. Let this strengthen more and more the basic objectives and actions, fix them with greater precision, like signposts along a road. As for the details, the small component parts with their adaptations and their execution, do not think too much about them; rather do them impromptu each time.

"Do not be afraid of this. You have plenty of material prepared with which to execute them and you will constantly be developing them more fully, profoundly, so as to make them more *attractive.* After all the only good objectives and actions are those which excite an actor and impel him to be creative. When we reach this point of going deeper into the development of the basic objectives and actions of the scheme we meet a new phase in the creation of a role."

*　　*　　*

"Now I come back to our point of departure, the thing for the sake of which we made our last experiment in forming the physical life of a role: the question of how to find new ways and means to a more natural, direct, intuitive, inner approach to a play and a part.

148

"The creation of the physical life is half the work on a role because, like us, a role has two natures, physical and spiritual. You will say that the main purpose of our art does not consist of externals, that the creation of the life of a human spirit is what it looks to in order to inform what we do on the stage. I quite agree, but precisely because of this I begin our work with the physical life of any part.

"Let me explain the reason for this unexpected conclusion. You know that if a part does not of its own accord shape itself inside an actor he has no recourse except to approach it inversely, by proceeding from externals inward. That is what I do. You did not feel your parts intuitively, so I began with their physical life. This is something material, tangible, it responds to orders, to habits, discipline, exercise, it is easier to handle than elusive, ephemeral, capricious feeling which slips away. But that is not all. There are more important factors hidden in my method: The spirit cannot but respond to the actions of the body, provided of course that these are genuine, have a purpose, and are productive. This state of things is particularly important on the stage because a role, more than action in real life, must bring together the two lines— of external and of internal action—in mutual effort to achieve a given purpose. The favorable condition in acting is that both are drawn from the same source, the play, which makes them congenial to each other.

"Why then do we often see the opposite effect on the stage— the inner line of a role truncated and replaced by the personal line of the actor, who has been diverted from creativeness by trivial preoccupations while he continues to move along automatically, by habit? This is caused by a formalistic, hack attitude toward acting.

"The physical approach to a part can act as a kind of storage battery for creative feeling. Inner emotions and feelings are like electricity. Scatter them into space and they disappear. But fill up the physical life of your part with feelings, and the emotions aroused will become rooted in your physical being, in your deeply felt physical actions. They will seep in, be soaked up, they will gather up feelings connected with each instant of the physical life of your role and in this way lay hold of the ephemeral sensations and creative emotions of an actor. Thanks to this approach the cold, ready-made physical life of a part acquires inner content. The two natures of a part, the physical and the spiritual, merge in each other. External action acquires inner meaning and warmth from inner feeling, and the latter finds its expression in physical terms, external embodiment.

"Here is another no less practical reason why I began our work from the physical angle. One of the most irresistible *lures* to our emotions lies in the *truth* and our *faith* in it. An actor on the stage need only sense the smallest modicum of organic physical truth in his action or general state and instantly his emotions will respond to his inner faith in the genuineness of what his body is doing. In our case it is incomparably easier to call forth real truth and faith in it in the region of our physical than of our spiritual nature. An actor need only believe in himself and his soul will open up to receive all the inner objectives and emotions of his role. If, however, he forces his feelings he will never believe in them; and without that faith he will never really feel his part.

"To permeate external physical actions with inner essentials, the spiritual life of a part, you must have appropriate material. This you find in the play and in your roles. Therefore we now turn our attention to the study of the inner content of the play."

CHAPTER SIX

Analysis

TODAY OUR LESSON began with a placard on which was inscribed: *The Process of Studying the Play and the Role (Analysis).*

Tortsov said:

"Let me repeat that the best thing that can happen to an actor is to have his whole role form itself in him of its own accord. In such instances one can forget about all 'systems,' techniques, and give oneself up wholly to the power of magic nature. This, alas, did not happen to any of you. So we tried all possible means available to nudge your imagination, attract your feelings, in order to get you to put natural, direct, intuitive life if not into your whole role at least into a part of it. Some of this work was successful; in different spots in the play there were flashes of life. Now evidently we have gone through all the paths of direct, immediate, intuitive approach to Shakespeare's work. What else can we do to produce new patches of light in the places that have no life in them; how can you be brought forcibly closer to the inner world of the characters shown on the stage? For this we need the process of *analysis*.

"What does this analysis consist of and what is its purpose? Its purpose is to search out *creative stimuli to attract the actor*, lacking which there can be no identification with a part; the purpose of the analysis is the *emotional deepening of the soul of a part* in order to comprehend the component elements of this soul, its external and internal nature, and indeed its whole life as a human spirit. Analysis studies the external circumstances and events in the life of a human spirit in the part; it searches in the actor's own soul for emotions common to the role and himself, for sensations, experiences, for any elements promoting ties between him and his part; and it seeks out any spiritual or other material germane to creativeness.

"Analysis dissects, discovers, examines, studies, weighs, recognizes, rejects, confirms; it uncovers the basic direction and thought of a play and part, the superobjective and the through line of action. This is the material it feeds to imagination, feelings, thoughts, and will.

"As you see, analysis has many missions to perform, but in the first instance, at the beginning of our work, it tries to seek out, understand, and put the right value on the most precious pearls, the creative stimuli set in the work of a writer of talent or genius, pearls which have remained unnoticed during our first casual approach to the play. The talent of an actor is sensitive, it reacts to all that is fine; creative stimuli naturally arouse a creative response in him. This response in turn throws areas of light in the dark stretches of the play and evokes genuine, if brief, sensations. These partial sensations serve to draw the actor closer to his role. Thus our first objective now is to seek out the creative stimuli the playwright embedded in his work to excite the actor.

"First, as you know, we turn to reason, which is far more subject to control than emotion. But we do not do this as a purely intellectual process. We use our mind first so that it will, like a scout, go out and reconnoiter. Reason begins by studying all planes, all directions, all the component parts of the play and individual roles. Like an advance guard it blazes new trails for new prospecting on the part of our feelings; then creative emotions follow along these paths prepared by the scout; and then, when the search is over, the mind comes in again, but this time in a narrowly confined new role. Now it acts like a rearguard, rounding up triumphant emotions, and consolidating what has been won.

"So analysis is not solely an intellectual process. Many other elements enter into it, all the capacities and qualities of an actor's nature. These must be given the widest possible field in which to manifest themselves. Analysis is a means of coming to know, that is, to feel, a play. Only through genuine emotional experience can one penetrate to the secret wellsprings of human nature in a role and there come to know, to feel, the invisible things hidden in the souls of people, those things inaccessible to hearing, sight, or conscious approach. It is a misfortune that reason is dry. Even though at times it does evoke a direct outburst of unconscious inspiration, it often kills it as well. By its conscious nature it often overwhelms and crushes feelings that are of the greatest value in creativeness. So that in the process of analysis one must use the mind with utmost caution and care.

"When as a boy I had to study the names of the cities along the Volga for the sheer purpose of memorizing them, I was bored and could not make them stick in my memory. But when I was older and my schoolmates and I made boat trips along the Volga, we learned the names not only of the big towns but of all the tiniest hamlets, landings, boat stops, and remembered them for all our lives. Today we can even recall who lived there, what you could buy, and what was produced there. Without wishing to do so we came in contact with the most intimate aspects of life, including some spicy details and local gossip. Everything we came to know was, without any effort on our part, carefully set on the shelves of our memories.

"There is an enormous difference between studying something just for the sake of knowledge and studying it for use. In the first case you find no room to store it; in the second case, the space is all prepared and what you learn goes immediately into it, as naturally as water flows into a pool or a channel which has been readied for it.

"The same is true of the analysis of a play. If we were making an analysis and looking for feelings experienced merely for the sake of sensations, we should find little space or use for them. But if the material derived from analysis is something we need to fill out, justify, or enliven the too shallow physical life of our roles, then the new material drawn from within the play and the roles themselves will find important application and will provide fertile ground for growth.

"The score for the physical life of a role is only the beginning of our work; the most important part lies ahead—the deepening of this life until it reaches the very depths, where the spiritual life of a role begins, to create which is the main objective of our art. This objective has now to a large extent been prepared and it will not be so difficult to achieve it. If you try to reach feelings directly, without preparation or support, then it is difficult either to grasp or to hold fast to the delicate substance of their pattern. But now that you have the firm support of a material, physical, tangible line for the physical life of your parts you will no longer be dangling in the air, you will be proceeding along a well-beaten path.

"The knowledge of one's physical being is a splendid and fertile field for growth. Everything planted here has a tangible basis in the material world. Actions based on it especially help to establish a role, because in this area it is easier to find large or small truths that produce faith in what one is doing on the stage. And you already know that faith and truth are powerful magnets for your emotions.

"Think back: Did your feelings remain unmoved when you sincerely lived in the physical being of your roles? If you probe deeper into this process and watch what happens in your soul at such a time, you will see that with faith in your physical actions on the stage you will feel emotions, akin to the external life of your part, which possess a logical bond with your soul.

"The body is biddable; feelings are capricious. Therefore if you cannot create a human spirit in your part of its own accord, create the physical being of your role."

*   *   *

"We have many ways of learning through the analysis of a play and its roles.

"We can re-tell the content of the play, make lists of facts and events, given circumstances proposed by the author. We can divide the play up into pieces—dissect it and divide it into layers, think up questions and provide the answers, read the text with exactly proportioned words and pauses and glance into the past and future of the characters, organize general discussions, arguments, and debates. We can keep close track of the appearance and merging of areas of light, weigh and estimate all facts, find names for units and objectives, and so forth. All these differing practical methods are part of the single process of analysis, or coming to know the play and your parts.

"I shall give you practical examples. But these cannot be done all at once and in the one scene we are rehearsing. That would confuse you; it would stick in your heads, remaining there to give an impression of extreme intricacy. Therefore I shall introduce the technical methods of analysis to you gradually, applying them in each scene."

*　　*　　*

At the end of our lesson Tortsov gave us work to do. He ordered us to go to Rakhmanov's class and sent word to return to us the copies of *Othello* which had been taken away. Each one of us was, without leaving the premises, to copy out the author's directions. He told us to choose besides and copy from the dialogues and soliloquies of the characters everything that was related to their characteristics, mutual relations, the explanation and justification for given facts, the places where the action takes place, the costumes, explanations of inner emotions, and so forth—everything we could mine from the text of the play. Out of all these excerpts we were to combine, under Rakhmanov's direction, a general list and enter it in the account of our lesson. Copies were to be given to each of us, but the texts of the play were again to be withdrawn.

"For my part," Tortsov announced, "I shall see the painter who is making sketches for the setting and costumes. I shall think about the general production plan for the first scene, and in addition to the author's indications I shall tell you my proposals at your next lesson. Then you will have all the necessary data at your disposal."

Rakhmanov read the play aloud to us and we stopped him whenever he came to anything which characterized the dramatis personae, their mutual relationships, or psychology, the author's notes concerning the production, direction, sets, and so forth. This all made notes adding up to several pages. These we sorted into groups (sets, costumes, author's notes, characterizations, psychology, thoughts, and so on). This constituted a new list which we are to present tomorrow to Tortsov.

*   *   *

"In order to obtain absolutely everything the author puts into his text and to round it out," said Tortsov today, "and also to clarify things he only hints at, information the actor needs to have, I suggest another technical means which we have adopted in our process of thinking about a play. What I have in mind is a series of questions and answers. For example:

"*When* does the action take place? At the time of the flowering of the Venetian Republic in the sixteenth century.

"In what season, and in the day or night? The first scene in front of Brabantio's palace takes place in the autumn or winter when there are heavy storms at sea. There are storm clouds in the sky and a tempest is brewing. The action takes place late in the evening when all Venice is sinking into deep slumber. If one wishes to apprise the audience of the hour, a clock in a tower can strike eleven. But since this effect is used very frequently in the theatre to induce a mood, one must exercise the utmost caution and not resort to it except in the case of extreme necessity.

"*Where* does the action take place? In Venice. In the aristocratic quarter not far from the Grand Canal, where the palaces of the grandees are located. A large part of the stage is devoted to water and only a small one to a narrow pavement—this is typical of the city built on water—and a landing in front of the water gate or entrance of the palace. It is desirable to have the upper and lower windows of the palace visible to the audience so that night lights, lanterns, and the scurrying around inside should convey the impression of a whole household aroused, of great excitement inside, behind the windows."

The students were doubtful about the possibility of reproducing the effect of real water and floating gondolas, but Tortsov said that the theatre was equipped for all such things. The ripple of the water is reproduced by a special kind of projector with a chromotrope mechanically revolving at various speeds. It sends out reflections of light flashes, rather like a magic lantern, and gives the absolute effect of rippling water. There are also mechanical devices for reproducing the waves. For example in Bayreuth, for the production of *The Flying Dutchman*, they show two large ships which sail, are maneuvered, turn around, and separate. One of them comes into port. In these maneuvers and turns, waves dash on board from different directions and lap the ships like real water.

*　　*　　*

"Now we have to train our telescope on the scarcely perceptible, quite unclear spots in the play so that you may be helped to breath life into it. How do we proceed?

"We must plow up the text again, which is to say reread it thoughtfully. You will, I dare say, protest: 'We've read it! We know!' But I shall prove to you by a number of instances that although you have read the play you still do not know it.

"Not only that, in some places you have not even succeeded in parsing the text. Besides, even in the bright patches, as we call them, you have only an approximate idea of what is said.

"Take as an example one of these large, bright spots—Othello's speech to the Senate:

> Most potent, grave and reverend signiors,
> My very noble and approv'd good masters,
> That I have ta'en away this old man's daughter,
> It is most true; true I have married her—
> The very head and front of my offending
> Hath this extent, no more. . . .

"Do you understand—do you feel—*all* the contents which have been put into this speech?"

"Yes. We think we do understand what he is talking about. It is the abduction of Desdemona!" asserted the students.

"No, it is not quite that," interrupted Tortsov. "He is speaking of stealing the daughter of a high official, and doing it from the position of a foreigner who happens to be in the employ of the Senate. Tell me, what is the service Othello is engaged in? He calls the Senators his 'masters.' What is the relationship between him and them?"

"He is a general, a military man," we decided.

"Is he, in our parlance, a kind of minister of war, and are they a council of ministers, or is he simply a mercenary soldier, and are they plenipotentiary governors who make all the binding decisions in the country?"

"We had not thought of that, and right now I don't see why actors have to know all those fine points," confessed Grisha.

"What do you mean, you don't see why you have to know such things?" exclaimed Tortsov with astonishment. "This is a question of a conflict not only between two different classes but also between nationalities. Besides it is also a question of the Senate's dependence on a black man whom they despise. Why, this is a terrible conflict for the Venetians—a whole tragedy! And you do not want to know about it? Are you not interested in the social status of the characters? How can you sense their interrelationship without it, or the poignancy of their clash, which plays such a tremendous part in the whole tragedy in general and in the love story of the two principals in particular?"

"Of course, you are quite right," we agreed.

"Let me go on," continued Tortsov.

> That I have ta'en away this old man's daughter,
> It is most true; . . .

"Now, tell me how this abduction took place. In order to judge the degree of his guilt it is necessary to know the details, and this not only from the point of view of the injured and affronted parties—Brabantio, the Doge, and the Senators—but also from the angle of the initiator of the crime—Othello—as well as from that of Desdemona, the heroine of the love story."

It had not occurred to us to think about this question and we could not answer.

"I shall continue," said Tortsov.

> . . . true, I have married her—

"Now tell me, who married them, where, in what church? Was it a Catholic church? Or because Othello is a Muslim was there no Christian priest to be found who would marry them? If that is so, to what ceremony would Othello give the name of marriage? Or was it a common-law marriage? For those times that would have been perhaps too bold, too brazen."

When we had nothing to say to that either, Tortsov expressed his opinion of us.

"Evidently," he concluded, "with certain exceptions you are able to read and acquire an almost formal understanding of what the words say, of what the printed letters in a copy of *Othello* indicate. But that is far from being what Shakespeare intended to say when he wrote his play. In order to comprehend his intentions you have to take the inanimate, printed letters and restore not only his thoughts but his visions, his emotions, feelings, in a word the whole subtext, which underlies the words in the formal text. Only then can we say that we not only have read but also know the play.

"The mistake you all made in re-telling the contents of the play was that you repeated what has long been well known to everyone—what the author wrote, the play as *in the present*.

"But what about its past and its future prospect? Who will tell us about them?

"Do not conceal from us the hints you yourselves get from beneath the words, between the lines, the things suggested by Shakespeare just as you yourselves see, hear, and sense the life of a human spirit in the play. Be creators, not mere narrators.

"Perhaps you, Grisha, will undertake this difficult task."

"Excuse me, please," replied Grisha, argumentatively, "but I will repeat what the author said. If you don't like that, if you are bored by it, well, let the author answer for it."

"Oh no," interrupted Tortsov. "The author wrote only what happens after the curtain is up. That is, so to speak, the *present* time of the play. But can the present exist without the *past*? Try taking away all the antecedents from your own present. Imagine for a moment that you are sitting here preparing to become an actor but there was nothing in your past leading up to this present work. You did not prepare yourself even in your thoughts to become an actor, you never acted, you never were in a theatre. Don't you feel that such a present would lose all value, that it would be like a plant without roots, doomed to wither and die?

"The present cannot exist without the past or without the future. You will say we cannot know or foretell the future. Yet we not only can but must desire it and have ideas about it.

"Of what good would your present, let us say your studies to become an actor, be if you were not preparing to go on the stage and devote your life to this profession?

"Naturally, our present occupations are the more interesting because they bear future fruit.

"If in ordinary life there can be no present without a past and a future, in the theatre, which mirrors life, it cannot be otherwise. The playwright gives us the *present* but in some ways he also gives us hints of the *past* and the *future*.

"A writer of books gives us more, in fact he actually gives us all three. He even writes prefaces and epilogues. No wonder; he is not restricted by the length of his book or by time considerations.

"But the case of the playwright is different. He is confined within the narrow limits of a play. These limits are fixed as to time, and very brief it is too. At most he can take four, four and a half hours, including three or four intermissions, each fifteen minutes long. He cannot hold the stage for more than forty or forty-five minutes at a time. That is the extent to which he can count on the attention of the public. What can he say in that brief time? And he has much to say. So this is where he looks to the actors for help. What the playwright does not have the time to say about the past and the future the actors should fill out.

"To this you will retort that they cannot put in more than the playwright's words. This is not exactly so. There are things which are conveyed in other ways than with words.

"When Duse, in the last act of *La Dame aux Camélias* just before she dies, read a letter Armand wrote her when she first knew him, her eyes, voice, intonations, her whole being were convincingly expressive of what she saw, knew, and was re-living down to the last detail of this moment in her past.

"Could Duse have achieved that result if she was not herself aware of all those minute details, if she had not thought of the things the heroine is seeing in her mind's eye as she dies?

"After the work we have done, it would seem that we could now say that we know all the written words of the text and whatever is hidden beneath them in the subtext—thoughts, feelings, things seen and heard.

"That is a great deal. But it is not all. We know by experience that the playwright does not spell out a great many things which are necessary to the actor. For example, Iago and Roderigo appear. From where have they come? What had happened five, ten, forty minutes, or a day, a month, a year earlier? Does not the actor have to know? Is it superfluous for the actor playing Roderigo to know where, when, and how he met, knew, courted Desdemona? If he is not aware of these facts and the images that correspond to them how can he speak the lines Shakespeare has given him? There are tiny hints in the text, and we shall take them into consideration, but what of the rest? Who will tell us about that? You cannot bring the author back to life and there is no other to be found. All you have left is your reliance on the director of the play. But not all directors are willing to proceed along the same line we do. Besides, what a director thinks up may prove quite alien to you as an actor. So nothing remains except to rely on yourselves. So, let's get to work. Let us do some dreaming and invent what the author did not spell out. You will have to become co-authors and round out what he did not do in his own name. Who knows, we may have to write a whole play! . . .

"Meanwhile, it is too bad that you talk and argue about the play so little among yourselves. How can I stir you up? Debates are the best means of stirring interest, of getting at essentials and clearing up misunderstandings."

We tried to explain to Tortsov why such conversations about the play did not take place outside of our classes.

"I see I shall have to help you," remarked Tortsov as he left the class.

*   *   *

Today we were scheduled to have a talk between teachers and students on the subject of *Othello*. We gathered in one of the lobbies of the theatre around a great table which was covered with a green baize cloth and on which lay sheets of paper, pencils, pens—

all the paraphernalia of a regular conference. Tortsov sat down at the head of the table and announced that the session was open.

"Who wishes to talk about *Othello* as he understands it?"

We were all embarrassed and sat there immobile and silent as if we had mouths full of water.

Thinking that perhaps the idea of the gathering was not exactly clear, Tortsov began to explain it. He said:

"At some time, somehow or other, you read *Othello* hastily, casually. From it you retained certain spots of recollection. Your second reading added something to these impressions. But all that is still too little inner material for your parts. Today's talk was planned in order to fill out that material. Therefore I am going to ask each one to express his opinion of the play quite frankly."

Evidently no one had any thoughts about it, because no one was willing to say anything. After a long and rather difficult pause, Rakhmanov asked for the floor.

"I have been silent up to now. I said nothing when Kostya asked to have *Othello* brought inside our walls, or when Tortsov confirmed the choice of the play for our work on a role. I have been silent despite the fact that I have not been in agreement with this at any time. Why do I oppose this choice? In the first place because this is not a play for students, and in the second place— and this is the principal reason—this tragedy is far from being the best work of Shakespeare. Really it's not even a tragedy but a melodrama. That is why the plot, the events in it, are so improbable that you cannot believe in them. Judge for yourselves—a black general! Where do we see any Negro generals? And I am speaking of our advanced times. So what can we say of the faraway Middle Ages, of Venice? And this nonexistent black general steals away the most beautiful, pure, naïve, fairy princess, Desdemona. That is absolutely improbable! Just let some savage steal the daughter of an Englishman or any other kind! Just let him try. It would be made very hot for any such Romeo."

Those present kept wanting to stop Rakhmanov but did not

quite dare to do so. After Tortsov however had expressed some
doubt and then, apparently somewhat embarrassed by his friend's
remarks, had stopped him, several of us attacked the speaker and
defended the play. All Tortsov could do then was throw up his
hands and keep saying: "That's enough! What are you saying?"

Each such remark only poured oil on the flames and the argument waxed hotter than ever. There was no way of giving it any
direction and Tortsov as chairman kept ringing his bell inces-
santly. Strangely enough, Rakhmanov found defenders in Vanya
and, who would have thought it, in Maria! This upset me and
caused me to enter the fray. Soon it developed that there was no
unanimity even among the opponents. On the contrary there were
many who were critical. It seemed to me (perhaps I was wrong)
that most of those who were protesting—like, say, Grisha and
Vasya—were against *Othello* not because the play was good or
bad but because it did not give each one a part to his taste. The
hall was filled with groans and cries, and all the more so when
Tortsov left his place as chairman and watched the scene from the
sidelines.

Can it be that all this uproar was provoked on purpose by our
teachers?—the thought flashed into my mind. If so it brilliantly
achieved its purpose, because the arguments about *Othello* were
burning and continued until well into the evening. Because of this
there were serious fines since the students were not at their
posts operating the sound board during the evening performance
—they were busy with *Othello* instead. Some of us were even re-
ported. Because of these arguments in which some of the actors
performing that evening participated and attacked Rakhmanov
fiercely, there was a delay in the intermission; they did not hear
the warning bell, they were so interested in the debate.

Now that I have come home after the evening performance is
over, in the quiet of the night, I am summing up what happened,
trying to write down everything I remember. This is difficult to

do; everything is so mixed up in my head and I am mortally tired. That is why there is no order in my notes.

* * *

"Now it's just the way it is after a fresh plowing and sowing; we have to examine what has come up and then gather the fruit," announced Tortsov as he came into class today. "Isn't there something new in your feelings after your long debates?"

"There is indeed," was the vociferous consensus. "But it's so chaotic you can't do anything with it."

"Nevertheless let us try to set it to rights," proposed Tortsov.

To our astonishment, after careful questioning, it appeared that we had not added any patches of light, although these now had clustered around them an infinite number of different sensations, hints, questions. So it is in the heavens when, alongside the brilliant large stars, the telescope discovers hosts of scarcely sparkling tiny stars. It is difficult for us to see that they really are stars at all; it seems as though the sky were shrouded in a milky white veil.

"An astronomer would call this a discovery!" was Tortsov's joyous exclamation. "Let us confirm our bright spots. Perhaps they will enhance the dull stars clustered around them. Let us begin with our first bright spot—Othello's speech to the Senate. How can we confirm and enlarge this spot in our memories?

"After all that has happened, let us now decide what the nature of our memories is: auditory, visual, or emotional."

"No, I do not hear the voice of Othello and the others," I said, "but I do feel and see something rather strongly, although it is indistinct."

"That's good. What is it you feel or see?" asked Tortsov.

"It turns out to be very little, much less than I thought," I confessed after testing myself at length. "I see some kind of banal, opera-singer figure and sense in it the nobility of a generalized character."

"That's not good because you will never feel anything like real life in that kind of 'vision,'" remarked Tortsov. "And yet in this part of the play there is such a clash of vivid, lifelike, human, social, national, psychological, and ethical excitements and passions that it would seem impossible not to be moved by them. Even the external plot is so fine, so unexpected, incisive that it compels your interest. What an interweaving of circumstances! Impending war, the country's painful need of its only savior, Othello; the brutal outrage perpetrated on the ruling class because blood has been mixed in the marriage of an aristocrat with a colored savage, a semi-brute. Try to believe all this and make a choice between the racial honor of the proud Venetians and the saving of their country by true patriots. How many varied threads are knotted together in this one scene. What a skilful theatrical technique of witty exposition and headlong action.

"If you wish to reinforce this scene still further, throw a bridge across from it to the two preceding ones. Imagine that they have been played so that you have felt the blowing up of a huge scandal, which has burst forth in the night like a clap of thunder and awakened the whole city. Just think, while you were sweetly sleeping there were sudden cries from a rushing mob, the splash of waves from hurrying gondolas filled with men in arms; meantime the windows in the Doge's palace are filled with lights, and add to this the dreadful rumors of a Turkish invasion, the abduction of the popular Desdemona by a black man, a hurricane blowing up. . . . Mix that all together and wake up. I am sure you will feel that your city of Venice is already in the hands of the infidels who will at any instant invade your home. See how one bright patch merges with another just as vivid and forms a large, bright area which now reflects light on the contiguous parts and puts life into them. Indeed the episode of war has now become intertwined with the episode of Desdemona's abduction. Yet have you forgotten that the abduction is strongly bound up with Iago's revenge on Othello because of his resentment over Cassio? Remember too that in all this boiling plot a large role is played by Roderigo, second only to Othello as a suitor for the hand of Desdemona. At the same time Roderigo is involved with Iago, and so forth.

"Do you sense how one character, one episode, affects another, and how therefore the simile of reflected light from stars is valid for the process of analysis we are now engaged in? We no sooner had begun to fix the scene of Othello's appearance before the Senate when we became involved with other episodes closely allied with it and they in turn threw light on the preceding scenes.

"After a rapid glance over what has remained in our memories, we see that some of the clear patches have already merged with others of the same kind, while a third group, although they have not yet merged, already show a tendency in that direction, and the fourth, fifth . . . tenth groups, having received reflected light from the first, are now becoming more distinct, while all the rest of these moments in our memories consist of scarcely perceptible hints, like the stars in the Milky Way.

"Yet to tell the truth, all we have done so far toward the creation of new light areas and their combination with our roles has been directed toward arousing our enthusiasm for certain spots in the play which had not intuitively entered our consciousness.

"Now that we have rediscovered these remarkable places, our actor's *enthusiasm* can in turn become an instrument in our *analysis* and help us to continue the work we have begun. Enthusiasm does more than act as a stimulus to creativeness. It is also a wise guide leading us to the secret wellsprings of the heart, it is a keen and penetrating searcher, a sensitive critic and appraiser."

* * *

"Gifted poets like Shakespeare give us plays which are full of genius, larded through with an infinite amount of fascinating food for thought, with interesting 'magic ifs' and proposed circumstances. In working out another person's theme for creative action we must mainly proceed along the *inner* line of a play because the external line of facts and events has already been laid down by the author. In order to understand and evaluate what is secreted in a piece of work we have to have imagination.

"Let us make an experiment. Vanya, you tell us the contents of *Othello*."

"A black Moor has stolen away a white girl. The father goes to the Senate but meantime a war has broken out. The Moor must be sent, the father does not count. Decide, says Brabantio, about us first. The Senators decide, they send the black man off to the war that very night. I'll go with him, I insist, says the daughter. So they go. The war ends in victory. They live in a palace. . . ."

"What do you think," asked Tortsov turning to the rest of us, "has Vanya really understood and appraised the new and fascinating theme for creativeness offered us by Shakespeare?"

We burst out laughing instead of replying.

"Perhaps you, Paul, can help us?"

"Othello stole the daughter of a Senator called Brabantio on the very night when the Turks staged an attack on one of the Venetian colonies," began Paul. "The only person who could lead a successful military expedition was Othello. But before entrusting him with the defense of their possessions it was necessary to settle the conflict between him and Brabantio, who demanded redress from defamation heaped on his family by this man from a black race scorned by the haughty Venetians.

"The abductor, the Moor, is called before the Senate, where a special session is being held."

"I'm already bored!" announced Tortsov. "That's the sort of libretto they give you in theatre programs. You try, Grisha, to tell us the contents of *Othello*."

"Cyprus, Candia, and Mauritania are conquered provinces, under the heavy heel of Venice," began our specialist in cliché acting. "The arrogant Doges, Senators, and aristocrats do not look upon the conquered people as human beings and do not allow intermarriage with them. But, you see, life does not pay any attention to such things and it forces people into difficult compromises. Then there is the unexpected war with Turkey. . . ."

"Excuse me, but I find this dull. It sounds like a history textbook. There is little in it to carry me away. And yet both art and creativeness are founded on the fact that they ignite our imagination, our passions.

"In what you say, you do not feel any of the warm interest of the material given us by Shakespeare. It is not easy to relate the essential part of a piece of writing."

I kept silent for I had no plan of my own.

After a while Tortsov undertook to tell the story himself, or rather to embroider imaginatively on Shakespeare's theme. He said:

"I see a beautiful young Venetian woman, who has grown up amid luxury and is spoiled, high-spirited, full of dreams, fantasies, the way young girls are who are brought up without mothers, raised on fairy tales and romances. This scarcely opened flower, Desdemona, is bored by being shut in with household responsibilities and catering to the whims of her proud and important father. No one is allowed to come and see her and her young heart craves love. There are suitors for her hand, arrogant and dissipated young Venetians. But they do not charm this young dreamer. She is looking for the unheard of, the things you read about in fine romances. She is waiting for a fairy prince or powerful potentate, a king. He will come from some wonderful far-off country. He must be a hero, handsome, bold, unconquerable. She will give herself to him and sail away in a fine ship to some fairy-tale kingdom.

"Now you go on from there," said Tortsov turning to me. But I was so intent on listening to him that I was not prepared and could say nothing.

"I can't," I said after a pause, "I'm not primed."

"Prime yourself then," urged Tortsov.

"I haven't the wherewithal," I admitted.

"I'll give it to you," said Tortsov. "Do you see in your mind's eye the place where the action is laid, where what you are telling about all happens?"

"Yes," I replied with quickened interest. "I imagine the action taking place in a Venice that looks exactly like our Sevastopol; for some reason I see the Governor's house from Nizhny Novgorod there too. This is where Brabantio seems to live, it is on the shore of the South Bay in which little steamers scurry around, as they do to this day. Yet this does not interfere with the antique gondolas darting in all directions, with their oars splashing."

"Let us assume that is so," said Tortsov. "Who can explain the caprices of an actor's imagination! It has no use for history or geography and is not afraid of anachronisms."

"It is even more curious," I continued with my fantasy, "that in my Venice, which looks like Sevastopol, there is a bluff on the shore of the bay exactly like the one in Nizhny Novgorod, on the banks of the Volga, where there are poetic and secluded places that I used to love and of which I have tenderly unhappy memories."

After I had finished telling what I saw with my inner vision, I was immediately tempted to criticize the foolish creation of my imagination, but Tortsov waved his arms excitedly and said:

"Don't do it, for goodness sake! It is not in your power to order yourself in accordance with your own wishes to bring up these or those memories. Let them come to life of their own accord and act as powerful stimulants to your creativeness as an actor. The only proviso is that they should not essentially contradict the basic plot of the play as written by the author."

In order to further my imaginings Tortsov then gave me another clue.

"*When* did all this happen, which you see with your inner vision?" was his new question.

When my source dried up he stimulated me again to further work.

"*How* did it all happen?" he asked, and then immediately clarified his question. "I mean that I would like to know the line of this inner action, its gradual progress and development. For the time being we only know that a spoiled young woman, Desdemona, lives in a Nizhny Novgorod palace on the shore of the Volga and does not wish to marry any of the dissipated young Venetians. Tell me what she dreams of, how she lives, and what happens next."

This new stimulus was to no avail, so Tortsov carried on in my stead, thinking up all sorts of fascinating rumors deriving from the talk about the popularity of the Moor that preceded his arrival.

Tortsov would have it that the Moor's feats and all the hardships he related to Desdemona must be like fairy tales, romantically beautiful and effective so that they would excite the overheated young brain of the girl who had been waiting for the hero in her dreams.

After another pause Tortsov tried once more to set me in motion. He advised me to tell in logical order what happened: Where did they meet, how did they fall in love, get married?

I was silent because I found it far more interesting and instructive to hear Tortsov's imagination at work.

So he went on, and described how Othello had arrived in Venetian Sevastopol in a great ship. The legends concerning the general's feats drew a huge crowd to the pier. The appearance and dark skin of Othello aroused curiosity. When he rode or walked through the streets little boys ran after him in crowds, the passersby whispered to each other and pointed their fingers at him.

The first meeting of these future lovers took place in the street and it made a great impression on the young woman. Othello fascinated her not only with his brave appearance but also and especially with his naïve ways of a savage, his modesty and his goodness, all of which shone in his eyes. This modesty and shyness joined with valor and imperviousness to fear made an unusual and beautiful combination.

Another time Desdemona saw Othello at the head of troops coming back from some military exercises. His easy seat on his horse made an even greater impression on her. That was the time she first saw Cassio riding with his general.

Desdemona's imaginings kept her from sleep. One day Brabantio announced to his daughter, as mistress of the household, that he had invited the celebrated Othello to dinner. At this name the girl almost fainted away.

It is easy to imagine with what care Desdemona dressed herself and had the dinner prepared, and how she waited for this meeting with her hero.

The look in her eyes could not but go to the Moor's heart. It embarrassed him and increased his shyness, which was so becoming in this hero with his name for invincibility.

The Moor, who had not been spoiled by womanly warmth, could not at first understand the exceptional amiability of his hostess. He was accustomed to being received and tolerated in the houses of highly placed Venetians as an official personage. Yet amid the honors heaped on him he always felt himself to be in the position of a slave. No pair of wonderful eyes had ever before looked with warmth on his black and, as he believed, ugly face, until suddenly on this day. . . .

Nor did Othello sleep for many nights, and he waited with impatience for another invitation from Brabantio. It was not long in coming. Probably at the instigation of the lovelorn girl he was invited again, and yet again, so that they could listen to his stories of his exploits, of the hard life during campaigns. After dinners, over the wine, and sitting out on the terrace with a view of Sevastopol harbor with the Nizhny Novgorod bluff, the Moor would modestly but truthfully tell about his exploits, as Shakespeare himself described him doing when the Moor speaks to the Senate, and as Tortsov imaginatively painted him.

I really came to believe that such a story could not but turn the head of a high-spirited young woman in a romantic frame of mind.

"Desdemona was not one to build her life like all the others on a narrowly bourgeois pattern," continued Tortsov. "She craved the unusual, the contents of a fairy tale. One could not have imagined a better hero than Othello for a girl of her flaming nature.

"The Moor began to feel more and more at home at Brabantio's. It was his first opportunity to see a real home at close quarters. The presence of a beautiful young woman lent an added charm, and so forth." Here Tortsov broke off his story.

"Do you not find," he asked, "that this kind of re-telling of the contents of a play is more interesting than the dry recounting of the facts? If you were to make me tell you still again the contents of this tragedy and I followed the inner pattern rather than the outer form, I'd think up something more. And the more often you made me tell the story the more material would be stored up for imaginative extensions to the words of the author, for the 'magic ifs' which you will use to justify the material given you by the author.

"So now follow my example, and as often as possible relate the contents of plays and sketches which you are given to act in, approaching them each time from a different angle, from your own point of view in your own person, or from that of one of the characters, that is to say putting yourself in his stead."

"All this is fine . . . but with one proviso: You must possess a brilliant natural or highly developed imagination," I said sadly. "We have to think about what leads to the development of an imagination which is still only in an embryonic stage."

"Yes, you will have to acquire methods for prodding your imagination, which has not yet warmed up," agreed Tortsov.

"That's it, that's what we need! That is exactly what we lack," I added to what he had said.

*　　*　　*

173

"We have begun our analysis layer by layer, working from the top down—from the things which are more accessible to our conscious feelings down to those which are less so.

"The topmost layer consists of the *plot*, the *facts*, and *events* of the play. We have already touched on these but limited ourselves to their enumeration for the purpose of reproducing them on the stage. Now we shall continue our study of them. The word 'study' in our language means not only that we state the fact, look at it, and understand it, but also that we appraise its worth and significance.

"This new aspect of analysis is what we call *appraising the facts*.

"There are plays (poor comedies, melodramas, vaudeville, revues, farces) in which the external plot represents the principal asset of the performance. In such works the very facts of a murder, a death, a wedding, or the process of dumping flour or water on the head of one of the characters, of losing a pair of trousers, of getting into the wrong room where a peaceful guest is taken for a robber, and so forth—all such facts constitute the principal moments of the production. It would be superfluous to appraise them; they are instantly comprehended and accepted by everyone.

"But in other works the plot itself and the facts contained in it sometimes do not have much significance in themselves. In such plays it is not the facts but the attitude of the characters toward them that provides the fulcrum, the central interest, which the audience follows with thumping pulse. In such plays facts are needed only to the extent that they provide motivation and occasion for revealing the inner content. Chekhov's plays are of this kind.

"In the best plays of all, form and content are in direct relationship with each other; then the life of the spirit is indivisible from the facts and the plot. In most of Shakespeare's plays, and among them *Othello*, this complete correspondence exists, this mutual interaction between the external, factual line and the inner line

"In such works, appraising the facts is of prime significance. As you examine the external events you come in contact with the given circumstances that give rise to the facts. As you study these circumstances you come to realize the inner reasons that relate to them. So you go deeper into the very thick of the spiritual life of a role, you reach the subtext, you come to the underlying current of the play which provokes the superficial waves of action.

"The technique of appraising the facts is very simple to start with. You begin by mentally canceling the fact to be appraised, and then you try to find out how that affects the life of the spirit in your role.

"Let us test this process in your roles," said Tortsov turning to Vanya and Grisha. "The first fact you come to in the play is your *arrival in front of Brabantio's palace.* Do I need to explain that if this fact were lacking the whole first scene would be nonexistent, and during the beginning of the tragedy you could sit quietly in your dressing room instead of moving around in excitement on the stage? It is obvious that the fact of your arrival at Brabantio's palace is an essential one and you must believe in it, and hence experience its impact.

"The second of the facts in the first scene which we have recorded is the *quarrel with Roderigo, Iago's defense of his innocence, the necessity of raising the alarm* and of starting the *pursuit of the Moor.* Remove all these facts, and what happens? The two characters would arrive on the scene in a gondola and immediately start to raise the alarm. In such a course of events we, the spectators, would be left in ignorance of the exposition of the play, that is to say of the relationship between Roderigo and Desdemona, Iago and Othello, of Iago's resentment against Othello, and the regimental intrigue which unlooses the whole tragedy.

"This would be reflected in the acting of the alarm scene. It is one thing to arrive somewhere, begin to yell, raise a racket to waken people who are sound asleep; it is quite another to do what you can to save your vanishing happiness, as in the case of Roderigo who is losing his bride, the eloping Desdemona. It is one thing to raise a row for the fun of it, and quite another when it is done in the spirit of revenge, as in the case of Iago who is venting his hatred of Othello. Every action which is carried out not merely because of some external reason but because of some inner impulse is incomparably more effective, better grounded, and therefore more moving to the actor who executes it.

"Appraising the facts is inseparable from another aspect of our analysis, namely, *the justification of the facts*. This is a necessary part of the process, because a fact without a basis dangles in mid-air. The fact which is not experienced, not included in the inner line of life in the play, not responsive to it, is of no use and indeed is a hindrance to proper inner development. Such an unjustified fact constitutes a blank, a break in a role. It is a spot of dead flesh in a living organism, it is a deep hole on a smooth road, it impedes free movement and the course of inner feelings. You must either fill up the hole or throw a bridge across it. That is why we need the *justification of facts*. Once a fact is justified it is automatically included in the inner line of the play, in the subtext; it promotes the free unfolding of the spiritual life of your part. Facts which are justified also promote logic and consecutiveness in feeling a part, and you already know what importance those two factors have in our work. . . .

"Now you know the facts of the first scene of the play. More than that, you have executed them more or less correctly. But you have not as yet plumbed the depths of their true validity, nor will you do this until you have *justified* them on the basis of new given circumstances, proposed by yourselves. These will compel you to visualize the course of events in the play as a human being, not just as an actor, as an initiator and author, not as a mere copyist. So let us now examine these facts and see whether you have appraised, from your own personal, human point of view, everything that happens in the first scene, putting yourselves in the place of Roderigo and Iago. As far as the external rendering of the facts is concerned, I believe what you did. They arrive, just s you did, at the landing and moor their gondola. Just as they do, you tied it up here, not just anyhow but with a purpose—*to raise the alarm*. In turn you raised the alarm with another and definite purpose in mind—to pursue and arrest the Moor, and rescue Desdemona.

"But yet you do not know—by which I mean you do not feel—why these actions were so urgently necessary to the two of you."

"I know! You bet I know!" Vanya practically burst out.

"Why then, tell me," suggested Tortsov.

"Because I'm in love with Desdemona."

"That means you know her. That's good. Tell us, what is she like?"

"You mean Maria? There she is!" Vanya exclaimed without stopping to think.

Our poor Desdemona waved her arms and flew out of the auditorium. The rest of us, including Tortsov, could not keep from laughing.

"Well, that fact has certainly been appraised from a human and not a theatrical point of view!" laughed Tortsov. "But if that is so, why don't you raise the alarm so as to rescue your beloved? Why has it been so difficult to convince you how necessary it is to do this?"

"Roderigo is capricious," was Vanya's rather confused reply.

"But there must be a reason even for being capricious, or else neither you nor the audience will put any faith in your caprice. On the stage nothing can happen irrelevantly," remarked Tortsov.

"He has quarreled with Iago!" was the reply Vanya now squeezed out of himself.

"Who is 'he'?"

"Roderigo; no, it's me."

"If it is you then you know better than anyone else the cause of the quarrel. Tell us about it."

"It's because he tricked me—he promised I'd marry her and he didn't keep his word."

177

"How and in what way did he deceive you?"

Vanya was silent. He was unable to invent anything.

"Don't you realize that Iago has twisted you around his little finger, has extorted large sums of money from you, and all the time was helping the Moor with his elopement?"

"So *he* was the one who arranged the elopement! The dirty dog!" exclaimed Vanya with genuine disgust. "I'll punch his face in! Why doesn't he, I mean, why don't I want to raise the alarm?" Here Vanya threw up his hands and again was silent because he could not think of any justification for the action.

"You see there is such an important fact for your part and you have not appraised it at all. That's a large blank space. And you cannot justify the action with any banal pretexts. What you need here is not simple but magic action which will really make you wild and push you into interesting movement. Any dry, formal pretexts will be harmful for your role."

Vanya had nothing to offer.

"Do you mean to say that you do not remember that Desdemona, through Iago, promised you her hand and heart, and that he in turn obliged you to purchase valuable wedding presents and to prepare a home; you actually went to all the trouble and furnished a place with mad luxury. How much did your friend and agent make out of all that! The day for the elopement was fixed, the church and the priest to marry you were prepared, all was ready for an intimate but lavish wedding, all paid for out of your generous purse. You were so full of excitement, anticipation, impatience you neither ate nor slept then suddenly . . . Desdemona elopes with a black savage. And this was done to you by that scoundrel Iago.

"You are convinced that they are being married in the very church prepared for your wedding, that the major part of the trousseau bought by you has gone to Othello. This is mockery, this is robbery! Now tell me, if things had happened in this fashion, what would you do?"

178

"I'd thrash the scoundrel!" Vanya decided and even flushed a little with resentment.

"What if Iago worsted you; you know he is a soldier and powerfully strong."

"What can I get out of him anyway, the fiend! I'd shut up and turn away from him!" By this time Vanya was bewildered.

"If that is so, why did you accede to his urging that you come to Brabantio's palace in your own gondola? Appraise this action," said Tortsov, giving Vanya fresh facts for his appraisal.

But our hot-headed young man was unable to solve the riddle.

"And here is one more fact not yet appraised, and one which you must examine down to the bottom if you are going to understand the interrelationship of these two important characters in the play.

"You, Grisha, what have you to say about Roderigo's arrival in front of Brabantio's palace? How did you, as Iago, accomplish this?" asked Tortsov with some insistence.

"I grabbed him, do you see, by the scruff of the neck, chucked him into the gondola, and brought him to where he had to go," decided Grisha.

"You suppose, then, that such brute force will help to stir your creative interest? If you do, all right; but I rather doubt your success. After all, analysis, appraisal of the facts, and their justification are necessary to us if we are to acquire faith in them and be carried away by interest aroused by them. If I were playing your part I could not achieve that end by the use of the coarse, primitive means you suggest. I'd be bored, and indeed I would find it repellent to act like a top sergeant; I would far rather accomplish my purpose by means of wiles that are worthy of Iago's diabolical mind."

"What would you do?" the students asked Tortsov.

"I would immediately turn myself into the most innocent, meek lamb who has been maligned by the most malicious gossip. I'd sit there with downcast eyes, and I would go on sitting there until Roderigo, that is you, Vanya, had finished pouring out all your anger, gall, and hatred. The worse things you said, the more unjust they were, the better for me. So there would be no need to interrupt you. Only when you had thoroughly vented your resentment, thrown off the burden on your soul, exhausted all your energy, would the time come to start action. Till then, my cue is to be silent. I should not argue, make any retorts, or you would be stirred to fresh accusations and excitement. I must knock the ground out from under your feet and let you fall flat on your face. When you had lost all support under you, then I would have you in my power and I could do what I wanted with you. That is why I should act that way. I'd stretch my immobility and silence to the proportions of a long, tiring, and awkward pause. After that I should walk over to the window, turning my back on you, and hand you a second even more distasteful pause.

"This awkwardness and misunderstanding is not what you, Vanya, expected to achieve by your Philippics. You probably expected that Iago would defend himself, as you would have done, beat his breast in despair. But instead of any outbreak you get— silence, immobility, a mysterious, rather sad, facial expression and look out of the eyes, embarrassment, misunderstanding. All this gives you the impression of having misfired; you are disillusioned, ill at ease, bewildered. These things cool you off quickly and put you in your place.

"After this I, as Iago, would go over to the table, near which you are seated, and begin to lay out the money and the valuables I happen to have with me. In the bygone days of friendship these were given to me by you, but now that the friendship is at an end they must be returned. This is the first moment when I can achieve a turnabout in my inner state. After this I would, while standing in front of you (since I no longer consider myself either as a friend or guest in the house), thank you warmly and sincerely for bygone favors, letting drop a few remarks about my memories of the better days of our friendship. Then I would take a sad leave, without touching your hand (I am no longer worthy of that), and as I go out I would almost casually yet quite clearly let drop the phrase: The future will show what I was to you. Farewell forever!

"Now tell me, if you were in Roderigo's place, would you have let me go? Here you have lost Desdemona and now your best friend, as well as all hope of the future. Would you not feel lonely, abandoned by all, helpless? Would not this prospect alarm you?"

*　　*　　*

"The *appraisal of facts* is a big and complicated piece of work. It is carried out not only by your mind but also and principally by your feelings and creative will. This work is done on the plane of the imagination.

"In order to appraise the facts by means of your own feelings, on the basis of your personal, living relationship to them, you as an actor must put to yourself this question: What circumstances of my own inner life—which of my personal, human ideas, desires, efforts, qualities, inborn gifts and shortcomings—can oblige me, as a man and actor, to have an attitude toward people and events such as those of the character I am portraying?

"For example, in *Othello*, Shakespeare gives us a whole series of facts and events. These must be appraised. The haughty, conceited, power-loving Venetians are well known to everyone. The colonies which have passed under the yoke of Venice by right of conquest—Mauritania, Cyprus, Candia—have all been enslaved. The tribes who inhabit these countries are not even considered by the Venetians to be human beings. And suddenly one of their number has dared to carry off Desdemona, brightest ornament of Venice, the daughter of one of the proudest and most influential men in its aristocracy. Appraise this scandal, this crime, shame, this insult to the family, indeed to the whole arrogant ruling class.

"And here is another fact: Suddenly, like a clap of thunder

from a clear sky, comes the news that a large Turkish fleet is heading for Cyprus, which formerly was one of the Turks' possessions and which they always dreamed of recovering.

"In order to make a more profound estimate of this fact let us make a comparison. Remember the terrible day when we woke up to hear that Russia was at war with Japan, and on top of that to learn that the major part of the Russian fleet had already been sunk.

"It was that kind of disturbance, only greater, which seized Venice and all its inhabitants on this fateful night.

"War has begun. Hurriedly they equip an expedition, at night, during a terrible storm. Whom to send, whom to choose to lead the expedition?

"Who else but the famous, the invincible Moor? He is called to the Senate.

"Think about this, weigh this fact, and you will sense with what impatience the arrival of the hero and savior is awaited in the Senate.

"Meanwhile fresh events, one after the other, are piling up in this fateful night.

"One new fact enters the picture, makes the situation more acute: Injured Brabantio demands justice, defense, and the clearing not only of his family honor but of the prestige of the whole ruling class of Venice.

"Take a thorough look at the position of the government and try yourselves to untie the knot of all these events. Weigh the fact of a father's sufferings, having lost at one blow his daughter and the fair name of his family. Weigh too the position of the Senators who are compelled by the pressure of events to curb their pride and effect a compromise. Appraise all these events from the point of view of the principal characters—Othello, Desdemona, Iago, Cassio. Passing from fact to fact, event to event, from one action to another, you will go through the whole play and only then will you be able to say that you know the plot and can tell it.

"After we have made this studied analysis of the line of the play, that is to say the author's work, we must repeat the process with all the circumstances proposed by the director, the scene designer, and all the others who contribute to the production. Their attitude and approach to the imagined life on the stage cannot but be interesting for us.

"Yet the most important circumstances are those with which we ourselves fill out our roles for the sake of our own creative state on the stage. At the same time, each one of us has to take into consideration too the circumstances imagined by those opposite whom we play and on whom we largely depend.

"Again it is easiest to begin with external facts, which for reasons you are now familiar with we do not give up while working toward the accretion of spiritual material."

*　　*　　*

"Let us turn from theory to practice," said Tortsov, "and go through the play on various levels, from the top down. Let us begin with the first scene. The top layer we have already examined sufficiently—the *facts* and the *plot*. On the next level, we come to *Venetian life*, manners and customs. What do you think about them?"

None of the students spoke up, because no one had even thought about this before; so Tortsov was obliged to intervene. As a result of his urging, suggesting, hinting, he managed to squeeze a small amount out of us, but as usual he contributed the lion's share.

"Who are they, this Roderigo and Iago? What is their social status?" he asked.

"Iago is an officer, and Roderigo an aristocrat," we volunteered.

"I think you are flattering them," replied Tortsov. "Iago is too coarse for an officer and Roderigo is too vulgar for an aristocrat. Would it not be wiser to reduce their rank somewhat and call

183

Iago a top sergeant who has risen, because of his exploits in the field, from the rank of simple soldier to petty officer? And count Roderigo simply as belonging to the class of wealthy merchants?"

Grisha, who always prefers to play noble characters, voiced a vigorous protest. He found that the psychology of his character was far too "subtly intellectual" for a person of low birth, and refused to look upon him as a simple soldier. We argued about this, we brought forward examples from life and literature, we pointed to Figaro, to Molière's Scapin, Sganarelle, and to the servants in Italian comedies who possessed the shrewd wits of the cleverest dodgers and rogues with whom the "intellectuals" always have to cope. As for Iago, he is a diabolical character from the outset, and the fiend in him is very subtle, quite apart from any social status or training.

We succeeded only in persuading Grisha that Iago is coarse albeit an officer. I, for my part, could see the cliché of "nobility" which Grisha had planted in his mind.

In order to push stubborn Grisha away from this mistaken position, Tortsov painted a picture of regimental life in which a soldier by hook or crook is determined to become an officer, an officer to become an "ancient" or adjutant, and so on up to the rank of general. By means of a true description he hoped to coax Grisha down off his stilts to come to grips with life. He said:

"Iago is by origin a simple soldier. His external appearance is rough, good-natured, sincere, honest. He is brave; in all the battles he fought side by side with Othello. More than once he saved his life. He is intelligent, shrewd; he has an excellent understanding of the battle tactics of Othello, who evolved them out of his military genius. Othello consulted with him constantly both before and during battle, and Iago more than once gave him intelligent and sound advice. There are two personalities in Iago: The one is what he appears to be, the other what he actually is. The one is pleasant, rather unrefined in manner, good-natured, the other wicked and repulsive. The exterior which he has assumed is so misleading that everyone (to a certain degree this includes his wife) is convinced he is the most sincere and best-natured of men. If Desdemona had had a little black son, the big, rough, good-natured Iago would have been the one to rear him in the place of a nurse. And when the boy grew up he would have looked upon this fiend with a good-humored face as his uncle.

"Although Othello has seen Iago in battle and knows how bold and ruthless he can be, he still shares the general view of him. He knows that men in battle become brutish, he is that way himself. Yet that does not keep him in private life from being soft, tender, almost shy. Besides, Othello has a high opinion of Iago's mind and shrewdness since he often gave him good advice in the war. During the campaign Iago was not only his counselor, he was also his friend. Othello poured out to him all his bitter thoughts, his doubts, and his hopes. Iago always slept in his tent. The great military leader, when he could not sleep, talked frankly with Iago. Iago was his servant, his orderly, and when need arose, his physician. Better than anyone else he could dress a wound, or when needed he could cheer, distract, sing bawdy but amusing songs, or tell stories of the same ilk. Because of his good humor he was allowed to say anything.

"How many times did Iago's songs and cynical anecdotes serve an important purpose! For example, when the army was worn out and the soldiers grumbling, along would come Iago to sing a song that would catch on with the soldiers even if it was cynical, and their whole mood would be altered. At another critical time when it was necessary to pacify the resentment of the soldiers, Iago would not hesitate to invent some horrible, cold-blooded torture or death for a prisoner, some savage taken in battle, and this would for a time allay the aroused feelings of the army. Of course this was done without Othello's knowledge, because the noble Moor did not tolerate wanton brutality, though when it was necessary he would instantly, at one blow, strike off a head.

"Iago is honest. He does not steal government money or property. He is too clever to take that risk. But if he can mulct a fool (and there are many of them around besides Roderigo) he never lets an opportunity pass. From such he wheedles money, presents, invitations to meals, women, horses, puppies, and so forth. These are his earnings on the side, and they provide him with the means of carousing and having a gay time. Emilia does not know about all this, although she may suspect it. Iago's closeness to Othello, the fact that he was raised from the ranks to be his lieutenant, that he sleeps in Othello's tent, and acts as his right-hand man, and so forth, all this, of course, gives rise to envy among the officers and affection among the soldiers. They all fear and respect Iago as he is a genuine soldier and fighting man who more than once has led his regiment out of difficulties, saved them from catastrophe. Campaign life suits him.

"Yet, in Venice, amid all the glitter, the starched and haughty manners at official receptions, or among the highly placed persons with whom Othello has to deal, Iago is not at home. In these matters Othello is not very well trained either—he needs to have someone at his side to fill in the blanks in his education, an adjutant whom one would not hesitate to send on an errand to the Doge himself, or to the Senators. He has to have someone versed in writing letters or able to explain aspects of military science he is not familiar with. Could he appoint to such an office a fighting man like Iago? Of course, the scholarly Cassio would be a far more suitable choice. He is a Florentine and at that time Florence was what Paris is today, a center of worldliness and exquisite arts. In his relations with Brabantio, in preparing secret meetings with Desdemona, could he use Iago as a go-between? For this you could not find anyone better than Cassio. So is there anything surprising in his naming Cassio adjutant to his person? Besides, Iago's candidacy for the post never once entered the mind of the Moor. Why would Iago want to play that role? Even without it he is an intimate of Othello, at home with him, his friend. Let him remain as such. Why should Othello put his friend into the awkward position of an untrained, unpolished, roughshod adjutant who would be the laughing stock of everyone! That is probably how Othello reasoned.

"But Iago's view was different. He supposed that his services, his bravery, the fact that he had on several occasions saved his general's life, that his friendship and devotion entitled him and no one else to be adjutant. It might have been all right to pass him over in favor of some distinguished person, some officer from his staff of comrades in battle; but to take the first smooth little underling of an officer who does not even know what it is to be in a battle, or what war is! Introduce this silly boy into a close relation to the general just because he can read a book, babble prettily with the young ladies, and cut a wide swath among the powerful in the land—this logic is incomprehensible to Iago. Therefore the appointment of Cassio was such a blow, insult, humiliation, such a piece of ingratitude that he cannot forgive it. The most offensive part of all is that he, Iago, was never considered by anyone for the post. And what completely annihilated him was that all Othello's secrets of the heart, his love for Desdemona and the elopement with her, were hidden from him and entrusted to that boy Cassio.

"There is nothing surprising in the fact that recently, ever since Cassio was named adjutant, Iago has been drinking heavily and carousing. It may have been during one of his drinking bouts that he met and made friends with Roderigo. The favorite theme of the heart-to-heart talks between these two new friends was, on the one hand, Roderigo's dream of eloping with Desdemona, which was something Iago was to arrange, and on the other hand, Iago's complaints about the unjust treatment dealt out to him by the general. In order to give vent to his resentment and also to feed it, he recalls and rehearses all the past—his own former services and the former ingratitude of Othello, to which he has earlier paid no thought but which now assumes criminal proportions. He even recalls camp stories about Emilia.

"The point is that while he was close to Othello, Iago was the butt of jealousy in many quarters. In order to have an outlet for their feelings these people invented all sorts of reasons for the closeness of Iago and Othello. They put out rumors, and saw to it that they reached Iago, to the effect that something had gone on, and might still be going on, between Othello and Emilia. At the time, he had not given these rumors the attention they deserved. This was because he did not bother much about Emilia and was unfaithful to her himself. He liked her buxomness, she is a good housewife, she can sing and play on the lute, she is gay, perhaps she has some money of her own, she comes of a good merchant family and is well educated for those days. Even if there had been something between her and the general (and he knew at the time that there was nothing) he would not have been too upset about it.

"But now, after the atrocious injury to him, he recalls the gossip about Emilia. Emilia is on good terms with Othello. He is a fine person, kindly, lonely, has no one to head his household, there is no feminine touch in his home; so Emilia as a housewife puts things to rights in the apartments of the bachelor general. Iago is aware of this. He has seen her often at Othello's and never given it a thought, but now he begins to accuse Othello. In a word, Iago has so hypnotized himself that he believes things which are not so. This enables him, wicked as he is, to rage at, slander, accuse innocent Othello more than ever and to inflame his own inner resentment and gall.

"This is the state of things when Iago learns the improbable, unexpected, to him incomprehensible news of the accomplished fact of Desdemona's abduction. He could not believe his eyes when he entered the general's apartment and saw the famous beauty almost in the embrace of the hideous black devil, as he now considers the Moor. The blow was so great that at first he was stunned. When they explained to him how the lovers, under the guidance of Cassio, had fooled everyone including himself,

Othello's close friend, when he heard gay voices laughing at him, he ran away to hide the resentment that boiled up inside him.

"The abduction of Desdemona not only offended him, it also put him in an embarrassing position in relation to Roderigo, because all the time he was swindling him, Iago kept swearing that he would get the beautiful girl for him and that he would steal her away if Brabantio refused his consent to their marriage. Then suddenly this affront! Even simple-minded as he was, Roderigo realized that he had been tricked by Iago. He even began to doubt that Iago was really close to Othello; he ceased to believe in his friendship. In short their relations were immediately ruined. Roderigo was enraged—blindly, stubbornly, like a child and like a fool. For the time being he even forgot that Iago saved him on one occasion from some drunken revelers who were intent on beating him.

"The abduction and wedding of Desdemona were beautiful and completely successful. Everything went simply and easily. Long before the appointed day, Cassio had entered into an affair with one of the maids in the house of Brabantio. More than once he lured her out to a rendezvous, taking her off in a gondola with a rear cabin, and then brought her back. For these lover's outings Cassio bribed Brabantio's servants heavily. One of the rendezvous had been fixed on this evening, but instead of her maid, Desdemona herself came out and vanished from her home forever. They had even used this same device before, when Desdemona slipped out to meet with Othello.

"Don't forget that Desdemona is not at all the way she is usually depicted on the stage. Actresses mostly make a timid, frightened Ophelia out of her. Yet Desdemona is not at all an Ophelia. She is decisive, bold. She does not want a conventional marriage planned out of social considerations. She has to have a fairytale prince.

"Incidentally, we shall come to her again later on. For the time being enough has been said to show clearly how she consented to the bold and dangerous plan of abduction.

"When Iago learned what had happened he decided not to give up. He believed all was not yet lost; if he could raise enough of a stir in the city Othello would be disapproved and, who could tell, perhaps even his marriage might be annulled on orders from higher up.

"Perhaps Iago was right; that might well have happened if the marriage and outbreak of war had not coincided. Othello was too necessary to the government; they could not even think of annulling his marriage at such a critical time. No time could be lost. When action was imperative Iago showed a diabolical energy. He was able to get everything done in time.

"Having cooled off, Iago returned to the young couple, congratulated them, laughed with them, called himself a fool; he even made Desdemona believe he had acted so stupidly when he first heard of the abduction and marriage because he was jealous of his adored general. Then Iago rushed off to find Roderigo. . . ."

Vanya (as Roderigo) proved to be more tractable than Grisha. He immediately, and with some relish, demoted his character to the rank of simple merchant, and he did it all the more readily because he could not give the slightest proof of any exalted origin for him. No matter how stupid an aristocrat may be, he will still show traces of a favored and refined society in which he was nurtured. As for Roderigo there is nothing to be gleaned from the play about him except his drinking, quarrels, and street brawls. Vanya not only followed the line laid down by Tortsov, he also added things out of his own imagination that were congenial to the life of a simple man. The life they projected made more or less this social picture:

Roderigo is probably the son of rich parents. They are landowners, they bring their produce in to Venice. There they barter it for velvet and other luxury items. Ships carry these things abroad, even to Russia, where high prices are paid for them.

But Roderigo's parents are dead. How can he manage such a large enterprise? All he knows how to do is to squander his patrimony. Thanks to their wealth both his father and he are received in aristocratic circles. Roderigo himself is rather simple-minded and always engaged in carousing; so he provides money (which, of course, is not returned) to young Venetians with similarly frivolous tastes. Where does he get it? Thanks to the previous good management and to loyal employees, the family enterprise is still running with the old momentum. But this cannot, of course, last for long.

Unfortunately one morning after a drinking bout, Roderigo was riding down a canal and saw, as in a dream or a vision, the beauteous young Desdemona getting into a gondola to ride to church accompanied by her nurse. His breath was taken away, he stopped his gondola and blearily watched her for a long time. This caught the attention of her nurse, who quickly threw a veil over Desdemona's face. Roderigo followed them, eventually, into the church. He was so excited that he became quite sober. Roderigo did not pray, he only watched Desdemona. Her nurse kept trying to shield her, but the girl herself was rather pleased with the attention, not because she found Roderigo to her taste, but because it was such a bore to sit at home or go to church, and also because she yearned for a little fun.

While Mass was going on Brabantio himself came in, found his daughter, and sat down beside her and her nurse. The nurse whispered something in his ear and pointed to Roderigo. Brabantio cast a stern look in his direction. But this did not faze as brazen a person as Roderigo. When Desdemona went back to her gondola, she found the bottom of it strewn with flowers. Brabantio ordered all the flowers thrown out into the water, handed his daughter into the gondola himself, and sent her and her nurse home. But Roderigo kept ahead of them all the way, strewing flowers in their path. The beautiful Desdemona was quite pleased with the attentions and by the young man's extravagance. Why?

Because it was gay, flattering to her self-esteem, and also because it annoyed her nurse.

After the first encounter Roderigo quite lost his head. He sat for whole nights in a gondola under her windows hoping that she would look out. She actually did do so once or twice, and even smiled at him out of mischief or coquetry. And he was simple enough to think he had made a conquest. He began to write verse, he bribed servants to convey his rhymed declarations of love to the beautiful lady. Finally, at Brabantio's instance, his brother went out and spoke to the importunate admirer and told him that if he did not desist from pursuing Desdemona he would take steps. But the pursuit did not end.

Then once he waylaid Desdemona's gondola in a dark canal and as he overtook it he threw into it a large bouquet and a madrigal he himself had composed. But, horrors, Desdemona did not even glance in his direction! With her own hand she threw the bouquet and madrigal into the water and turning away angrily, covering her face with a veil. Roderigo was crushed. He did not know what to do. To avenge himself on this cruel beauty the only thing he could think of was to go on a week-long spree. . . .

This is how matters stood when Othello appeared on the scene. Roderigo was in the crowd when Desdemona first saw the Moor in the street. With the return of the victorious Othello to Venice, military men became all the rage and the favorites of the courtesans during the nightly carousing. During these orgies Roderigo footed the bills. This endeared him to the officers and threw him together with Iago. On one occasion when there was a drunken brawl some of these officers nearly beat Roderigo to death, but Iago intervened with considerable warmth. Roderigo was so grateful he wanted to recompense him generously, but Iago assured him he had acted merely out of liking for him. This was the beginning of their friendship.

Meantime Othello's romance with Desdemona was developing more and more. Cassio, who was the go-between in this love affair of Othello and Desdemona, knew of Roderigo's infatuation—he had also made his acquaintance during one of the nightly brawls. Cassio was quite well aware of Roderigo's simple-mindedness. Since he knew the relations between Othello and Desdemona, Roderigo's hopes of having his love returned seemed quite ridiculous to Cassio. That is why he was constantly joking about it, teasing Roderigo, and inventing hoaxes. He would assure him that Desdemona would take a walk in a certain place or that she had fixed a rendezvous with him at such another place, and Roderigo would wait around in vain for hours on end expecting to see his beautiful lady. Insulted and humiliated he ran to Iago who took him under his protection and swore that he would avenge him and finally arrange the marriage because he never believed in any romance with the black fiend. This caused Roderigo to cling more and more to Iago and shower him with money.

When Roderigo learned about the marriage between Othello and Desdemona, the poor simpleton at first burst into tears like a child; then he heaped all the bad words in his vocabulary on his friend and decided to break off all acquaintance with him. Poor Iago had all the trouble in the world to persuade Roderigo to help raise a row throughout the entire city in order to accomplish a divorce or the nonrecognition of the marriage. We first see the two friends when Iago has practically forced Roderigo into a gondola (a luxurious one, trimmed with expensive materials, as is proper for a rich man) and has brought him to the house of Brabantio. . . .

CHAPTER SEVEN

Checking Work Done and Summing Up

"WHERE DOES the action take place?" asked Tortsov.

"In Venice."

"When?"

"In the sixteenth century. The year is not fixed, as we have not yet consulted with the scene designer," answered one of the theatre apprentices in charge of this matter.

"What is the time of year?"

"Late autumn."

"Why did you choose that season?"

"So that it would be harder to get up on a cold night and start off!"

"Is it day or night?"

"Night."

"What is the hour?"

"About midnight."

"What were you doing at this hour?"

"Sleeping."

"Who wakened you?"

"Petrushin," here he pointed at another apprentice.

"Why was he the one to do it?"

"Because Rakhmanov named him gate-keeper."

"What did you think when you became conscious?"

"Something untoward has happened and I shall have to go off somewhere, since I am a gondolier."

"What happened next?"

"I hurriedly dressed myself."

"What did you put on?"

"My tights, shorts, my jerkin, cap, and heavy shoes. I fixed my lantern, took my cape, and got my oar."

"Where are they kept?"

"In the entry, in the hall hanging on brackets fastened to the wall."

"And where do you sleep?"

"In the cellar, below water level."

"Is it damp there?"

"Yes, damp and cold."

"Evidently Brabantio keeps you on short rations."

"What else can I expect? I'm only a gondolier."

"Of what do your duties consist?"

"To keep the gondola and all that goes with it in order. The accessories are numerous: handsome cushions to sit or lie on, lots of them—those for special occasions, some for less formal occasions, and others for everyday use. There is also a gorgeous gold embroidered baldaquin. There are also dress-up oars and ornamented boat hooks. There are lanterns, too, for ordinary use and a lot of little ones for the *grande serenata*."

"What happened next?"

"I was surprised by the flurry in the household. Some said there was fire, others that the enemy was coming. In the vestibule a lot of people were listening to what was going on outside. Someone out there was yelling like mad. As we did not dare open the lower windows we rushed upstairs to the reception room. Up there the windows had already been opened and whoever was able to, stuck his head out. That's when I heard about the abduction."

"What did you feel about this?"

"Terrific resentment. You see I am in love with the young lady of the house. I take her out for rides or to go to church, and I am proud of this because everyone looks at her and admires her beauty. Because of her I already have a name in Venice. I am always, accidentally as it were, dropping a flower and am happy when she finds and keeps it. Or if she touches it and leaves it in the gondola I pick it up, kiss it, and keep it as a memento."

"Do you mean to tell me that rough gondoliers are as sensitive and sentimental as that?"

"Only on account of Desdemona, who is our pride and joy. This motive is especially valuable to me because it fires me with energy to go out on the pursuit to save her honor."

"What did you do next?"

"I rushed downstairs. The doors were already open, arms were being carried out, in the vestibule and corridors men were putting on armor and mail. I, too, put on some armor in case I had to fight. Then when we were all assembled, I took up my place in the gondola to await further orders."

"With whom did you prepare your role?"

"With Proskurov, and Rakhmanov checked it."

"Very good work. I have no corrections to suggest."

And this man was just an extra, drawn from the apprentices in the theatre, I thought to myself. What about us? How much work we still have to do!

After he had listened to everything that had been prepared by the apprentices Tortsov said:

"This is all logical and consecutive. I accept your preparations and surmise what your plan is." Then he called the rest of us to join the apprentices on the stage and showed us all the fixed out-line of the production for the entire first scene.

It appeared that all during the time that we were doing the first exercises based on this scene, Tortsov had made notes of the moments most successful in expressing the excitement of the alarm and pursuit, the mood necessary for this scene, and the images that naturally derived from it. Now he showed us his mise-en-scène, adapted to the play, with all his notes on our exercises. He pointed out that this proposed plan for the scene, the movements and places of action, all were produced by us and therefore spontaneous with us.

I wrote out his production plan as follows:

"Iago and Roderigo arrive in a gondola. There is a gondolier at one end. The scene begins with the sound of two muffled voices on the left of the audience and the splash of a gondolier's oar (not in rhythm with the words). The gondolier is first seen on the left.

"The first six lines are spoken with great heat as the gondola floats up to the landing at Brabantio's home.

"There is a pause after the words: 'if ever I did dream.' Iago hushes Roderigo. Pause. They reach the landing. The gondolier lands, rattles some chains. Iago stops him. Play the pause out. They look around. No one is at any of the windows. Begin the hot debate again as before the pause, but in subdued voices. Iago makes sure they do not speak too loudly. Iago keeps under cover as much as he can so that he will not be too visible from the windows.

"Iago says his line: 'Despise me if I do not . . . ,' but not in order to underline his evil feelings and character as is usually done. He is hot under the collar, angry, and is trying to paint his hatred of Othello in a way to achieve his immediate purpose—to force Roderigo to shout and raise a racket.

"Roderigo has come around a little. He has even turned his face half-way toward Iago. The latter stands up in a decisive way and holds out his hand to help Roderigo up. He hands him the oar from the gondola so that he will bang it on the side of the boat. Iago himself hurries off to hide under one of the archways in front of the house.

"With Roderigo's words: 'What, ho, Brabantio! Signior Brabantio, ho!' the scene of raising the alarm begins. It must be played to the hilt, not hurried, but so that each thing will be justified and one can believe that they really have roused the entire sleeping household. This is not any too easy. Do not be afraid of repeating lines several times. Interlard the lines with pauses (to extend the scene) consisting of noises; for example, Roderigo banging his oar, and the sound of chains rattling at the mooring post. The gondolier can be told by Roderigo also to rattle the chains. Iago, under the colonnade, is hammering away at the door with a knocker such as they used then instead of a bell. . . .

"*The scene of rousing the household*: (a) Voices are heard far off backstage; a window on the second floor is opened; (b) a servant's face is pressed against a windowpane; he tries to look out and see what is going on; (c) a woman's face (Desdemona's nurse) appears at another window; she looks sleepy, is dressed in a nightgown; (d) a third window is opened by Brabantio. In the pauses between their appearance there are growing sounds inside the awakening house.

"As the scene progresses all the windows are gradually filled with people. They all look sleepy and are only half dressed. This is the *scene of the alarm in the night*.

"*The physical objective of the crowd* is to make every effort to look around and try to understand the cause of the noise.

"*The physical objective of Roderigo, Iago, and the gondolier* is to make as much noise as possible, to frighten everyone and get their attention.

"So the first crowd-scene interlude comes before Brabantio appears. The second one is after the words:

BRABANTIO: Not I. What are you?
RODERIGO: My name is Roderigo.

Pause. Crowd scene: general indignation. After what has been said earlier about Roderigo's pursuit of Desdemona and after we know that this same Roderigo has been pelted with orange peels and garbage to chase him away, this general indignation is understandable. Indeed what brazen conduct is this for a good-for-nothing drunken creature to raise the whole house in the middle of the night? It is as if they said to each other: What a brazen fellow! What shall we do with him?

"Brabantio reviles Roderigo, and all the rest believe the disturbance is because of some trifling thing. Many leave the windows, the crowd thins out, and some of the windows are closed. This excites Roderigo and Iago to an even greater pitch.

"The servants who remain at the windows scold at Roderigo and they all talk at once. In another moment the whole place will be shut up.

"Roderigo is frantic because Brabantio has already half closed his window and is turning away. But before he closes the window entirely, Brabantio says his lines beginning with the words:

> But thou must needs be sure
> My spirit and my place have in them power . . .

You can imagine the nervousness, the rhythm and tempo of Roderigo and Iago as they do everything in their power to hold back Brabantio.

"Iago's line begins: 'Zounds, sir, . . . ' But he must find some unusual means of putting an end to the misunderstanding. He carefully pulls his hat down so he will not be recognized. All who are still looking out of the windows, and several who have returned to them, crane their necks to see who the unknown man under the colonnade can be. . . .

"After the words: 'You are—a Senator!' there is a slight interlude and the crowd scene. The indignant household, angered by Iago's sally, rush to Brabantio's defence; but he at once stops them with his retort.

"Roderigo with the words: 'Sir, I will answer anything, . . . ' begins with extreme nervousness and precision to relate the events of the night. He does not do this for the sake of revealing the plot to the audience, he does it to paint as terrible and scandalous a picture of the abduction for Brabantio as possible and thus precipitate him into taking energetic measures. He tries to put the marriage in the light of a forced abduction and, when he can, he lays the colors on thick; or else he speaks ironically, doing in short everything he can think of to accomplish the objective he has set himself: *To rouse the whole city before it is too late and separate Desdemona from the Moor.*

"After the words: 'Let loose on me the justice of the state,' there is a pause of consternation. *This pause is a psychological necessity.* A tremendous inner overturn is taking place in the souls of these people. For Brabantio, for the nurse, and all the rest of the household, Desdemona is no more than a child. It is a commonly known fact that a household never realizes just when a little girl has become a young woman. To feel these things, to come to look upon Desdemona as a woman, the wife not of some Venetian grandee but of a dirty, dark-skinned Moor; to come to understand the horror of the loss, the sense of vacancy in the house; to grow accustomed to the idea that the most precious thing they had has been taken from father and nurse; to balance out all these new horrors that are besetting their souls and to find a new modus vivendi—all this takes time. It will be a catastrophe if those playing Brabantio, the nurse, and the personal servants skip quickly over this moment as they hurry on to the dramatic scene.

"This pause is the transitional step leading the actors to the dramatic scene if they feel it logically and consecutively, that is, if they visualize Desdemona in the embraces of the black devil, the room she had as a young girl now empty, the effect of the scandal that has fallen on the family and its repercussions in the whole city. If Brabantio sees himself compromised in the eyes of the Doge himself and all the Senators, sees those and all the other things that can upset a man and a father ... As for the nurse she may be thrown out or even haled into court.

"The objective of the actors is to remember, understand, and determine what they should do at such a time so that they can live as if the things described in the play had happened to them, that is to say to living human beings, and not just to characters in a play. In other words *let the actor never forget* that especially in dramatic scenes he must always *live in his own self and not take his point of departure from his role more than finding in it the given circumstances in which it is to be played*. Therefore the objective to be reached amounts to this: *Let each actor give an honest reply to the question of what physical action he would undertake, how he would act (not feel, there should for heaven's sake be no question of feelings at this point) in the given circumstances created by the playwright, the director of the play, the scene designer, the actor himself by means of his own imagination, the lighting technician, and so forth*. When these physical actions have been clearly defined, all that remains for the actor to do is to execute them. (Note that I say execute physical actions, not feel them, because if they are properly carried out the feelings will be generated spontaneously. If you work the other way around and begin by thinking about your feelings and trying to squeeze them out of yourself, the result will be distortion and force, your sense of experiencing your part will turn into theatrical, mechanical acting, and your movements will be distorted.

"I continue to discuss a little longer this important pause following the words: 'Let loose on me the justice of the state,' and I shall give you a small stimulus, a hint as to what a person such as Brabantio does at such a time: (1) He tries to understand, from the terrible news he has been told, all that he can accept; (2) In the next moment, as the teller of the news comes to the most terrible point of all, he hastens to stop him as though he were putting up a shield to ward off the impending blow; (3) He looks around for help from others; his eyes search their hearts to fathom how they take the news—do they accept or credit it?—or he looks pleadingly at them as if he begged them to say such a thing is absurd and unfounded; (4) Then he turns toward Desdemona's room and tries to imagine it empty; next his thoughts run like lightning through the whole house, trying to imagine the future and looking for some object in life; they turn then to some other place which they see as an unkept room, and in it a filthy fiend his imagination no longer pictures as a human being but as a beast, a gorilla. To all this he is unable to reconcile himself, therefore there is only one way out—as quickly as possible and at whatever cost to save her! After feeling all this in logical sequence, Brabantio spontaneously bursts out with the lines:

Strike on the tinder, ho!
Give me a taper! Call up all my people! . . .

"After the words: 'Light, I say! Light!' there is a pause for the commotion. Do not forget that this commotion takes place inside the house, so the sounds are muted—that is why Iago can speak against this background.

"Iago makes the speech: 'Farewell, for I must leave you' very hurriedly. It would be a disaster if he were discovered now, for it would disclose his plot.

"What does a person do when he gives his last instructions in a great hurry? He speaks with exceptional vividness, precision, color, and deliberation. It is important that he should not slur or speak too rapidly, even though inside he is trembling and trying to get away as quickly as possible. But he curbs his nervousness and tries to appear as equitable and comprehensible as possible. Why? Because he knows there is no time for him to repeat anything.

"And here I put the actor who plays Iago on notice that he must act out of his own right and carry out the simplest human objective, which consists of explaining everything clearly and coming to an agreement about the subsequent steps to be taken.

"The crowd scene is now an interlude for the gathering of forces. At Iago's last words, when the exposition has been clearly conveyed to the public, there is a nervous moving around in the house behind the windows of the night lamps and lanterns. These nervously intermittent flashes of light, if well rehearsed, can create an atmosphere of great disturbance. Meantime down below, the great iron latch is drawn, the lock and the metal hinges creak an the main door is opened. Out comes the gatekeeper with a lantern, other servants pour out. They rush out into the colonnade, putting on odd pieces of clothing as they go, quickly fastening themselves up; some run to the right, others to the left; then they come back and explain things to each other which they have not understood, then they run off again. (Actually these extras go back into the house and put on, let us say, some helmets or hauberks, armor, and thus transformed come out of the same door without being recognized by the public. This cuts down the number of extras needed.)

"Meantime people in the process of dressing themselves keep pouring out of the house. They carry halberds, swords, arms; they swarm into gondolas moored at the landing (not Roderigo's); they put down the things they are carrying, turn back into the house, and return carrying more stuff, completing their toilets as best they can on the run.

"A third group can be seen upstairs in the palace. They have opened all the windows and are obviously dressing themselves, putting on doublets and hose, and meantime calling down to the people below in an exchange of questions and directions which, because of the noise, no one can hear. They repeat the questions, they yell, they are angry, excited, quarrel with one another. The old nurse in a state of panic and screaming hysterically rushes out into the colonnade. Another woman, probably a maid, and in the same state, is with her. Up in one of the windows there is a woman whimpering and watching what is going on below. Perhaps it is the wife of one of the men going off—who knows if he will ever come back?—after all there will be a fight. . . .

"After the words: 'O unhappy girl!—With the Moor, say'st thou?' Brabantio comes forward armed with a sword. In a businesslike way he cross-examines Roderigo who is having his gondola brought around for Brabantio and is giving orders. . . .

"After the words: 'Some one way, some another,' there is a pause. Brabantio is giving the orders. With 'some one way' he points to the canal the gondola should take to the left of the audience and leading off stage, and with 'some another' he points to the street which runs to the left behind Brabantio's house.

"The gondolas cast off, chains rattle.

"After the words: '. . . get good guard and go along with me,' Brabantio quickly goes over to one of his servants in a gondola and says something to him. The servant jumps out of the boat and races down the street to the right along Brabantio's house.

"At the words: 'Pray lead me on,' Brabantio joins Roderigo in his gondola.

"During the words: '. . . Get weapons, ho!' the soldiers in a gondola choose and display pikes and halberds.

"At the line: 'And raise some special officers of night,' the maid who was with the nurse runs off along the street to the right.

"At the last line of the scene: 'I'll deserve your pains,' Roderigo's gondola, with Brabantio in it, and the gondola laden with soldiers begin to move away."

*　　*　　*

"The first scene of *Othello*" Tortsov said to us, "has now been prepared far enough for you to play it, and play it in order to get the feel of the life of both spirit and body in your parts in accordance with the line we have tested. As you repeat it try to put in more and more of your own life, try to draw more and more on your own nature.

"But it is not the acting itself we are so concerned with. We chose *Othello* in order to study methods and techniques to apply to roles. So that now, having finished our experiments on the first scene, let us try to understand the method and principle on which this scene of alarm and pursuit was based. Let us say that we move to theory so that we know what our practice had as its basis.

"You will recall that, to begin with, I took away from you all copies of the play and made you promise not to look at it again for the time being.

"However, to my astonishment, it turned out that without the text you were unable to relate the contents of *Othello*. Yet something of the play must have remained with you despite your unfortunate first contact with it. And indeed there remained in your memories something like oases in a desert, bright patches you recalled from various parts of *Othello*. I attempted to emphasize these and establish them more strongly.

"After that the whole play was read to you in order to refresh your memories. This reading did not create new areas of light but it did clarify the general line of the tragedy. You all recalled certain facts and later on certain actions in their logical and consecutive order. You wrote them down after you had given an acceptable account of the contents of *Othello*, and then you played the first scene according to the facts given and in terms of physical actions. But there was no truth in your acting, and the creation of that truth was the hardest part of the work.

"What absorbed the most attention and work were the simplest and most familiar things in real life: to walk, look, listen, and so forth. You impersonated them on the stage better than many professionals, but you could not do it like human beings. It was necessary to study things you are perfectly familiar with off the stage. What a difficult job it was! But in the end you accomplished it, you carried the scene to the point of complete truthfulness, at first only in spots but later all along the line. When you could not encompass a large piece of truth, small pieces popped up, which then merged into larger units. Along with truth came its invariable concomitant—faith in the reality of the physical actions and faith in all the physical being of your parts. Thus we created one of the two natures inherent in each character of the play. Thanks to frequent repetitions of this physical being it was strengthened: 'The difficult became habitual, the habitual, easy.' In the end you were in possession of the physical side of your parts, and the physical actions pointed out to you by the author and the director of the play were transmuted into your own. That is why you repeated them with such relish. . . .

"It is not surprising that you soon felt the need of using words, and because you did not have the author's text at hand you had recourse to your own. You needed them not only to help you carry out your external objectives but also to express thoughts and to convey the experiences which were welling up in you. This need obliged you to turn again to the play in order to make excerpts of thoughts from it and also, imperceptibly to you, of feelings. Unnoticed by you I grafted them on you in logical and consecutive order by means of suggestion, frequent repetition, and the hammering down of the line of the scene; until finally you gained possession of the whole first scene as rehearsed. Now the alien actions set down by the author and indeed the spiritual life in your parts have grown into being your own, and you soak them up with pleasure.

"Yet would we have achieved this result if, side by side with the physical being, the spiritual being of your parts had not grown?

"Inevitably the question then arises: Can the first exist without the second, or the second without the first?

"More than that, both aspects of life are drawn from the same source, the play of *Othello;* therefore, they cannot be alien to one another by nature; on the contrary their kinship and congruence are mandatory. I have laid particular emphasis on this law because that is the basis of our psychotechnique.

"This law is of great practical significance for us because in the instances when a role does not come to life spontaneously, intuitively, it is necessary to build it by psychotechnical means. It is lucky that this psychotechnique is practical and available. We can even, in case of need, reach the spiritual life of a role reflexively through its physical life. This is a valuable resource of creative acting.

"But the greatest advantage of our method has to do with the thoughts, words, and diction of a role.

"You recall that when I obliged you to use your own words to express the thoughts in your parts, I often reminded you of or suggested whatever thought came next. You seized upon my suggestions with increasing eagerness because you grew more and more accustomed to the logic of the thoughts which Shakespeare himself laid down in his play.

"Exactly the same thing happened with the words of your parts. At first you chose, as you would in real life, the words that came to your mind and tongue, whatever helped you best to carry out your intended objective. In this way your speech and your part developed in normal conditions and was active and effective. I kept you under these conditions for a long time, indeed until the whole score of your parts was established and the right line of objectives, actions, and thoughts was hammered out.

"Only after this preparation did we return to you the printed text of the play. You scarcely had to work on your lines because for some time in advance I had been suggesting to you Shakespeare's own words when you had to have them, when you were reaching out for them for the verbal accomplishment of this or that objective. You grabbed them hungrily because the author's text expressed a thought or carried out a piece of action better than your own. You remembered the Shakespeare words because you fell in love with them and they became necessary to you.

"What happened as a result of this? Another person's words became your own. They were grafted on to you by natural means, without any forcing, and only because of that they retained their most important quality—liveliness. Now you do not rattle off your part, you act by means of the words for the sake of carrying out an objective basic to the play. That is the very thing for which we are given the play.

"Please think this over well and then tell me: Do you suppose that if you had begun your work by slaving away to learn the lines, as is done in the majority of the theatres of the world, you would have achieved what you did by means of our method?

"I can tell you in advance that the answer is—no. You would have forced yourselves to memorize the text mechanically, trained the muscles of your speech organs to reproduce the sounds of words and phrases. In this process the thought contained in your parts would have evaporated and the text have become cut off from objectives and actions.

"Now let us compare our method with what is done in any theatre of the ordinary type. There they read the play, hand out the parts with the notice that by the third or the tenth rehearsal everyone must know his role by heart. They begin the reading, then they all go up on the stage and act, while holding the script. The director shows them the business to do and the actors remember it. At the predicted rehearsal the books are taken away and they speak their lines with a prompter present until they are letter-perfect in their parts. As soon as everything is in order—and they hurry because they do not want to wear down or talk out their parts—they schedule the first dress rehearsal and put out the notices. Then there is the performance—a success with the critics. After that their interest in the play fades and they repeat their performances in a routine way."

*   *   *

"To sum up: the point of the physical actions lies not in themselves as such but in what they evoke: conditions, proposed circumstances, feelings. The fact that the hero of a play kills himself is not so important as the inner reason for his suicide. If that does not appear or is lacking in interest, his death as such will pass without leaving any impression. There is an unbreakable bond between the action on the stage and the thing that precipitated it. In other words there is complete union between the physical and the spiritual being of a role. That is what we invariably make use of in our psychotechnique. That is what we have been doing now.

"With the help of nature—our subconscious, instinct, intuition, habits, and so forth—we evoke a series of physical actions interlaced with one another. Through them we try to understand the inner reasons that gave rise to them, individual moments of experienced emotions, the logic and consistency of feelings in the given circumstances of the play. When we can discover that line, we are aware of the inner meaning of our physical actions. This awareness is not intellectual but emotional in origin, because we comprehend with our own feelings some part of the psychology of our role. Yet we cannot act this psychology itself nor its logical and consecutive feelings. Therefore we keep to the firmer and more accessible ground of physical actions and adhere rigorously to their logic and consistency. And since their pattern is inextricably bound up with that other inner pattern of feelings, we are able through them to reach the emotions. That pattern becomes part and parcel of the score of a role.

"By now you have experienced this interplay. This is the approach from the exterior to the interior. Make this bond a firm one, repeating your pattern of the physical being of your part many times over. This will confirm the physical actions but at the same time strengthen the emotional response to them. Some of them may in time become conscious in character. Then you can make use of them as you choose to recall physical actions which are naturally tied up with them. But there are many of the inner stimuli which you will never fully hold in your grasp. Do not regret this. Consciousness might destroy their effectiveness.

"Still the question will remain: Which of the inner appeals can one keep hold of and which should one not touch?

"This is not a question you should raise. Leave that to nature. Only nature can find her way around in this process which is not accessible to our consciousness.

"Your job is to seek help in the method I have described to you. When you reach the moment of creation do not seek the path of inner stimulation—your feelings know what to do better than you can tell them—but stick instead to the physical being of your role."

Part III

Gogol's *The Inspector General*

This latest of the three studies in this volume was written around 1934. As the frequent references in this text to passages in *An Actor Prepares* testify, the latter work was already finished and the manuscript, as Stanislavski intended, was in the United States for its first publication. *Building a Character* was as finished as Stanislavski would ever make it. Thus this section not only culminates Stanislavski's explorations in *Creating a Role* but serves as a natural bridge between this volume and the two earlier publications.—EDITOR

CHAPTER EIGHT

From Physical Actions to Living Image

"HERE IS MY APPROACH to a new role," said Tortsov. "Without any reading, without any conferences on the play, the actors are asked to come to a rehearsal of it."

"How is that possible?" was the bewildered reaction of the students.

"More than that. One can act a play not yet written."

We were at a loss even for words to express our reaction to that idea.

"You do not believe me? Let us put it to the test. I have a play in mind; I shall tell you the plot by episodes and you will act it out. I shall watch what you say and do in your improvisation, and whatever is most successful I shall jot down. So that by our joint efforts we shall write and immediately act out a play not yet in existence. We shall share the profits equally."

The students were even more astonished by this and did not know what it was all about.

"You are all familiar, through your own experience, with how an actor feels on the stage when he is in what we call the 'inner creative state.' He gathers up into a single whole all the elements that alert him and orient him toward creative work.

"It would seem that that state should be sufficient to enable him to approach a new play and part and study them in detail. But that it is not enough; to study and come to know the essentials of a playwright's work, to form ideas about it, something is still lacking, something the actor needs to stir and set his inner forces

213

to work. Without this something his analysis of the play and part is purely intellectual.

"Our mind can be set to work at any time. But it is not sufficient. We must have the ardent and direct cooperation of our emotions, desires, and all the other elements of our inner creative state. With their help we must create inside ourselves the actual life of our role. After that the analysis of the play will proceed not only from the intellect but from an actor's whole being."

"Excuse me, please," said our argumentative Grisha, "but how can that be? In order to feel the life in a role you have to know the text of the play, you have to, don't you see, study it. Yet you assert that you mustn't study it without first feeling it."

"Yes," confirmed Tortsov, "you do have to know the text, but you must not in any circumstances come to it cold. *You must beforehand pour into your prepared inner creative state the actual feelings of the life of your part, not just the spiritual but also the physical sensations.*

"Just as yeast causes fermentation, so the sensing of the life of his role imparts the kind of inner warmth, the ebullition necessary to the actor in the process of creative experience. It is only when he has reached that creative state that he can think of approaching a play or role."

"How does one come by the actual spiritual and physical feeling of the life in a role?" asked several students who had been surprised by Tortsov's remarks.

"Today's lesson will be dedicated to that question. Kostya, do you remember Gogol's *Inspector General?*" said he suddenly turning to me.

"I do, but only in general outline."

"So much the better. Go up onto the stage and play for us Khlestakov's entrance in the second act."

"How can I play it since I don't know what I have to do?" said I with surprise and objection in my tone.

"You do not know everything but you do know some things.

So play the little that you know. In other words, execute out of the life of the part those small physical objectives which you can do sincerely, truthfully, and in your own person."

"I can't do anything because I don't know anything!"

"What do you mean?" objected Tortsov. "The play says: 'Enter Khlestakov.' Don't you know how to go into a room in an inn?"

"I do."

"Well then go on in. Later on Khlestakov scolds Ossip because he has been lolling around on the bed. Don't you know how to scold?"

"I do."

"Then Khlestakov wants to make Ossip go out and try to get some food. Don't you know how to approach a difficult subject with another person?"

"I know that too."

"Then play what is available to you, the things you feel the truth of, what you yourself can believe in."

"What is available to us at first in a new role?" I asked in an effort at clarification.

"Very little. You can convey the externals of the plot with its episodes, with its simplest physical objectives. At first that is all you can execute sincerely. If you attempt anything more you will run into objectives beyond your powers, and then you run the risk of going astray, of overacting and doing violence to your nature. Beware of too difficult objectives to start with—you are not yet ready to penetrate deep into the soul of your part. Keep strictly inside the narrow confines of physical actions, search out their logic and consecutiveness, and try to find the state of 'I am.' "

"You say convey the plot and the simplest physical actions," I argued. "But the plot is conveyed by itself as the play unfolds. The plot was made by the author."

"Yes, by him and not by you. Let his plot remain. What is needed is your attitude toward it. Go onto the stage and begin

215

with Khlestakov's entrance. Leo will play Ossip for us and Vanya the tavern waiter."

"With pleasure!" Leo and Vanya answered in unison.

"But I don't know any words, I haven't anything to say," I was still being stubborn.

"You don't know the words, but you do remember the general drift of the conversation, don't you?"

"Yes, more or less."

"Then tell us that in your own words. I'll prompt you as to the order of the thoughts in the dialogue. Besides you will soon catch on to their logic and consecutiveness."

"But I don't know what the image is that I have to show!"

"Nevertheless you do know an important rule: Whatever part an actor plays he must always act in his own right, on his own responsibility. If he does not find himself in his part he will kill off the imaginary character because he will have deprived him of live feelings. Those live feelings can be given to the character he has created only by the actor himself. So play every part in your own right in the circumstances given you by the playwright. In this manner you will first of all feel yourself in the part. When that is once done it is not difficult to enlarge the whole role in yourself. Live, true human feelings—that is the good soil for accomplishing your purpose."

Tortsov showed us how to mark off a room in an inn. Leo lay down on the divan and I went into the wings and prepared myself to appear, as is customary, looking like a half-starved young member of the gentry. I entered slowly, handed Leo my make-believe cane and top hat—in other words I repeated all the good old clichés which cluster around this part.

"I don't understand. Who are you?" asked Tortsov when we had finished.

"I—it was I, myself."

"It didn't look like you. In real life you are quite different from what you were just now on the stage. That's not the way you yourself would walk into a room."

"How should I?"

"With something on your mind, with an object inside, with curiosity, but not empty as you were. Off the stage you are completely aware of all periods and phases of natural communication. You gave me the entrance of an actor onto the stage, but what I want is the entrance of a human being into a room. Off the stage there are other stimuli for action. Find them now on the stage. If you enter with a purpose or—as is the case with Khlestakov—without any purpose, just because you have nothing to do, what actions would best stimulate the corresponding inner state?

"Your entrance just now was theatrical, done 'in general'; in your movements there was neither logic nor consecutiveness. You missed a number of necessary points. For instance, in real life, wherever you go, you are obliged first of all to orient yourself and discover what is going on there, and decide how to conduct yourself. But you did not even look at Ossip or the bed before you said: 'You've been lying around on my bed again.' Also, you slammed the door the way they do in the theatre when the sets are made of canvas. You did not remember and you did not convey the weight of the door. The door knob was handled like a toy. All these little physical actions call for a certain amount of attention and time. After all the work you have done on actions with imaginary objects* you should really be ashamed of allowing yourself to make such mistakes."

"They were caused by my not knowing where I came from," I said, trying to excuse myself in my embarrassment.

"You don't say! How can you not know on the stage where you came from and where you arrived at; that is one thing you must absolutely know. Entrances from 'outer space' are never to be achieved in the theatre."

* See *An Actor Prepares*, pp. 51ff.

"Well, where did I come from?"

"That's nice! How should I know? That's your affair. Besides Khlestakov himself tells where he has been. But since you do not remember that, so much the better."

"Why is it better?"

"Because it will enable you to approach the role in your own person, from life and not from the author's directions, not from all the rubber-stamp conventional forms. This will allow you to be independent in your ideas of the image to be projected. If you were going to be guided only by printed instructions you would not be carrying out the objective I gave you, because you would be doing blindly what the author said, you would be staking everything on him, you would parrot his lines, ape his actions which are not akin to yours—all instead of making your own image analogous to the one created by the author.

"Envelop yourself in the given circumstances of the play and then answer this question sincerely: What would you yourself (not Khlestakov whom you are not acquainted with) do if you had to extricate yourself from a hopeless situation?"

"Oh yes," I sighed, "when one has to get out of a situation by oneself and not follow the author blindly, it takes a deal of thinking."

"Now that was well said," remarked Tortsov.

"But this is the first time that I have transposed myself into the situation and the circumstances into which Gogol put his characters. For the public their situation is comic but for Khlestakov and Ossip it is hopeless. I felt this today for the first time, and yet how many times I have read *The Inspector General* and seen it performed!"

"This came about because you took the right approach. You carried Gogol's situation and circumstances for these characters over into your own terms. That is important. That is splendid! Never force your way into a part; don't begin to study it with a sense of compulsion. You yourself must choose and carry out even the small fractions of the part which are to begin with accessible to you. Do that now, and you will in some small measure *feel yourself in the part.*

"Now tell me, how would you in real life, here, today, now, get out of the situation in which Gogol had placed you?"

I was silent because I was somewhat confused.

"Try to think. How would you spend your day?" prodded Tortsov.

"I got up late. The first thing is that I would persuade Ossip to go to the proprietor of the inn and take steps to get some tea. Then there would be a long ado making my toilet, washing, brushing my clothes, getting dressed, fixing myself up, drinking tea. Then . . . I'd stroll along the streets. I would not sit in the airless room. I have the feeling that on my stroll my citified appearance would attract the attention of the provincial men."

"And especially the provincial ladies," said Tortsov in a tone of banter.

"So much the better. I should try to scrape an acquaintance with someone and scrounge an invitation for dinner. Then I'd look in at the shops and the market."

As I said all this I suddenly began to feel a little like Khlesta-kov.

"Whenever possible I would not be able to resist tasting some tempting bit displayed on a hawker's tray near the shops or at the market. Of course this would not sate but rather whet my appetite. Afterwards I would go to the post office to inquire whether a money order had arrived for me."

"It hadn't," croaked Tortsov, and egged me on.

"By now I am worn out and my stomach is empty. I have no recourse except to go back to the inn and try once more to send Ossip down and negotiate dinner for me."

"Now that is what you bring with you when you make your entrance in the second act," interrupted Tortsov. "In order to come on the stage like a human being and not like an actor you had to find out who you are, what has happened to you, under what circumstances you are living here, how you have spent your day, where you came from, and many other supposed circumstances you have not yet invented but all of which influence your actions. In other words, just to walk onto the stage it is necessary to sense the life of the play and your relation to it."

*　　*　　*

Tortsov continued his work with me on the role of Khlestakov. "Now you know what you have to have before you make your entrance," he said. "Establish properly the natural process of communication so that you can carry out your actions not for the entertainment of the public but for the sake of the object of your attention, and then go on with your physical objectives.

"Ask yourself what it means to you to go into your hotel room after your fruitless walk through the town. Then put another question: What would you do in Khlestakov's place after you came back? How would you deal with Ossip when you discovered he had been lying on the bed again? How would you persuade him to go to the proprietor to wheedle dinner out of him? How would you wait for the result of this maneuver and what would you do in the intervening time? How would you accept this bringing of food? And so forth, and so forth.

"In brief, call to mind each episode in the act; realize what actions each one consists of; follow through the logic and consecutiveness of all these actions."

This time when I repeated the scene I did not miss even the tiniest secondary detail, and thus proved that I understood the nature of each of the planned physical actions. In this way I was able to rehabilitate myself after my lack of success yesterday.

Tortsov recalled our first trials of actions without props, a lesson memorable for me because he first made me count thin air instead of money.

"How much time was spent then just on this work," said Tort-sov, "and how quickly you accomplished an analogous job today."

After a small interruption he said:

"Now that you have grasped the logic and the consecutiveness of these physical actions as well as felt their truth and established your faith in what you were doing on the stage, it will not be diffi-cult for you to repeat this same sequence in different given circum-stances, which the play will set for you, and which will be en-larged and enhanced by your own imagination.

"So now, what would you do here, now, today in this supposed hotel room if you had returned to it after a fruitless expedition through the town? Begin, only do not act; simply and honestly decide and say what you would do."

"Why not act? That would be easier for me."

"Of course. It is always easier to act in the old rubber-stamp ways than to move about truthfully."

"But I was not speaking of clichés."

"For the time being that is the only way you can talk. They are ready-made; but truthful action, action with a useful purpose, prompted by inner impulses, has to live first, and that is what you are trying to achieve."

Leo lay down on the bed, Vanya began to prepare himself for his entrance as the hotel waiter.

Then Tortsov put me on the stage and obliged me to talk out loud to myself:

"I remember the given circumstances of my part, the past, the present," I said to myself. "As for the future, that is related to me, not to my part. Khlestakov cannot know the future but I am obliged to know it. It is my job as an actor to prepare that future from the first scene I play. The more hopeless my situation is in this awful hotel room the more unexpected, extraordinary, in-credible will be my moving to the home of the Mayor, the com-plications, the matchmaking.

"I shall recall the whole act according to episodes."

I then enumerated all the scenes and quickly based them on circumstances invented by me. When I had finished this work, I concentrated my attention on it and then went into the wings. As I went I said to myself:

"What would I do if, when I was returning to my hotel room, I heard the voice of the proprietor behind me?"

I had scarcely mentioned the "magic if" when I felt as though something had struck me from behind. I began to run, I scarcely knew what I was doing, and suddenly found myself in my imaginary hotel room.

"That was original!" laughed Tortsov. "Now repeat the action in some new given circumstances," he ordered.

I walked off slowly into the wings and after a pause to prepare myself I opened the door and stood there in an agony of indecision, not knowing whether to come in or go downstairs to the dining room. But I came in and my eyes kept searching for something in my room or through the crack of the door. When I realized what I was after, I adapted myself to the situation and left the stage.

A little later I came on again in a capricious, difficult mood, like some spoiled creature. I looked around nervously for some time. Then thinking and again adapting myself to the situation, I left the stage.

I did a whole series of entrances until finally I said to myself:

"Now it seems to me that I know what I would bring with me when I came in, if I were in the place of Khlestakov."

"What do you call the thing you have been doing?" asked Tortsov.

"I was analyzing, I was studying myself, Kostya Nazvanov, in the given circumstances in which Khlestakov is placed."

"Now I hope you realize the difference between approaching and judging a role in your own person and in that of another, between looking at a role with your own eyes instead of those of the author, or director, or drama critic.

"In your own person you live your role, in the person of someone else you simply toy with it, play-act it. In your own person you grasp the role with your mind, your feelings, your desires, and all the elements of your inner being, while in the person of another, in most cases, you do it only with your mind. Purely reasoned analysis and understanding in a part is not what we need.

"We must take hold of the imagined character with all our being, spiritual and physical. That is the only approach I am willing to accept."

*　　*　　*

"What can I do about it?" said Tortsov meditatively as he came into class today, as if he were talking over something with himself. "Oral transmission is boring, dry, unconvincing for a practical matter. It would be better to make you do and feel things in your own persons than to have me give explanations. But unfortunately you are not yet so versed in the technique of handling imaginary objects that you can do what I believe is necessary. I'll have to go up on the stage myself and show you how, by beginning with the simplest objectives and actions, you move on to create the *physical life of a part,* and from that you again move forward and create the spiritual life of a part, and how they together engender inside you the *actual sense of life in a play and part,* which in turn transmutes itself into the inner creative state with which you are familiar."

Tortsov went up on to the stage and disappeared into the wings. There was a long pause in which we heard the sound of Leo's bass voice. He was arguing about where it is best to live, in St. Petersburg or in the country.

Suddenly Tortsov ran onto the stage. Such an entrance for Khlestakov was so sudden and unexpected that I actually trembled. Tortsov slammed the door and then stood looking into the corridor through the crack. Obviously he imagined that he had run away from the proprietor of the hotel.

I cannot say that I was too well pleased by this new angle, but he certainly made his entrance with sincerity. Then Tortsov began to reflect aloud about what he had just done.

"I overdid it!" he confessed to himself. "It should be done more simply. Besides, would that be right for Khlestakov? After all he, as a resident of St. Petersburg, felt himself superior to anyone in the provinces.

"What suggested that entrance to me? What memories? I can't think. Perhaps in this mixture of braggadocio with cowardice and callow youth lies the key to the inner character of Khlestakov? Where did I get the sensations I experienced?"

After thinking about this for a moment Tortsov said to us:

"What did I just do? I analyzed what I accidentally felt and what I accidentally did as a result of those feelings. I analyzed my physical actions in the given circumstances of the role. But I made this analysis not purely with my cold mind; all the elements in me contributed. I made the analysis with my body and soul.

"I shall now develop my work of analysis and tell you what prompted me. Logic suggested: If Khlestakov is a braggart and a coward, then in his heart he fears to meet the proprietor, but outwardly he wants to put on a brave appearance and be calm. He even exaggerates his calm, although he feels the look of his enemy behind him and has chills up and down his spine."

Tortsov then went into the wings, prepared himself, and then executed brilliantly the proposition he had just set forth. How did he do it? Can it be solely that by sensing the truthfulness of his physical actions, all the rest, that is to say the emotions, followed naturally? If so, his method must be accounted miraculous.

Tortsov stood there for a long time and then he began to speak:

"You saw that I did not do this by means of purely intellectual analysis, but that I studied myself in the conditions set by the part, and with the direct participation of all human inner elements, and through their natural impulse to physical action. I did not carry the action through to the end because I was afraid of falling into clichés. Yet the principal point is not in the action itself but in the natural evocation of impulses to act.

From my everyday human experience and life I seek to cull physical objectives and actions. In order to believe in their validity, I have to give them an inner basis and justify them in the circumstances set by the play. When I find and feel this justification then my inner being to a certain extent merges with that of my role."

Tortsov then went through the same operation with each bit of the scene—persuading Ossip to go get some dinner for him, the monologue after Ossip goes out, the scene with the waiter and with the dinner.

When all this had been accomplished Tortsov withdrew into himself and seemed to be mentally reviewing the work done. Finally he said:

"I feel that we have made a pale outline of impulses to physical action in the circumstances of life and the conditions proposed by the role! Now these must be recorded in writing, just as we did after the scene of dramatic inaction.* Do you remember how we attributed all that to physiology? I shall do the same thing with this scene of Khlestakov."

Tortsov began to recall all the impulses to action he had remarked in himself, and I wrote them down. Grisha at this point found a reason to object to one of the actions noted. "Excuse me please, but this is purely psychological and not physical action at all."

"I thought we had agreed not to argue about words. Besides we decided, you know, that in every psychological act there is a great deal of the physical, and in the physical—a great deal of the psychological. At this time I am going over the role in terms of physical actions; so that is why I am listing only them. What will come of this we shall see in the near future."

* See *An Actor Prepares*, pp. 131-32.

225

And Tortsov went back to the interrupted recording. When this was finished he explained:

"One can also make a list of physical objectives taken from the text of the play. If we compared both lists we would find them coincident in some places (where the actor and the part naturally merge), and in others disparate (this is where there is a mistake, or where the actor's individuality breaks through in ways that diverge from his part).

"The further work is up to the actor and the director—enhancing the moments when the actor merges with his part and bringing him back from the places where he diverges from it. We shall talk about this in detail later on. For now the important thing is only the points at which the actor merges with his part. These lively contacts draw an actor into the play; he no longer feels himself to be an outsider in its life, and certain places in his part are very close to his feelings.

"As I look over this list," explained Tortsov, "I test my objectives, as it were, by a common denominator, by asking myself: Why did I do this or that?

"When I have analyzed and summed up what I did, I reach the conclusion that my basic objective and action was: I wanted to get something to eat, to allay my hunger. That is why I came here, that is why I made up to Ossip, was on my best behavior with the waiter, and later quarreled with him. In the future all my actions in these scenes will be directed toward the one objective—to get something to eat.

"Now I shall repeat all the actions confirmed on this list," decided Tortsov. "And in order not to get into routine habits (I have not yet prepared my actions with content, purpose, and truth) I shall simply move from one proper objective and action to the next without executing them in physical terms. For the time being I shall limit myself to arousing inner impulses to action and shall fix them through repetition.

"As for the actions themselves, they will develop of their own accord. Our miracle-working nature will attend to that."

After that Tortsov went over and over the sequence of his physical actions, or rather he repeatedly aroused his inner impulses necessary to such action. He tried not to make any movements, but conveyed what was going on inside him through his eyes, his facial expression, and the ends of his fingers. He repeated that the actions would develop of their own accord, that they cannot indeed be restrained once you have established the inner impulses to action.

I followed the list we had written down and reminded him of any oversight.

"I feel," said he without interrupting his work, "that the individual, separate actions are shaping into larger periods, and that out of these periods a whole line of logical and consecutive actions is emerging. They are pushing forward, creating movement, and that movement is generating a true inner life. In feeling this life I sense its truth, and truth engenders faith. The more often I repeat the scene the stronger the line becomes, the more powerful the movement, the life, its truthfulness, and my faith in it. Remember that we call this unbroken line of physical actions the *line of physical being*.

"This is no small matter, but it is only half (and not the more important half) of the life of a role."

After a rather long pause Tortsov continued:

"Now that we have created the physical being of a part we must think about the more important task—creating the spiritual being in a role.

"Yet it would seem that it had begun to exist in me already, of its own accord and outside my will and consciousness. The proof of this lies in the fact that I, as you yourselves confirmed, executed my physical actions just now not drily, formally, lifelessly, but with liveliness and inner justification.

"How did this come about? Quite naturally: The bond between

the body and the soul is indivisible. The life of the one engenders the life of the other, either way around. In every *physical action*, unless it is purely mechanical, there is concealed some *inner action*, some feelings. This is how the two levels of life in a part are created, the inner and the outer. They are intertwined. A common purpose brings them closer together and reinforces the unbreakable bond between them.

"In your improvisation on the theme of the madman,* for instance, your over-all effort to save yourselves and your truthful action along the line of self-preservation were indivisible and ran parallel with each other. But imagine a different combination of these two levels. The one would be making an effort at self-preservation and the other, simultaneously, would be tending to increase the danger, that is to allow the violently insane man free access into the room. Can one possibly unite two such mutually destructive lines of inner and outer action? Need I prove to you that this is not possible because the bond between the body and the soul is indivisible?

"I shall prove it in my own person by repeating the scene from *The Inspector General*, not mechanically but completely justified as to the physical being of the part."

Tortsov began to act and at the same time to explain his feelings.

"While I am playing I listen to myself and feel that, parallel with the unbroken line of my physical actions, runs another line, that of the spiritual life of my role. It is engendered by the physical and corresponds to it. But these feelings are still transparent, not very provocative. It is still difficult to define them or be interested in them. But that is not a misfortune. I am satisfied because I sense the beginnings inside me of the spiritual life of my part," said Tortsov. "The more often I re-live the physical life the more definite and firm will the line of the spiritual life become. The

* See *An Actor Prepares*, pp. 42ff.

228

more often I feel the merging of these two lines, the more strongly will I believe in the psycho-physical truth of this state and the more firmly will I feel the two levels of my part. The physical being of a part is good ground for the seed of the spiritual being to grow in. Scatter more of such seeds."

"What do you mean by scattering?" I asked.

"Create more 'magic ifs,' proposed circumstances, imaginative ideas. They will immediately acquire life and merge with the physical being of your part, both giving a basis for and also evoking more physical actions."

Tortsov repeated many times the physical actions we had listed. I did not have to correct or prompt him as he already knew them in their order of sequence.

In doing this work Tortsov did not seem to realize how much his truthful, purposeful, productive actions, not just physical but psychological as well, were being given outward form through his facial expression, his eyes, his body, the intonation of his voice, and the expressive gestures of his fingers. With each repetition the truthfulness of what he was doing was enhanced, hence his faith in it too. Because of this his acting became more and more convincing.

I was amazed by his eyes. They were the same and yet not the same. They were stupid, capricious, naïve, blinking more than necessary because of shortsightedness—he could not see beyond the end of his nose. He made no gestures. Only his fingers worked involuntarily and very expressively. He spoke no words, but now and then some funny intonations escaped him, and they too were expressive.

The more often he repeated this sequence of so-called physical actions—or, to be more exact, the inner stimuli to action—the more his involuntary motions increased. He began to walk, to sit down, to straighten his cravat, admire his boots, his hands, to clean his nails.

As soon as he noticed any of this he instantly cut it out, evidently fearing to get into a routine.

By the tenth repetition his acting took on the aspect of being finished, thoroughly felt, and, thanks to the paucity of movements, very restrained. He had created life with its true, productive, purposeful actions. I was entranced by this result and could not help applauding. The others all joined in.

This quite sincerely astonished Tortsov. He stopped acting and asked: "What's the matter? What happened?"

"What happened was that you never played Khlestakov, never rehearsed the part, but went on the stage and both played and lived the part," I explained.

"You are mistaken. I did not feel anything, I did not play and never shall play Khlestakov, as that is a role quite outside my powers. Yet I can carry out correctly the inner stimuli to action and invent truthful, productive, purposeful actions in the circumstances proposed by the author. Even that small amount gives you a sense of real life on the stage.

"If the whole company were so prepared it would be possible by the second or third rehearsal to take up the real analysis and study of the roles—not the intellectual mulling over of each word and movement, which takes the life out of a part, but the increasingly real sense of life in the play, the thing you feel with your body as well as your soul."

"But how do you accomplish this?" All the students were interested to hear.

"By constant, systematic, and absolutely valid exercises of actions without props.

"Take me, for instance. I have been on the stage for a long time; yet every single day, not excluding today, I spend ten or twenty minutes on such exercises in the most varied circumstances I can imagine and always do them in my own person, on my own responsibility, so to say. If it were not for this, how much time do you think I should have had to spend on getting to understand the nature and the component parts of the physical actions in that scene of Khlestakov!

"If an actor keeps in constant exercise of this sort he will come to know practically all human actions from the point of view of their component parts, their consecutiveness and logic. But this work must be done daily, constantly, like the vocalizing of a singer, or the exercises of a dancer.

"From what I showed you today you must realize how very important this is. It is not without reason that I insist on your putting your special attention on these exercises. When you have worked out a technique such as has been developed in me through long training, then you will be able to do what I did. And when you achieve this, the same inner creative life beyond the range of your consciousness will stir in you of its own accord. Your subconscious, your intuition, your experiences from life, your habit of manifesting human qualities on the stage will all go to work for you, in body and soul, and create for you.

"Then your playing will always be fresh, you will have a minimum of clichés in your acting, and a maximum of truth.

"Go through the entire play in this same way, all the given circumstances, all the scenes, the units, objectives, everything that is accessible to you to begin with. Let us assume that you find in yourselves corresponding actions; then accustom yourselves to executing them with the logic and consecutiveness of your role, right through the play from beginning to end, and you will have created the external physical being of your part.

"To whom will these actions then belong? To you or to your role?"

"To me!"

"The physical being is yours, the movements also, but the objectives, the given circumstances, these are common to you both. Where do you end and where does your character begin?"

"There's no possible way of saying," exclaimed Vanya, who was all confused.

"But don't forget that these actions you have found are not simply external, they are inwardly justified by your feeling, they are reinforced by your faith in them, they are brought to life by your state of 'I am.' Moreover inside of you, and running parallel with the line of your physical actions, there has naturally been created a continuous line of emotional moments reaching down into your subconscious. Between these lines there is complete correspondence. You know that you cannot act sincerely, with directness, and be feeling something quite different inside you.

"To whom do these feelings belong—to you or to your part?"

Vanya merely waved his arms in despair.

"There you see, you are quite dizzy. That is a good thing because it goes to show that a great deal that is in your part and a great deal that is in you have become so intertwined that you cannot easily distinguish where the actor begins or his character ends. When you are in that state you come closer and closer to your part, you feel it inside you and feel yourself inside of it.

"If you work on your whole role that way you will get an inkling of its life—not in any purely intellectual or formal way but realistically, physically and psychically, because the one cannot exist without the other. No matter if this life is at first superficial, shallow, not filled out, nevertheless it does have flesh and blood in it and a bit of quivering, live soul, the soul of the human-being-actor-character.

"If you take this attitude toward your character you can speak of his life in the first and not the third person. This is of great importance in relation to further systematic and detailed work on your part. As a consequence of it everything that you acquire will immediately find its right place, its own shelf, its own hanger, instead of rambling around senselessly inside your head, as happens with actors who are mere word-eaters. In other words you must handle yourself so that you do not approach your character abstractly, as you would a third person, but concretely, as you would address your own self. When you achieve the sense of being inside your part and its being inside of you, when it merges by itself with your inner creative state, which borders on the subconscious, then go forward with assurance.

"Write down the list of the physical actions you would undertake if you found yourself in the situation of your imaginary character. Do this same work with the textual role, that is to say write down the list of actions which your character undertakes in accordance with the plot of the play. Then compare the two lists or, as it were, superimpose the one on the other as you put tracing paper over a design to see where the lines coincide.

"If the work of the playwright is done with talent, and if he has drawn his play from the living sources of human nature and human experience and feelings, and if your list of actions was also prompted by your own living human nature, then there will be a coincidence at many points between the two lists, especially in all the basic and principal places. These will be moments for you of rapprochement with your part, moments bound together by feelings. To feel yourself even partly in your role and your role even partly in you—that is a great accomplishment! That is the initial step of merging with and living with your part. Even for the other parts of the role, in which an actor still does not feel himself, there will be some manifestations of human nature; because if the role is well made it will be human as we are, and one human being senses another."

* * *

Tortsov spoke to us again today about his psychotechnique for creating the *spiritual life* of a role through the *physical being*. As usual he explained his thoughts in a picturesque example:

"Have you ever traveled? If you have, you know all about the changes that take place along the way, both inside the traveler and outside. Did you ever notice that even the train is transformed both inwardly and externally depending on the countries through which it is hurrying?

233

"When it first pulls out of the station it is all new and glittering in the frosty air. Its roof is covered with white snow, like a fresh table cloth. But inside it is dark because the winter light filters with difficulty through the frozen windows. The farewells of those seeing you off affect your feelings. Sad thoughts fill your mind. You think of those you have left behind.

"The swaying of the train, the pulse of the wheels, has the effect of a lullaby. You incline to sleep.

"A day and a night pass. You are traveling southwards. Outside everything is changing. Already the snow has melted. Other scenery flashes by. But inside the railway car it is close because the winter heat is still turned on. The passengers are all different; they speak with different accents, and their clothing is different. Only the railway tracks remain the same. They run on and on to infinity.

"It is not the rails, however, but what surrounds you outside or inside the train that is of interest to you as a traveler. Moving along the railway you come to ever new places, you receive more and more new impressions. You experience them, they raise you to a pitch of enthusiasm or plunge you into a sadness; they excite and momentarily alter the mood of the traveler, altering him as well.

"The same thing happens on the stage. What takes the place of the rails? How do we move on them from one end of a play to the other?

"At first it would seem that the best material we could use would be genuine, live feelings. Let them lead us. But things of the spirit are evanescent; it is difficult to fix them firmly. We cannot make sound 'rails' out of them; we need something more 'material.' Most appropriate for this purpose are physical objectives, for they are executed by the body, which is incomparably more solid than our feelings.

"After you have laid your rails of physical objectives, get aboard and start off to new lands—in others words, the life of the play.

You will be moving along, not staying in one place or thinking about things with your intellect; you will take *action*.

"This unbroken line of physical actions, fastened in place with strongly fixed objectives in lieu of bolts and ties, is just as necessary to us as the rails are to the traveler. Like him too the actor moves through many lands which are the varying given circumstances, through the 'magic ifs' and other inventions of the imagination. Again like him we come upon changing conditions which evoke in us the most varied moods. In the life of the play, the actor meets new people—the other characters who play opposite him. He enters into a common life with them and that also stirs his feelings.

"And just as the traveler has little interest in the rails themselves but only in the new countries and places through which they run, so too the creative urge of the actor is not absorbed in the physical actions themselves but rather in the inner conditions and circumstances which offer justification for the external life of his role. We need the beautiful fictions of our imagination, which give life to the characters we are playing, that is, the feelings which surge in the heart of the creative actor. We need attractive objectives which loom ahead of us as we move through a whole play."

Here Tortsov stopped speaking. There was a pause. Suddenly amid the silence we heard the grumbling voice of Grisha:

"That's just fine. Now we know all about the problems of transportation in art," he growled in scarcely audible tones.

"What are you saying?" Tortsov asked him.

"I'm just saying, don't you see, that true artists don't ride around in railway carriages on the ground, they soar in airplanes, above the clouds," said Grisha with great warmth and emotion, almost in a declamatory tone.

"I like your comparison," said Tortsov with a slight smile. "We shall go into that at our next lesson."

*　　*　　*

"So our tragedian needs an airplane in which to soar above the clouds, and not a railway carriage traveling down on the surface of the earth," said Tortsov to Grisha on entering the classroom.

"Yes, don't you see, an airplane!" repeated the "tragedian."

"Nevertheless, unfortunately, before an airplane can take off it has to run along the firm surface of a runway for a specified distance," remarked Tortsov. "So, as you see, even to soar you cannot do without the earth. The airplane pilots need it as much as we actors need a line of physical actions before we can take off in higher regions.

"Or could you, perhaps, fly straight up into the clouds in a vertical line without using a runway? They say that mechanics are so far developed that it can be done, but our actor's technique is not yet aware of any means of direct penetration into the realm of the subconscious. If, to be sure, you are caught up in a whirl of inspiration, it can carry your 'creative airplane' above the clouds in a vertical line without any preliminary run down the airstrip, but unfortunately these inspired flights do not depend on us and we cannot make rules about them. The only thing we have in our power is to prepare the ground, lay our rails, which is to say create our physical actions reinforced by truth and faith.

"With an airplane its flight begins when the machine takes off from the ground; with us the elevation begins when the realistic or even the ultranaturalistic ends."

"How did you put that?" I asked so that I could gain time to write it all down.

"What I mean to say," explained Tortsov, "is that I use the word ultranaturalistic to define the state of our spiritual and physical natures which we consider *entirely natural* and *normal* and in which we believe sincerely, organically. *It is only when we are in that state that our spiritual wellsprings open wide*, that scarcely perceptible emanations from them reach the surface: hints, shades, the aroma of that true, organic, creative feeling which is so timid and easily upset."

"You mean then that those feelings are engendered only when an actor believes sincerely in the normality and rightness of the actions of his physical and spiritual nature?" I asked.

"Yes! Our deep spiritual wellsprings *open wide only when the inner and outer feelings of an actor flow in accordance with the laws fixed for them, when there is absolutely no forcing, no deviation from the norm, when there is no cliché or conventional acting of any kind. In short, when everything is truthful to the limits of ultranaturalism.*

"But if you infringe upon the normal life of your nature, it is sufficient to annihilate all the intangible *subtleties* of the subconscious experience. That is why even seasoned actors with well-developed psychotechnique are afraid, when they are on the stage, of the slightest slip into false feeling or falseness in physical actions.

"In order not to frighten away their feelings these actors do not put their minds on their inner emotions but center their attention rather on their *physical being*.

"From all I have said it must be clear," said Tortsov summing up, "that the truth of our physical actions and our faith in them are not needed by us for the sake of realism and naturalism but rather to affect, in a reflexive way, our inner feelings in our roles, and to avoid frightening away or forcing our emotions, in order to preserve their pristine quality, their immediacy and purity, to convey on the stage the living, human, spiritual essence of the character we are portraying.

"That is why I advise you not to forsake the earth before you make your flights into the empyrean, not to abandon your physical actions when you sail into your subconscious," said Tortsov to Grisha to wind up the argument between them.

"It is not enough just to soar upwards, you must also orient yourself up there," Tortsov went on. "There, in the regions of the subconscious, there are no highways, no rails, no signals. It is easy to lose your way or take the wrong turn. How can you orient yourself in this unknown region? How can you direct your feelings since your consciousness does not penetrate there? In aviation they send out radio waves from the earth to guide planes that fly in inaccessible spheres without pilots. In our art we do something similar. When our feelings soar into a region inaccessible to our consciousness we work on our emotions obliquely, with the aid of stimuli, lures. They contain something in the nature of radio waves, which affect intuition and call forth responses in our feelings."

*　　*　　*

Today's lesson was devoted to a discussion of Tortsov's experiment with the role of Khlestakov.

Tortsov gave this explanation:

"People who do not understand the line of the physical being in a role laugh when you explain to them that a series of simple physical, realistic actions has the capacity to engender and create the more elevated life of a human spirit in a role. The naturalistic quality of this method upsets them. But if they would stick to the derivation of the word from 'nature' they would realize there is nothing to be worried about.

"Besides, as I have already told you, the point does not lie in these small, realistic actions but in the whole creative sequence which is put into effect thanks to the impulse given by these physical actions. What this sequence is I want to discuss with you today.

"I shall use for this purpose the experiments I made with the role of Khlestakov.

"You saw that neither I nor Kostya could come out onto the stage, either as human beings or as actors, until we had found a justification beforehand for our simple physical act in a whole series of imaginary circumstances, 'magic ifs.' You also saw that these simple actions required us to break up the scenes into units and objectives; we had to evolve a logic, a consistency, in our actions and feelings, we had to search out the truth in them, establish our faith in them, our sense of 'I am.' But to accomplish all this we did not sit at a table with our heads in a book, we did not divide up the text of the play with a pencil in hand—no, we remained on the stage and acted, we searched in our action, in our own natural life, for whatever we needed to promote our object.

"In other words we did not analyze our actions through our reason, coldly, theoretically, but approached them in practice, from the angle of life, human experience, our own habits, our artistic or other senses, our intuition, our subconscious. We ourselves searched for whatever was needed to help us execute our actions; our own nature came to our aid and guided us. Think about this process and you will realize that it was *an internal and external analysis* of ourselves as human beings in the circumstances of the life of our role.

"The process I am talking about is carried out simultaneously by all the intellectual, emotional, spiritual, and physical forces of our nature; this is not theoretical but practical research for the sake of a genuine objective, which we attain through physical actions. Absorbed by the immediate physical actions, we do not think about nor are we aware of the complex inner process of analysis, which naturally and imperceptibly goes on inside of us.

"Therefore the new secret and new quality of my method of creating the physical being of a role consists of the fact that the simplest physical action when executed by an actor on the stage obliges him to create, in accordance with his own impulses, all sorts of imaginary fictions, proposed circumstances, and 'ifs.'

"If such a tremendous effort of the imagination is needed for the execution of the simplest physical action, then for the creation of the line of the physical being of an entire role, there must be a long and unbroken series of imaginative fictions and proposed circumstances for the whole play. These can be prepared only by the aid of detailed analysis carried out by all the internal forces of creative nature. My method arrives at this analysis by natural means.

"This new and fortunate quality of a naturally induced self-analysis is what I wish to stress."

Tortsov did not have the time to finish his examination of his experiment with the role of Khlestakov so he promised to do it at our next lesson.

*   *   *

As he came into class today Tortsov announced:

"I shall continue the examination of my method for creating the physical being of a role.

"To answer the question I put to myself ('What would I do if I found myself in Khlestakov's situation?'), I have to invoke the aid of *all the inner as well as physical nature of an actor*. This is what helps not only to understand but to feel, if not the whole play at once, at least its over-all mood, its atmosphere.

"By what means can we induce our creative nature to go to work with entire freedom of action? Here too my method can be of help.

"As you are *drawn* to physical actions you are *drawn away from* the life of your subconscious. In that way you render it free to act and *induce* it to work creatively. This action of nature and its subconscious is so subtle and profound that the person who is doing the creating is unaware of it.

"Thus when I was making my experiment with Khlestakov and started off with physical actions as a way of creating the physical being in my role, I was not aware of what was going on inside of me. I was naïve enough to imagine that I was creating the physical actions, that I was managing them. But actually it turned out that they were merely the external reflections of the creative work which, beyond my consciousness, was being carried on inside me by the subconscious forces of my nature.

"It is not within the range of human consciousness to carry out this occult work, and so what is beyond our powers is done in our stead by nature itself. And what induces nature to do this work? My method of creating the life of the physical being of a part. *My method draws into action by normal and natural means the subtlest creative forces of nature which are not subject to calculation.* This is a new quality of my method, and I wish to stress it."

The students, and I among them, understood Tortsov's explanation but nevertheless did not know how to apply it to themselves. We begged him to give us a more concrete, technical explanation.

To this request Tortsov made the following reply:

"When you are on the stage, carrying out certain physical actions, adapting yourself to the object of your attention in accordance with the terms of the play, keep your mind entirely on projecting what you have to convey in the most vivid, true, and pictorial form. Put yourself firmly to the task of making the person playing with you think and feel as you do, see the things you are talking about with your eyes, hear them with your ears. Whether or not you succeed in this is another question. The important thing is that you earnestly desire it and that you believe in the possibility of achieving your objective. If you do so, your attention will be wholly centered on your prepared physical actions. Meantime your own nature, freed from supervision, will do for you what no psychotechnique can consciously accomplish.

"Take a firmer hold of physical actions. They are the key to freedom for that marvelous artist—creative nature—and they will protect your feelings from all force.

"Just think: You prepare with logic and consistency a simple, accessible line for the physical being of your role, and as a result you suddenly feel inside yourself the life of a human spirit. To find in yourself the same kind of human material as the author took from life, from the human nature of other people, when he wrote your part—isn't that a wonderful piece of conjuring!

"Such a result is all the more important because in the creative work we do here we are looking not for conventional and theatrical but for genuinely human material. And this can be found only inside the soul of the creative actor.

"And did you notice that when I began to feel inner impulses to action in the part of Khlestakov, no one was exerting any pressure on me externally or internally, no one was giving me any directions? More than that, I was myself making an effort to get rid of the old barnacles of tradition that have clustered around the performance of this classic role.

"I was trying, besides, for the time being, to protect myself from the influence of the author, and on purpose did not look at the text of the play. I did all this in order to remain uninhibited and independent, to pursue my own human experience.

"As time goes on, as I get deeper into my part, I shall call for much and most varied kinds of information about the play. All advice and information, anything of practical application in solving the given question or in accomplishing the projected action, all this I will accept with gratitude and put into immediate use, so long as it does not run counter to my feelings. But at my first approach, until I have created some kind of a firm base from which I can operate with assurance, I am afraid of anything that might distract me and complicate my work unduly.

"Remember the importance of this fact that to begin with it is the actor himself who, because of his own needs, necessities, impulses, seeks the help and directions of others, and this help is not *forced* on him. In the first case he maintains his independence, in the second he loses it. Any creative material taken over from another person and not experienced in one's own person is cold, intellectual, not organic.

"In contrast, one's own personal material immediately falls into place and begins to work. Anything which an actor takes from his own life experience, the thing to which he responds inwardly, can never be alien to him. It does not have to be artificially produced. It is already there, it wells up of its own accord, it begs to be manifested in physical actions. I do not need to repeat that all these 'own' feelings of an actor must be analogous to the feelings inherent in his part.

"For a better evaluation of the method I recommend, compare it with the approach to a new role in most of the theatres throughout the world.

"There the director of the play studies it in his office and comes to the first rehearsal with a ready-made plan. Indeed many of them do not make any serious study of it but rely on their own experience. At one wave of the hand, out of sheer ingrained habit, these 'experienced' directors lay down the line the play is to follow.

"Other, more serious, directors with a literary bent will formulate an intellectual line after detailed study in the quiet of their offices. It will be a true line, but it will have no appeal and therefore be of no use to a creative actor.

"Finally there is the director of exceptional talent who shows the actors how to play their parts. The more gifted his demonstrations, the deeper the impression he makes, the greater the actor's enslavement. Having seen the brilliant handling of his part, the actor will wish to play it just as he has seen it demonstrated. He will never be able to get away from the impression he has received, he will be compelled awkwardly to imitate the model. But he will never be able to reproduce it for this objective is beyond his native powers. After such a demonstration an actor is shorn of freedom and of his own opinion about his role.

"Let every actor produce what he can and not chase after what is beyond his creative powers. A poor copy of a good model is worse than a good original of mediocre pattern.

"As for the directors, one can only advise them not to foist anything on their actors, not to tempt them beyond the range of their capacities, but to enthuse them and make them ask of their own accord for the information they need in order to execute simple physical actions. A director should know how to stimulate in an actor an appetite for his part.

"Now then, I have explained to you what is done in the majority of theatres and also the particular secret of my method which *preserves the freedom of the creative artist.*

"Compare and choose."

*   *   *

Today an interesting conversation took place in the green room. It was a discussion among some experienced actors about Tortsov's new method. It seems that a number in the company do not accept this attitude toward art.

"It is easier for me to talk with you established actors by beginning at the end and working backwards," said Tortsov. "You are very familiar with the feelings of a creative actor in a fully-made, finished part. These are sensations beginners do not know. Now if you dig down in yourselves, your thoughts, your feelings, and recall any one of your roles which you have played many times, one that is firmly set, then tell me: What are you preoccupied with, what are you preparing yourself for, what do you foresee, what objectives, what activity draws you, when you leave your dressing room and go out on the stage to play a familiar part? I am not talking now to actors who compose the score of their roles out of simple craft, tricks and special 'turns.' I am speaking to serious, creative actors."

"I think about my first objective when I go onto the stage," said one of the actors. "When I have achieved that the second follows of its own accord; when I have played out the second, I think of the third, the fourth, and so forth."

"I begin with the through line of action. It unrolls in front of me like an endless highway at the end of which I see the sparkling cupola of the superobjective," added another, older actor.

"How do you try to attain your ultimate goal, or to approach it?" asked Tortsov.

"By logically accomplishing one objective after another."

"You act, and by your action you advance nearer and nearer to your ultimate goal?" Tortsov pressed him for further explanation.

"Yes, of course, as one would with any score."

"What is your concept of these actions in a familiar part? Are they difficult, complex, intangible?" queried Tortsov.

"They used to be, but finally they were resolved into about ten very clear, realistic, comprehensible, accessible actions, what you might call the marked channel of the play and part.

"What are they—subtle psychological actions?"

"Of course they are of that nature. But thanks to frequent repetition, and the indivisible bond between them and the life of the role, their psychology has to a large extent put on flesh, and through it one can reach the inner essence of feelings."

"Tell me, why is that so?" insisted Tortsov.

"I imagine because it is natural. The flesh is tangible, accessible. All one has to do is act with logic and consistency, and feeling follows of its own accord."

"Then," said Tortsov catching up his expression, "what you really end up with is simple physical action, and that is what we begin with. You say yourself that external action, the physical being, is most accessible. Then would it not be better to begin your creative work on a part with what is accessible, that is to say physical actions? You say that feeling follows action in a finished, well-prepared part. Yet in the beginning, even before the part is created, feeling also follows the line of logical actions. So why not coax it out from the very start, when you take your first steps? Why sit at a table for months and try to force out your dormant feelings? Why try to force them to come to life divorced from actions? You would do better to go out on the stage and at once engage in action, that is to say to do what is accessible to you at the time. Following that action, whatever is accessible to your feelings at the time will naturally emerge, in harmony with your body."

It seemed strange to me as a student that the older actors should find it difficult to grasp such a simple, normal, natural truth.

"How can it be?" I asked one of them.

"The tempo of work, the launching of plays, the repertory, rehearsals, performances, understudying parts, replacements, extra recitals, half-prepared work—all this encumbers the life of an actor. You cannot see through it to what is being done in art any more than you can see through a curtain of smoke. Whereas you, lucky devils, are immersed in it." This was said to me by a young pessimist who is active in the repertory of the theatre.

And yet we students envy him!

*   *   *

"Let us sum up our work in investigating my method.

"The result is to be looked for in the creative state which is formed in the actor when he has created the line of the physical and spiritual being in his role. Many of you have already, either accidentally or with the aid of psychotechnique, succeeded in establishing a true *inner creative state while on the stage*. But as I have already pointed out that is not sufficient. You must be able to pour into your inner creative state a *genuine sense of the life in your role in accordance with the given circumstances of the play*. This produces a miraculous transformation in the feelings of an actor, a transfiguration or metamorphosis.

"Now listen to this: When I was young I was fascinated by the life of antiquity. I read about it, talked with experts, collected books, engraving, drawings, photographs, postcards, and it seemed to me that not only was I familiar with that epoch but that I also really felt it.

"Then . . . I came to Pompeii. There I walked in the same streets as did the people in ancient times, I saw with my own eyes the narrow little alleys of the city, I went into homes that were still intact, I sat on the marble slabs where ancient heroes had rested, my hands touched objects which once upon a time they had handled, and for a whole week I was deeply aware both spiritually and physically of this past life.

"Because of that all my odd books and bits of information fell into place, they came to life in a different way, in a common, integrated existence.

"Then I really understood what the great difference was between nature and postcards, between an emotional realization of life and a bookish, intellectual comprehension of it, between a thought image and physical contact.

"Almost the same thing occurs when we first approach a part. A superficial acquaintance with it offers only a pale result from the point of view of emotional perception, no more than what a book, a vicarious view of an epoch, can give you.

"After our first acquaintance with the work of a playwright our impressions live on within us in something like patches, separate moments, often vivid, unforgettable, which lend color to all our further work on the play. Yet these separate and distinct points which have no interrelation except the external one of the play, which lack inner cohesion, do not give us the sense of the whole play.

"When you reach the point beyond the intellectual concept of the play, when you execute physical actions analogous to your part, in given circumstances analogous to those set up by the playwright, then and only then can you understand and feel the pulsing life of your character and do it with your own whole being.

"If you carry the line of the physical being through your whole part and if, thanks to that, you feel the living spirit in it, then all the separate and distinct points and sensations fall into place and acquire a new and genuine meaning.

"That state forms a solid foundation for creative work.

"When you have achieved that foundation, then any information received from the outside, from your director or from other sources, no longer rolls around in your head and your heart like some superfluous supplies in an overfilled storeroom; it falls into its predestined place or else it is rejected.

"This work is not done by the intellect alone but by all your creative forces, all the elements of your inner creative state on the stage together with your real sense of the life in the play.

"I have taught you to create in yourselves a physical as well as a spiritual sense of the life in a play. This acquired feeling of its own accord merges with your inner creative state already in existence and together they form the *lesser working creative state*. It is only when you are in this state that you are able to undertake the analysis and study of your role with the participation of all your spiritual and physical creative forces, and not merely those of your intellect.

"I lay great significance on this: Your first steps in approaching a new play must not be taken with your mind as much as with your feelings, while your subconscious and intuition, both as an actor and a human being, are still fresh and free. The soul of your part will be shaped from the bits of your own living soul, your desires, yearnings, imagination. If you accomplish this creative work, then your every character will live on the stage and will possess its own individual colors.

"When I was demonstrating Khlestakov I myself at times felt that I was inside the very soul of Khlestakov. This feeling alternated with another when I found part of the soul of the role in me. This happened too to Kostya when he felt that he really could snatch a bit of something to eat from a hawker's tray. That was a moment when he merged completely with his part, finding in himself some of Khlestakov's instincts. As I probed deeper I found fresh points of contact in conditions of external and internal life similar to those of my character. These moments of congeniality became more and more frequent, until they formed a whole unbroken line of both physical and spiritual being. Now that I have been through this preliminary creative period I can assert that if I were to find myself in Khlestakov's situation I would act in real life just the way he does in the physical being I have created for him.

"When I feel this way, I am very close to the state of 'I am,' and nothing frightens me. Standing thus on a firm base, I can manipulate both my physical and my spiritual nature without fear of becoming confused and losing my ground. And if I do slip off into a false direction I can easily come back and direct myself again along the right path. On this same basis, when I am on the stage I can assume my external characterization with the help of my trained habits. And in the framework of given circumstance and logical feelings I can use the inner material I have acquired to produce any inner characterization desired. If both those external and inner characterizations are based on truth they will inevitably merge and create a living image.

"Thus my method of creating a physical being automatically analyzes a play; it automatically induces organic nature to put its important inner creative forces to work to prompt us to physical action; it automatically evokes from inside us live human material with which to work: it helps, when we are taking our first steps toward a new play, to sense its general atmosphere and mood. All these are the new and important possibilities of my method."

Appendices

A. Supplement to *Creating a Role*

A Plan of Work

1. *Tell* the story of the plot (in not too much detail).

2. *Play the external plot* in terms of physical actions. For example: enter a room. But since you cannot enter unless you know where you came from, where you are going and why, seek out the external facts of the plot to give you a basis for physical actions. This should all be in rough form and constitutes the justification of an outline of *given circumstances* (just rough, external ones). Actions are drawn from the play; what is lacking is invented in line with the spirit of the play: What would I do if here, today, this very minute, I found myself in the situation analogous to that of the plot?

3. *Act out improvisations dealing with the past and the future* (the present occurs on the stage): Where did I come from, where am I going, what happened between the times I was on the stage?

4. *Tell the story* (in greater detail) of the physical actions of the plot of the play. Produce subtler, more detailed, more profoundly based proposed circumstances and "magic ifs."

5. *Draft a temporary definition*, in approximate terms, and *rough outline* of the superobjective.

6. On the basis of the acquired material shape a rough, approximate *line of through action*, always saying: What would I do "if . . . ?"

7. For that purpose break up the play into *large, physical units* (there is no play without these large physical units, large physical actions).

8. *Execute* (act out) these roughly sketched physical actions based on the question: What would I do "if . . . ?"

9. If the larger units are too difficult to encompass, *break them up temporarily into medium-sized units, or even, if necessary, into smaller and smaller units. Study the nature of these physical actions.* Adhere strictly to

the *logic* and *consecutiveness* of the large units and their component parts and combine them in whole large actions, always without props.

10. *Shape a logical, consecutive line of organic, physical actions.* Write it down and fix it firmly by frequent repetition. Clear it of all superfluity—cut ninety-five percent! Go over it until it reaches the stage of being true enough to be believed in. The logic and consecutiveness of these physical actions will lead to *truthfulness* and *faith*. But this is achieved by being logical and consistent, not by trying to achieve truth for the sake of truth.

11. Logic, consecutiveness, truth, faith, set in the state of being "here, today, this very minute," is now further grounded and fixed.

12. All this taken together produces the state of "I am."

13. When you have achieved the "I am" you will also have arrived at *organic nature* and its subconscious.

14. Up to now you have been using your own words. Now you have the *first reading of the text*. Seize on the separate words and phrases which you feel the need of; write them down and add them to your own free text.

When you come to the second and later readings, take down more notes, cull more words to be included in your own invented text of your parts. Thus gradually with small bits and then whole phrases your role becomes supplied with the playwright's own words. The blanks are soon filled in with the actual text of the play according to its style, language, and diction.

15. Study the text, fix it in your minds, but avoid saying it aloud so as not to jabber mechanically or build up a series of word acrobatics. Repeat many times and fix firmly your line of logical, consecutive physical actions, truth, faith, "I am," organic truth, and the subconscious. By giving these actions a basis of justification you will find always fresh, new, subtler given circumstances coming into your mind and a more profound, broad, all-embracing sense of concerted action. As you do this work, go over and over in constantly increasing detail the contents of the play. Imperceptibly you will acquire a basis for your physical actions which is psychologically more subtle because of your proposed circumstances, the through line of action, and your superobjective.

16. Continue to act the play along the lines now set. Think about the words, but when you act, replace them with *rhythmic syllables* (tra-la-la-la).

17. The true inner pattern of the play has now been laid down by the process of justifying your physical actions. Fix it even more firmly, so that the spoken text will remain subordinate to it and not be jabbered mechanically and independently from it. Continue to act the play using rhythmic syllables. *Go over in your own words* (1) the pattern of thought,

(2) the pattern of visualization of the play; (3) explain them both to those playing opposite you in order to establish intercommunication with them and also a pattern of *inner action*. These basic patterns form the subtext of your role. *Ground them as firmly as possible and maintain them constantly.*

18. After this pattern has been fixed, while you are still sitting around the table, *read the play in the author's own words, and without moving even your hands, convey as accurately as you can to those playing opposite you the patterns worked out, the actions, all the details of the score of the play.*

19. *Do the same thing, still sitting around the table but with your hands and bodies free, using some of the business blocked out for provisional production.*

20. *Repeat the same on the stage with the business as blocked out provisionally.*

21. *Work out and fix the plan of the stage sets (inside four walls).* Each person to be asked: Where would he choose (in what setting) to be and to act? Let each one suggest his own plan. The plan for the sets will be taken from the consensus of the plans proposed by the actors.

22. Work out and record the stage business. Set the stage according to the agreed plan and introduce the actors into it. Ask the actors where they would choose to make a declaration of love; where they would choose to work on the person playing opposite to engage in a heart-to-heart talk, and so forth; where it would be more convenient to cross over in order to hide some embarrassment? Let the actors cross and carry out their physical actions as required by the play—hunt for books on the bookshelves, open windows, light a fire, and so forth.

23. *Test the pattern of the stage business by opening arbitrarily any one of the four walls.*

24. Sit down at a table and carry on a series of conversations concerning the literary, political, artistic, and other aspects of the play.

25. *Characterization.* All that has been done so far has achieved inner characterization. Meantime the external characterization should have appeared of its own accord. But what is to be done if this does not occur? You should go over what has already been established but add a game leg, terse or drawling speech, certain attitudes of arms or legs, position of the body in keeping with certain mannerisms, habits. If the external characterization does not appear spontaneously, it must be grafted on from the outside.

B. Improvisations on *Othello*

These two short studies in *Othello* appeared in the Russian edition of *Creating a Role*. They are printed here for their interest, although their context relates less to the discussion in this volume than to that in *An Actor Prepares* (pp. 280 ff.). Thus Paul here plays the part of Iago as he did in *An Actor*, and the scene under discussion, as then, is the third scene of Act III, and not, as in this volume, the opening scene of the play.—EDITOR

Objectives; Through Line of Action; The Superobjective

TODAY TORTSOV decided to return to work on improvisations and to have us play for him our whole repertoire of sketches.

But since some of the students were detained we had to begin with the improvisations of *Othello*.

At first I refused to act without preparation, but then I agreed to do it because I really wanted to.

I was so excited that I did not know what I was doing. I could not hold myself in.

Tortsov's comment was:

"You make me think of a motorcyclist whizzing down a highway and yelling: 'stop me or I'll have an accident!' "

"When I am excited I am so wrought up I can't control myself," I said in self-defense.

"That is because you lack creative objectives. You play tragedy 'in general.' And any generality in art is dangerous," Tortsov said with conviction. "Be honest, what were you aiming at today?" he queried.

"It is best," he continued, "to limit yourself in any part to one and only one superobjective which contains in itself all the other units and objectives, large and small. But probably only a genius can encompass that.

256

To feel in a superobjective all the complex spiritual content of a play is no easy thing! It is beyond the powers of ordinary mortals. If we can limit the number of our objectives to five in each act with a total of twenty or twenty-five for the whole play, and they taken together contain the essence of that whole play, that is the best result we can hope to achieve.

"Our creative path is like a railway with its large and small stations, flag stops—which are our objectives. We have our capitals of provinces and our provincial cities, down to the one-horse towns, which require more or less attention, longer or shorter stops. We can whizz by all these stations with the speed of an express or plod like a mail train. We can stop at all stations or only the largest ones. We can make longer or shorter stops. Today you whizzed by like a fast express making no stops at any intermediate objectives. They flashed by like so many telegraph poles. You did not even notice them, nor did they interest you because you did not really know your destination."

"I didn't know because you haven't told us anything about this," I said in self-justification.

"I have not spoken about it because the time had not yet come. But today I have spoken of it because it is time you knew about it.

"First of all we must see to it that the goal we set ourselves is clear, true, and well-defined. It must rest on a solid basis. It is the first thing to think about. Toward it we must direct all our desires and efforts. Otherwise we shall go off the tracks as you did today.

"The goal or the objective must not only be definite, it must also be attractive, and exciting. The objective is a live bait which our creative will hunts down like a fish. The bait must be tasty; just so an objective must have substance and charm. Without them, it will not draw your attention. The will is powerless until it is inspired by passionate desires. An exciting objective is what will stimulate it. It is a powerful motive force behind our creative will, it is its greatest magnet.

"Moreover, it is of extraordinary importance that the objective be a true one. That kind of an objective will stir true desires; this in turn calls for true effort, and true effort ends up in true action.

"Shchepkin said that you can act well or badly—that is not important. What is important is that you play truly. In order to play truly you must follow the path of true objectives; they are like signposts showing you the way.

"Before we do anything else we must correct your mistake; so please play the whole scene over again. But first let us divide it up into large, medium, and small units and objectives.

"In order not to get bogged down in details, do your scene according to the largest of your units and objectives. What are Othello's and what are Iago's?"

"Iago provokes the jealousy of the Moor," said Paul.

"What does he do to that end?" asked Tortsov.

"He uses slyness, slander, disturbs his rest," answered Paul.

"And does it, of course, in a way to make Othello believe him," added Tortsov. "Now you go and accomplish this objective as best you can and convince, not Othello because he is not here yet, but this very much alive Kostya who is sitting in front of you. If you can do that nothing more will be asked of you," said Tortsov firmly.

"And what is your objective?" asked Tortsov turning to me.

"Othello does not believe him," I said.

"In the first place Othello does not yet exist. You have not created him. So far there is only Kostya," Tortsov corrected me. "In the second place if you are not going to believe what Iago tells you, there will be no tragedy. There will be a happy ending instead. Can't you think of something more consonant with the play?"

"I try not to believe Iago."

"In the first place that is not an objective, and in the second place you do not have to make any effort. The Moor is so sure of Desdemona that his normal reaction is to believe his wife. That is why it is so hard for Iago to destroy his confidence in her," explained Tortsov. "It is difficult for you even to understand what the villain is saying. And if you had heard the terrible news from any other source than Iago, whom you hold to be the most honest and devoted of men, you would laugh him to scorn and chase him away as an intriguer, and the incident would be closed."

"In that case perhaps the Moor's objective is to try to understand what Iago is saying," said I offering a new objective.

"Of course," approved Tortsov; "before you can believe it, you have to try to understand this improbable thing that is being said to the trusting Moor about his wife. It is only after he has considered the slander that he is seized with the need of proving the falseness of the accusation, the purity of Desdemona's soul, the injustice of Iago's view, and so forth. So to begin with try only to understand *what* and *for what purpose* Iago is saying these things.

"Thus," said Tortsov summing up, "let Paul try to upset you and you try to understand what he is saying to you. If you both carry out these two objectives I shall be very well satisfied.

"Take each one of the secondary, auxiliary objectives and string it on one general one, which we shall call the *through line of action* and at the end, like a clasp, put the *superobjective* you are trying to attain. When you can do this your sketch will have homogeneity, beauty, sense, and power."

After these explanations Tortsov made us play the sketch over again, as he put it, according to *objectives*, with a *through line of action* and in consonance with the *superobjective*. After we finished playing we were given a criticism and some explanations. This time Tortsov said:

"Yes. You played the sketch according to objectives, thinking all the time about the through line of action and superobjective. But . . . thinking does not yet mean action for the sake of a basic goal. You cannot reach the superobjective by means of your thoughts, your mind. The superobjective requires complete surrender, passionate desire, unequivocal action. Every bit, every separate objective, is needed for the sake of getting closer to the fundamental purpose of the play, that is to say the superobjective. There you must head straight for your goal and never allow yourselves to go off on tangents or deviate from your through line.

"To create means to head for your superobjective with passion, effort, intensity, purpose, and justification.

"As for the subsidiary objectives, of course they must be filled out carefully and completely, but only to the extent necessary and helpful to the superobjective and through line of action, never as today, taking each objective separately.

"Try to understand and fix in your minds to the best of your ability this line: From the superobjective to desire, effort, the through line of action, and back to the superobjective."

"But how can that be," we exclaimed in bewilderment, "from the superobjective you come back in the end to it again?"

"Yes, that is just how it is," explained Tortsov. "The superobjective which expresses the main, basic essence of the play should arouse the actor's creative desire, his efforts, and his action, so that in the end he will master the superobjective which to begin with initiated his creative process."

Through the Text to the Subtext

"Now that you know the principal secret of our creativeness let me see you play an excerpt from *Othello*," said Tortsov to us today.

Paul and I went up on the stage and began to play a scene between Iago and Othello.

How long had it been since Tortsov went over this scene with me and corrected it? In any case I did not believe his work had been entirely in vain. But it was. I had scarcely begun to say my lines when I went off again on the same old track.

Why did this happen?

Because while I was acting, and I was not conscious of it, I had in mind some former, casual objectives which, to tell the truth, amounted to no more than playing a fixed image. This resulted in exaggerated acting, and I did my best to justify it by inventing given circumstances and actions.

As for the words and thoughts, I pronounced them mechanically, unconsciously, the way you sing a song while you are working or when you are hauling a barge. Could this coincide with the author's intentions?

The text called for one thing, my objectives for something else. The words impeded the action and the action interfered with the words.

In a minute Tortsov stopped us.

"You are just contorting yourself and not living," he said.

"I know it! But what can I do!" I replied in a hysterical voice.

"What?" exclaimed Tortsov. "You ask what you should do? And this after I unveiled to you the principal secret of our creativeness?"

I remained stubbornly silent, angry at myself.

"Answer me this," began Tortsov. "Where were your feelings just now? Did they respond instantly, intuitively to your creative challenge?"

"No," I admitted.

"If not what should you have done?" said Tortsov, pressing his cross-examination.

Again I was silent and sulky.

"When feelings do not respond to a creative challenge of their own accord, you must leave them alone because they will not bow to force," Tortsov answered his own question. "In such cases you must turn to the other members of the triumvirate, your will and your mind. The most accessible is your mind. So begin with it."

I did not speak or move.

"With what do you begin your acquaintance with a play?" said Tortsov patiently and persuasively. "You begin with a careful reading of the text. There it is in black on white, in permanent form, and it represents, in this case, a marvelous work of art. The tragedy of *Othello* is splendid material for creative acting. Is it reasonable not to use this material, and is it possible not to be enthralled by such a theme? You know you yourself could not invent anything better than Shakespeare created. He was not a bad writer at all. No worse than you. Why refuse to give him a trial?

"Would it not be simpler, more natural, to start on your work by using the text of this play by a genius? He traces the right creative path for you with clarity and beauty and points out the necessary objectives and actions; he gives you the right hints in building the proposed circumstances; and above all he has put into his words the spiritual essence of the play.

"Therefore begin with the *text* and put your *mind* to work on reading its depths. Your *feelings* will not hesitate to join your mind and lead you deeper down into the *subtext* where the writer has concealed the motives which prompted him to create the play. The text thus gives birth to the subtext in order to have it recreate the text."

After these explanations Paul and I stopped acting and began to say over the lines. Of course all we did was repeat the words without taking the time to penetrate into their underlying meaning.

Tortsov was not long in putting an end to this.

"I suggested that you resort to your mind and thought, so that by means of them you would reach your feeling and the subtext," he said to us. "But where is the mind, where is the thought in what you are doing? You don't need them to scatter the words around like so many peas. For that all you need is a voice, lips, and tongue. Mind and thought have nothing in common with such mechanical action."

After this lecture we started to make ourselves penetrate into the meaning of the words we were pronouncing. The mind is not as skittish as the feelings and it does admit of more direct pressure.

" 'My noble lord . . . ' " Paul began with calculated tone.

" 'What dost thou say, Iago?' " I replied with an expression of deep thought.

" 'Did Michael Cassio, when you woo'd my lady, know of your love?' " asked Paul, looking as if he were trying to solve a brain-teaser.

" 'He did, from first to last . . . ,' " I replied with calculated pauses, the way one speaks in translating from a foreign tongue.

Here Tortsov interrupted our arduous labor.

"I don't believe either of you. You never tried to win Desdemona's hand and you know nothing about your past," he said to me. "As for you," turning to Paul, "you have really very little interest in the questions you are putting. You don't really need the answers to them. You put a question and do not even listen to Othello's reply."

Apparently we had not realized the simple truth that every word spoken must have its basis, its justification, in some imaginary given circumstance, some "magic if."

We had done this kind of work more than once, preparing objectives and actions, but this was the first time we were called upon to do it in conjunction with the actual words of another person. Besides in our improvisations, when we were acting, we used any thoughts and words that came along. They popped into our minds and slid off our tongues as part of the particular objective and action, whenever words became necessary.

But it is one thing to use your own words and thoughts, and quite another to adopt those of someone else, which are permanently fixed, cast as it were in bronze, in strong clear shapes. They are unalterable. At first they are alien, strange, remote, and often even incomprehensible. But they have to be reborn, made into something vitally necessary, your own, easy, desired—words you would not change, drawn from your own self.

For the first time we were being faced with the process of assimilating the words of another person. And our amateurish babbling of inanimate sounds, which was what Paul and I were doing with the magnificent words of *Othello*, certainly did not count.

I realized that we had come to a new phase in our work—the creation of the living word. The roots of this run down into one's soul, they feed on one's feelings; but the stem reaches up into consciousness where it puts forth luxuriant foliage of eloquent verbal forms, conveying all the deep emotions from which they draw their vitality.

I was excited and embarrassed by the importance of this occasion. In such a state it is difficult to gather in one's attentions and thoughts, to fire one's imagination to produce a long series of given circumstances, justifying and breathing life into each thought, each phrase, the entire verbal text of the playwright.

In the distracted condition in which we found ourselves, I felt incapable of coping with the problem put to me. So we asked Tortsov to postpone our work until the next lesson so that we could have time and opportunity to think about it and make preparations at home, that is to say to invent all the necessary fantasies, given circumstances which would justify and enliven the lines which up to now had been so many inert words.

Tortsov agreed.

*　　*　　*

This evening Paul came to see me and together we thought about various circumstances which would justify the words of our roles in *Othello*.

In accordance with Tortsov's prescription we first went through the entire play, and after that we addressed ourselves to the careful study of the thoughts contained in our scene.

In this way we harnessed to our task, as we were taught to do, the most biddable of our creative triumvirate—our *minds*. We read:

IMPROVISATIONS ON OTHELLO

IAGO: My noble lord . . .
OTHELLO: What dost thou say, Iago?
IAGO: Did Michael Cassio, when you woo'd my lady,
    Know of your love?

How much fantasy one must bring into play to give the Moor occasion to recall the past. One knows something of his earlier life, the period of his first acquaintance with Desdemona, his falling in love, the abduction, all this is in the first acts and Othello's speech to the Senate. But how much more the author left unsaid concerning what happened before the play begins, also in the intervals between scenes or at the same time as the action but off stage.

It was what Shakespeare left unsaid that Paul and I undertook to fill out.

I have neither the time nor the patience to set down here all the many combinations, permutations of imagination, we thought up concerning how, with Cassio's aid, secret meetings with Desdemona were contrived. Many of the things we invented excited us and seemed in our eyes both poetical and beautiful. For young men like ourselves, who were keen for love, such themes are always emotionally exciting no matter how many forms they may take.

We also talked at length on the subject of Othello's feelings with regard to the woman who did not scorn the love, the kisses, the secret embraces of this black slave.

On this we broke off our work for it was after one o'clock. Our heads were tired and our eyes drooping.

We parted with the satisfaction of knowing that we had made what we could call a sound beginning for the scene, built on a foundation of proposed circumstances.

* * *

Again today, on the eve of our lesson with Tortsov, Paul and I met to go on with our work of inventing proposed circumstances for our scene in *Othello*.

Paul demanded that we work on his role as he had nothing to show Tortsov, whereas for mine I had already imagined a few things.

Yes, it was just a few things and far from enough, for I hoped to build all my scene on a basis of proposed circumstances. It is so much more pleasant to work on the stage if you have that basis. However, there was nothing to do but go to work on Iago.

263

Again we called our *minds* into play. In other words we went through the text carefully, analyzed it, and decided that we wished to look into the past of this classic Shakespearean villain. Little is said about him in the play. This, however, had its silver lining, because it left a clear field for our imagination.

I do not intend to record anything which did not have a direct bearing on my part. Why should I? Yet anything that does influence my imaginary character I am bound to enter in this diary.

I feel a great urge to see Iago with an attractive exterior, not a repulsive person at all. Without this it would be impossible to account for the confidence I as Othello have to feel in him. To achieve this there must be a visual basis for taking Iago, the genuine villain, for a simple-hearted man. If he appears before me in the guise of an operatic villain with viperish eyes, and makes grimaces, which is how he is usually played, I would be obliged deliberately to turn away from him or else feel myself in a foolish position.

The trouble is that Paul is naturally a person who will excuse or forgive anything. In this case he tends to excuse and forgive Iago. In order to do this he tries to make him jealous of his wife Emilia and Othello who is supposedly having an affair with her. To be sure, there are hints of this in the text. Using them as a point of departure you can, to a certain degree, use them to justify the malice, hatred, thirst for revenge, and all the other vicious qualities with which the soul of Iago is impregnated. However, this throwing of a shadow on Othello does not suit me. It does not fall in with my plans. My fairy-tale hero is pure as a dove. He must be innocent of relations with women. Iago's suspicions must be false. They cannot have any basis in fact.

Therefore, if Paul feels this is necessary, let Iago rage with jealousy; but I demand of the actor playing the part that he persistently and skilfully keep from me any external signs which might reveal these wicked feelings festering in his soul.

I also need to feel that Iago, for all his great mind, is rather simple. Otherwise how can I laugh at what would seem naïve suspicions? I want to see in Iago a huge, immovable, rough, naïve, loyal soldier, to whom one forgives anything for the sake of his devotion. It is easy to hide a villain under the rough good-natured exterior of a simple-minded soldier, and it would be difficult for me to unmask him.

I think I persuaded Paul at least partly to this view.

* * *

I was just undressing to go to bed when this question arose in my mind: Previously, in all our improvisations without the lines of the play, we started with the proposed circumstances and arrived at the physical objectives, or the other way round, from the objectives to the proposed circumstances. Today we acted quite differently, we began with the playwright's own text and finally reached the proposed circumstances just the same. Does this mean all roads lead to Rome? And therefore does it make any difference from which end you make a start—from the *objective* or from the *text*? From the *mind* or from the *will*?

* * *

I went to Tortsov's lesson today with less than wings on my feet, for I felt that I was far from properly prepared.

He called on Paul and me first but did not hurry us, that is to say, he gave us time to get ready, to go over in our minds the pattern of proposed circumstances we had prepared.

As we are supposed to do, we called on our intellect as the most responsive of our three motive powers. It produced the facts, the thoughts encased in the lives, the circumstances of Othello's and Iago's lives, all the things Paul and I had gone over in our two sessions. This put us on our rails at once and provided a direct and natural approach to what underlies the text.

I felt at ease. It was pleasant to be on the stage and I also felt I had the right to be there, to speak the words and do what came naturally to me from the unrolling of the ribbon of proposed circumstances and from the text itself. Earlier, when I had played Othello in our improvisations I had only occasionally had this feeling. Now I was completely at ease and for much longer.

The main point is that when this had happened earlier it was purely unconscious, accidental. Now it was brought about consciously with the help of an inner technique and a systematic approach. Was this not to be called a success?

I shall try to define the charms of this sensation and what the steps were which led me to it.

To begin with, Paul as Iago was rather skilful in assuming the exterior of a simple-minded person. At any rate I believed in his transfiguration.

Iago says:

Did Michael Cassio, when you woo'd my lady,
Know of your love?

As I pondered his question I involuntarily recalled my Venice-Sevastopol-Nizhny Novgorod house, on the banks of the Volga; I remembered coming to know Desdemona, her charming, affectionate, playful ways, the wonderful secret meetings arranged with the help of Cassio who knew our secrets "from first to last."

With these thoughts and pictures in my mind I was glad to answer Iago because I had so much to tell him; I was glad to have him question me at length. It was difficult to restrain the smile that rose to my lips from some inner source. Perhaps I was not experiencing what the live Othello did, but I understood the character of his thoughts and sensations and I believed in them.

That is the great thing on the stage—belief in thoughts and feelings.

It is also a great satisfaction to speak phrases and thoughts which cover a multitude, an unbroken line, of inner visualizations unrolling like a moving picture.

To convey this to anyone else you have to use every available form of communication and, above all, words. The most suitable and expressive ones will prove to be Shakespeare's. First, because he is a poet of genius, and second, because what I now need to know I find in those very words. What better can convey their own inner essence than they themselves? Under such circumstances another's words are necessary, dear, and close to me, they become my own. They come out of their own accord, naturally.

Words which had been empty up to now had been filled out with artistic invention and imagined pictures in which I was able to believe. In short, I sensed the spiritual essence of the play, it made me feel akin to it, and it required once more its own forms in order to be made manifest.

What a remarkable process! And how close to the creative ways of nature itself!

Really it was as though I had plucked a seed from a ripe fruit and from it had raised fruit exactly like that from which it originally came. I had taken the kernel substance from the playwright's text and then expressed it freshly with his words which now were my own. They had become a necessity to me, not because this time I was determined to get at their core but because I needed to put that essence in verbal form. The text had bred the subtext and the subtext had resurrected the text.

This is what happened throughout the beginning of the well-prepared and well-imagined scene Paul and I worked on in my apartment. What would now happen to the part I had not yet succeeded in filling out and justifying with sufficient proposed circumstances?

I collected all my attention in order to take in all of Iago's lines. I was well aware of the villainy underlying his poison-laden questions. I realized, I mean I felt, their diabolical power, the irresistibility of their logic and consecutiveness leading inevitably to catastrophe. I could sense what slander and intrigue could be in the hands of a virtuoso.

For the first time I could follow and feel how by cleverly phrased questions and a whole series of logically plotted thoughts the villain imperceptibly cut away the firm ground under his victim's feet, poisoned the pure atmosphere, leading him to astonishment and bewilderment, to doubt; then awoke suspicion, horror, grief, jealousy, hatred, execration, and finally vengeance.

This terrifying spiritual transformation of Othello is told in only ten small printed pages! The genius of the inner pattern of Shakespeare's masterpiece now struck me with full force for the first time.

I do not know whether I played well or badly, but I had no doubt about the fact that for the first time I played the text, for the first time I took a close look into it and saw into the subtext. Perhaps my emotions did not reach that far, perhaps it was only my attention. Perhaps the creative stage I felt was not really living my part but only a presentiment of it. Nevertheless the undoubted fact was that this time the actual lines of the play hooked me and dragged me along, logically, consecutively, down into their soul.

Paul and I had a clear and great success today. We were praised not only by Tortsov and Rakhmanov but also by our fellow students.

The most indicative thing was that not even Grisha objected or criticized. That was more important than praise. I was happy about this.

Can it be that our success was due just to the author's lines?

"Yes," said Rakhmanov as he went by me, "today you believed Shakespeare. Before, you hid his words, but today you were not afraid to relish them. Shakespeare held up his end. You can be sure of that!"

* * *

Elated by our success Paul and I sat by the Gogol monument for a long time and rehearsed in detail, step by step, everything that happened today at our lesson.

"All right," he said, "let's begin from the beginning when Iago teases Othello, and my line is:

But for a satisfaction of my thought;
No further harm.

Or, I added more specifically,

> . . . By Heaven, he echoes me,
> As if there were some monster in his thought
> Too hideous to be shown. . . .

That's it exactly," agreed Paul. "It seemed to me," he went on, "that just then you felt at ease and light-hearted."

"Yes, that's true," I answered taking up his hint; "and do you know why? It was thanks to you. What happened was that I suddenly felt you were the good-natured soldier whom I had always wanted to see in Iago. I believed you and instantly I had that feeling of 'having the right to be on the stage.' Then later, at the lines:

> And didst contract and purse thy brow together
> As if thou then hadst shut up in thy brain
> Some horrible conceit. . . .

I felt quite gay and like cracking some kind of a joke, saying something funny to cheer you up and myself as well," I confessed.

"Tell me once more," asked Paul with interest, "just where the place is where I succeeded in winning you away from joking and in making you be serious?"

"I began to listen to your words, or rather to take in Shakespeare's thoughts, at the place where you say:

> Men should be what they seem;
> Or those that be not, would they might seem none!

and then later, where you speak in riddles:

> Why then, I think Cassio's an honest man.

or when, pretending to be noble, you seem to be trying to avoid questioning:

> Good my lord, pardon me.
> Though I am bound to every act of duty,
> I am not bound to that all slaves are free to—

At these points I felt a hint, already tinctured with fiendish poison, and I thought: What a snake this Iago is! He is pretending to be offended so that he will be more easily believed! Moreover, I realized that although an an-

268

swer like that could not go unchallenged, yet the more explanation is required the deeper you bog down in the quicksands of his plot. And again
I was amazed at Shakespeare's genius."

"I have the feeling that you philosophized and mulled over the play more
than lived it," said Paul doubtfully.

"I think I did both," I agreed. "But what harm was there in that as
long as I was at ease when I was questioning you?"

"And so did I when I was squirming out of your questions and be-
wildering you," said Paul, relieved. "That was my objective."

"Objective?" I thought. "Eureka!" I exclaimed suddenly. "Listen carefully! This is what happened to us," and I painstakingly tried to recover
all the sensations and thoughts which I had not yet succeeded in clarifying
and collating. "In all our exercises and improvisations, such as those with
the mad dog and lighting the fire, we started from the *objective* which
spontaneously generated thoughts and words, a kind of accidental *text*
which became vital to us in carrying out the given objective.

"Today we started from the author's *text* and arrived at our *objective*.

"Wait; let us trace the path of this: The day before yesterday, when we
were working in my apartment, we went from the *text* to the *proposed circumstances*. Isn't that so?" I asked thoughtfully. "Today however, without
our having been conscious of it, we went from the text via the proposed
circumstances and reached our creative objective!

"Let us test this and see how it happened."

We began to recall our induced emotions as we were playing the scene.
It turned out that Paul was trying at first only *to draw my attention to him*.
Next he wanted me to feel that he was a good-natured soldier, which was
what I too wanted to see in him. To accomplish this he tried to *represent*
himself in that light as well as he could. When he succeeded in this he began
to drop one thought after another in my mind, all of which were compromising to Cassio and Desdemona. Meantime his thoughts were strongly
fixed on the subtext.

As for me, my objectives were evidently as follows: At first I only
clowned, I *poked fun* at myself and Iago. Then when he agitated me I
turned the conversation into serious channels, I wanted to gain a closer
comprehension of the words or rather the thoughts of the villain. Later, I
recall, I tried to make a mental *picture* of Othello in his complete loneli-
ness, a joyless prospect. Finally, when I was able to a certain extent to
achieve this, I realized that the deceived Moor, frightened by the visions
conjured up, would hasten to *get rid of, send away* this villainous, poison-
ous Iago.

All these were objectives engendered by the text. Following it along through the play we came to other deeper lines, other proposed circumstances and objectives that naturally, spontaneously, and inevitably arose from the text. In this approach there can be none of that regrettable divergence between the text and subtext as occurred during the first period of my work on the role of Othello, I mean during my test performance.

So it was, we decided today, that the right, you might say classic, course of creativeness operates from the *text* to the *mind;* from the mind to the *proposed circumstances:* from the proposed circumstances to the *subtext;* from the subtext to *feeling (emotions)*; from emotions to the *objective, desire (will)* and from the desire to *action*, the clothing in words, gestures and so forth, of the subtext of the play and its parts.

* * *

Tomorrow we have a lesson with Tortsov. So today Paul and I worked some more on the proposed circumstances and objectives in our scene from *Othello*.

We not only succeeded in going through it to the end but were also able to repeat what we had done earlier. As a result the line of proposed circumstances and objectives was sufficiently filled out.

What a big piece of work! Tortsov must see it.

Can we fail to put it across when we play for him at our lesson?

It would be a pity if all this work should go for nothing and we should be unable to clarify completely this thing on which we seem to be getting a hold!

* * *

We did not have to ask Tortsov to let us play. He suggested himself that we repeat our scene from *Othello* and we did.

To our complete bewilderment, however, this time we had no success with it, despite the fact that we felt ourselves to be in a splendid creative state while we were playing!

"Do not be upset," said Tortsov when we confessed to him how disillusioned we were. "That happened because you overloaded the text. A long time ago at your test performance, I scolded you because you spat out your text like bits of unnecessary peel. Today, by contrast, you overburdened the text, made it too heavy by reason of a too complicated and detailed subtext.

"When a word has substantial inner content it becomes heavy and is spoken slowly. This happens when an actor begins to stress the text to use it as a vehicle to convey the multitude of his inner emotions, thoughts, visualizations, in brief the whole inner content of the subtext.

"An empty word rattles like a pea in a dry pod; an overstuffed word is slow to be turned, like a sphere filled with mercury.

"But I repeat, do not let this distress you. On the contrary it should be the cause of joy in you," he said approvingly to us both. "The most difficult thing we have to do is to create a substantial subtext. That caused the overloading for you, but in time the inner essence of the text will settle, be padded down, will crystallize, become more compact and so, without losing its substance, will gain in lightness and fluency."